Congress and the Politics of Foreign Policy

REAL POLITICS IN AMERICA

Series Editor: Paul S. Herrnson, *University of Maryland*

The books in this series bridge the gap between academic scholarship and the popular demand for knowledge about politics. They illustrate empirically supported generalizations from original research and the academic literature using examples taken from the legislative process, executive branch decision making, court rulings, lobbying efforts, election campaigns, political movements, and other areas of American politics. The goal of the series is to convey the best contemporary political science research has to offer in ways that will engage individuals who want to know about real politics in America.

Congress and the Politics of Foreign Policy

EDITED BY

Colton C. Campbell
Florida International University

Nicol C. Rae
Florida International University

John F. Stack, Jr.
Florida International University

UPPER SADDLE RIVER, NEW JERSEY 07458

Library of Congress Cataloging-in-Publication Data

Congress and the politics of foreign policy/edited by Colton C. Campbell, Nicol C. Rae, John F. Stack, Jr.
p. cm.—(Real politics in America)
Includes bibliographical references and index.
ISBN 0-13-042154-5
1. United States—Foreign relations—Law and legislation. 2. United States—Foreign relations.
I. Campbell, Colton C. II. Rae, Nicol C. III. Stack, John F. IV. Real politics in America series.

KF4651 .C657 2002
327.73—dc21

2002010542

Senior acquisitions editor: Heather Shelstad
Associate editor: Brian Prybella
Editorial assistant: Jessica Drew
Marketing manager: Claire Bitting
Marketing assistant: Jennifer Bryant
Editorial/production supervision: Kari Callaghan Mazzola
Prepress and manufacturing buyer: Ben Smith
Electronic page makeup: Kari Callaghan Mazzola and John P. Mazzola
Interior design: John P. Mazzola
Cover director: Jayne Conte
Cover design: Kiwi Design
Cover photos: photo of White House by Marc Anderson;
    photo of Washington, D.C.—Capitol Hill by Getty Images, Inc./PhotoDisc, Inc.;
    photo of Washington, D.C.—Supreme Court by Corbis Digital Stock

This book was set in 10/12 Palatino by Big Sky Composition
and was printed and bound by Courier Companies, Inc.
The cover was printed by Phoenix Color Corp.

Real Politics in America
Series Editor: Paul S. Herrnson

© 2003 by Pearson Education, Inc.
Upper Saddle River, New Jersey 07458

Printed in the United States of America
10   9   8   7   6   5   4   3   2   1

ISBN 0-13-042154-5

Pearson Education LTD., London
Pearson Education Australia PTY, Limited, Sydney
Pearson Education Singapore, Pte. Ltd
Pearson Education North Asia Ltd, Hong Kong
Pearson Education Canada, Ltd., Toronto
Pearson Educación de Mexico, S.A. de C.V.
Pearson Education—Japan, Tokyo
Pearson Education Malaysia, Pte. Ltd
Pearson Education, Upper Saddle River, New Jersey

To our mentors, Roger H. Davidson and Eric R. A. N. Smith,
Byron Shaffer, and Richard B. Finnegan.
They have probably forgotten what they said, but we haven't.

CONTENTS

PREFACE

Despite the end of the Cold War in the early 1990s, the dictum that the U.S. Constitution is an invitation to struggle for the privilege of directing American foreign policy is still an accurate description of political reality in contemporary politics. This is the central theme of the essays collected in this book. Accommodation among the three branches of government is made more difficult by the apparent absence of a clear doctrine or paradigm to guide U.S. foreign policy in the post–Cold War era, and the habitual division of partisan control among the branches during the past decade has made such a consensus even more difficult to attain.

There still remains a strong consensus between the political parties and between the branches of government that the executive should generally predominate on national security matters. The chief executive's capacity to deploy U.S. forces and Congress's fear of being perceived as undermining those forces has been a particularly powerful weapon in this regard, as the domestic debates over deployments in Bosnia and Kosovo have indicated. Several of the included chapters delineate the rise of presidential power in terms of executive assertiveness, congressional acquiescence, and judicial sanction.

Nevertheless, Congress can—and does—use its powers and prerogatives to remain an active partner and effective obstacle to presidential ambitions when it chooses to do so. This is perhaps best illustrated by the rise in "message politics" that now pervade the floors of both chambers of Congress, and has also intruded on the foreign policy process. Even in the august Senate, message politics filters into deliberation as with the Comprehensive Nuclear Test Ban Treaty. Perhaps "playing politics" with such ostensibly critical matters as nuclear testing is symptomatic of the generally low salience of foreign and defense policy issues in American politics since the fall of the Soviet Union.

The increased influence of "ethnic" lobbies in U.S. politics since the demise of communism is also on the rise. In the absence of an overriding global foe, these groups are now better able to assert that their particular interest is also the national interest. Several ethnic lobbies, most notably the Israeli, Irish, and Cuban lobbies, have had particular influence on congressional debates over their respective areas of interest, and have often prevailed, as national public opinion remains generally unmobilized or unmotivated by these issues.

Is a new U.S. foreign policy doctrine emerging? Some have argued that the global economy and democratization have become the new guidelines for U.S. foreign policy. There appears to be a consensus among elite opinion on these issues in the abstract, but in Congress globalization must contend with many state and local interests, to which members of both parties are electorally committed to give attention. Human rights issues will arouse U.S. concern, but only when other U.S. security interests—such as the preservation of NATO and containment of conflict—are present will America become militarily involved. The higher degree of internationalism prompted by globalization and the end of the Cold War also raises issues of sovereignty and institutional prerogative, of which Congress is jealous. Yet as a global superpower, militarily and economically, the U.S. federal government is unlikely to find its powers compromised by supranational bodies that rely on U.S. participation for their effectiveness.

The terrorist hijackings and assault on the World Trade Center and the Pentagon on September 11, 2001 brought the congressional–presidential relationship once more into focus. As is traditional in a national security crisis, partisan disagreements on Capitol Hill were immediately minimized. The two House leaders, J. Dennis Hastert (R-Ill.) and Richard Gephardt (D-Mo.), who had rarely been seen together, appeared jointly on television, while Senate leaders Tom Daschle (D-S.Dak.) and Trent Lott (R-Miss.) held joint press conferences throughout the first week after the attack. All members of Congress, with the exception of Representative Barbara Lee (D-Calif.), supported an open-ended resolution authorizing the president to "use all necessary and appropriate force" to combat the terrorists. "When America is threatened, Americans come together," charged Senator Wayne Allard (R-Colo.). "That's true in the Senate as it is everywhere."[1] Pointedly summarized by Senator John F. Kerry (D-Mass.), the tragedy "wipes away many of the differences of just forty-eight hours ago."[2]

All this bipartisanship initially translated into a string of legislative victories for the Bush administration in the aftermath of the September 11 terrorist attacks. But while Congress may remain united on stamping out terrorism, the strain of bipartisanship was evident among the stalwarts of both parties as the president's "war on terrorism" infringed on the normal partisan agenda that had sharply divided lawmakers before September 11. Some Democrats expressed concern about giving the president a blank check in authorizing force. "We know we must bring those responsible to justice," declared Representative Lynn Woolsey (D-Calif.). "But my constituents also ask, 'Do we know what means are appropriate to accomplish that?'"[3] Other lawmakers urged a more deliberate approach to devising an antiterrorism package, especially as it pertained to definitions of terrorism and limitations on civil liberties.[4] Representative Henry J. Hyde (R-Ill.), chair of the House Committee on International Relations, had scheduled a meeting to act on the administration's antiterrorism measure but postponed the committee's session a week after demands by committee members from both parties that major elements of the bill be eliminated or revised.[5] And Democrats in the Senate urged patience, delaying a scheduled vote on the president's legislation by weeks, not days as the administration had hoped. Still others quickly called for the use of a parallel-track strategy to allow Congress to work simultaneously on legislation related to the Pentagon and World Trade Center attacks in addition to economic and social domestic issues not related to terrorism such as education, energy, the Patients' Bill of Rights, a prescription drug benefit for seniors, and appropriation bills.[6]

A president's advantage in directing U.S. foreign policy is magnified in times of warfare or crisis, largely because such instances tend to centralize authority.[7] It is not uncommon then for the normal lawmaking process to be short-circuited, or for Congress to delegate authority to the president immediately following recent events. But by nature Congress is a deliberate institution, hesitant to extend presidential power without good reason. With the legislative process moving at double speed in the days following the terrorist attacks, many House Democrats grew increasingly frustrated at being kept on the sidelines while Minority Leader Gephardt and a small cadre of key Democratic lawmakers cut deals with Republican counterparts and President Bush. Rank and file members complained that the Democratic Caucus had not been fully consulted on several key decisions, and that Gephardt's desire for bipartisanship allowed Republicans to coax him into agreements that contradicted the party's interests.[8] Such criticisms also underscored the strains placed on congressional leaders as they worked to accommodate the president's demands in the aftermath of a national security problem.

How long congressional leaders can continue to keep their caucuses in line remains a guessing game, contingent on public approval for or against the president. The Constitution is "an invitation to struggle" in the area of foreign policy,[9] and if hostilities are prolonged (or cease), presidential powers and bipartisanship are likely to dissipate. "People are hoping we can work together," Representative Robert Menendez (D-N.J.) said. "But democracy is based on a conflict of ideas. Ultimately, I don't think that you will find a willingness to capitulate simply for the sake of appearing bipartisan."[10] The framers created the presidency to deal with direct threats to the national security of the United States such as that posed by the assault of September 11, 2001, and in such situations the natural disposition of citizens and Congress is to rally around the national leader, the president. The limitations and the maintenance of that consensus will remain contingent, as ever in a pluralistic system, by the perception of presidential success in dealing with the crisis. But in the absence of such a perception the legislative branch will inevitably become more significant.

This book would not have been possible without the cooperation and generosity of many individuals at Florida International University. The Jack D.

Gordon Institute for Public Policy and Citizenship Studies made enormous contributions. The steady support and encouragement by Provost Mark B. Rosenberg is especially appreciated. We gratefully acknowledge the contributions of Thomas Breslin, Vice President for Research, Arthur W. Herriott, Dean of the College of Arts and Sciences, Ivelaw L. Griffith, former Associate Dean of the College of Arts and Sciences and now Dean of FIU's Honors College, and Joyce Shaw Peterson, Associate Dean of the Biscayne Bay Campus. We appreciate Timothy J. Power, director of the graduate program in political science at FIU, for facilitating the interest of our graduate students. And we would like to thank Elaine Dillashaw of the Gordon Institute for providing invaluable support, assistance, and, above all, unwavering patience in the production of this book.

A special acknowledgement goes to Paul Herrnson, series editor as well as director of The Center for American Politics and Citizenship at the University of Maryland, College Park, who made a number of constructive suggestions that greatly improved the book's conceptualization and organization. Heather Shelstadt and Jessica Drew at Prentice Hall shepherded the book through the production process. Kari Callaghan Mazzola provided editorial/production supervision, and Dana Chicchelly provided careful copyediting; both Kari and Dana contributed significantly to the volume's clarity. Last, but not least, we are thankful to our families—old and new—who continue to make life a joy and whose love is not contingent on this book's success.

To the reader, we hope our efforts and those of the contributing authors will advance your understanding and appreciation for the role of three U.S. institutions in the crafting of foreign policymaking—the U.S. Congress, the U.S. Presidency, and the U.S. Supreme Court—institutions that are never short of excitement.

Colton C. Campbell
Nicol C. Rae
John F. Stack, Jr.

NOTES

1. Quoted in Mary Lynn F. Jones, "Congress United—For Now," *Roll Call*, 19 September 2001, p. 1.
2. Quoted in ibid.
3. Quoted in Betsy Rothstein, "Lawmakers Bare Raw Feelings in Wake of Tragedy," *The Hill*, 19 September 2001, p. 1.
4. Neil A. Lewis, "Lawmakers Tap Brakes on Bush's Hurtling Antiterrorism Measure," *New York Times*, 25 September 2001, p. B-7.
5. Mark Preston, "Agenda Split Emerges," *Roll Call*, 24 September 2001, p. 1 and Kerry Kantin, "Uncertain Situation Leads to Agenda Conflicts," *The Hill*, 26 September 2001, p. 1.
6. Noelle Straub and J. P. Cassidy, "Anti-terrorism Legislation Hits Snag," *The Hill*, 26 September 2001, p. 1.
7. Roger H. Davidson and Walter J. Oleszek, *Congress and Its Members*, 8th ed. (Washington, D.C.: CQ Press, 2002), p. 399.
8. Ethan Wallison, "Gephardt Faces Heat Over Bipartisanship," *Roll Call*, 24 September 2001, p. 1.
9. Edward S. Corwin, *The President: Office and Powers, 1787–1957*, 4th ed. (New York: New York University Press, 1957), p. 171.
10. Quoted in Lewis, "Lawmakers Tap Brakes on Bush's Hurtling Antiterrorism Measure," p. B-7.

About the Contributors

DAVID P. AUERSWALD is Professor of National Security Strategy at the National War College. He is author of *Disarmed Democracies: Domestic Institutions and the Use of Force*. He served as an APSA Congressional Fellow on the Senate Foreign Relations Committee.

COLTON C. CAMPBELL is Assistant Professor of political science at Florida International University. He is author of *Discharging Congress: Government by Commission* and coeditor of *New Majority or Old Minority? The Impact of Republicans on Congress*; *The Contentious Senate: Partisanship, Ideology, and the Myth of Cool Judgment*; and *Congress Confronts the Court: The Struggle for Legitimacy and Authority in Lawmaking*. He served as an APSA Congressional Fellow in the office of U.S. Senator Bob Graham (D-Fla.).

CHRISTINE A. DEGREGORIO is Professor of government at American University. She is author of *Networks of Champions: Leadership, Access, and Advocacy in the U.S. House of Representatives*.

CHRISTOPHER J. DEERING is Associate Professor of political science at George Washington University. His books include *Committees in Congress, Second Edition* (with Steven Smith) and *Congressional Politics*. He served as an APSA Congressional Fellow in the office of Senate Majority Leader George J. Mitchell (D-Maine), and is a former Brookings Institution research fellow.

C. LAWRENCE EVANS is Professor of political science at the College of William and Mary. His books include *Leadership in Committee: A Comparative Analysis of Leadership Behavior in the U.S. Senate* and *Congress under Fire: Reform Politics and the Republican Majority* (with Walter J. Oleszek). He served as an APSA Congressional Fellow in the office of U.S. Representative Lee Hamilton (D-Ind.).

LOUIS FISHER is Senior Specialist in American national government at the Congressional Research Service. He is author of numerous books, including *Presidential War Power*; *American Constitutional Law*; *The Politics of Shared Power: Congress and the Executive*; *Constitutional Dialogues: Interpretation as Political Process*; *Constitutional Conflicts between Congress and the President*; and *Congressional Abdication of War and Spending*.

JONATHON MOTT is an instructional Internet-technology consultant. His articles appear in *Social Science Quarterly* and *Public Integrity*, and he has taught courses at the University of Oklahoma and at Brigham Young University. He served as a Carl Albert Congressional Fellow in the office of U.S. Representative J. C. Watts (R-Okla.).

DAVID M. O'BRIEN is Leone Reaves and George W. Spicer Professor of Government and Foreign Affairs at the University of Virginia. He is author and coauthor of several books, including *Supreme Court Watch* (annual); *Constitutional Law and Politics* (two volumes); *Struggles for Power and Governmental Accountability and Civil Liberties and Civil Rights, Second Edition; Storm Center: The Supreme Court in American Politics, Third Edition; The Politics of American Government; The Public's Right to Know: The Supreme Court and the First Amendment; What Process Is Due? Courts and Science-Policy Disputes; Judicial Roulette; Privacy, Law, and Public Policy; Abortion in American Politics; The Politics of Technology Assessments;* and *Views from the Bench: The Judiciary and Constitutional Politics.* He served as a Judicial Fellow at the U.S. Supreme Court.

WALTER J. OLESZEK is Senior Specialist in American national government at the Congressional Research Service, and adjunct professor of political science at American University. His books include *Congressional Procedures and the Policy Process, Fifth Edition* and *Congress and Its Members, Seventh Edition.* He served as policy director of the Joint Committee on the Organization of Congress.

NICOL C. RAE is Professor of political science at Florida International University. He is author of *The Decline and Fall of the Liberal Republicans: From 1952 to the Present; Southern Democrats;* and *Conservative Reformers: The Freshman Class of the 104th Congress.* He is coauthor of *Governing America* and coeditor of *New Majority or Old Minority? The Impact of Republicans on Congress* and *The Contentious Senate: Partisanship, Ideology, and the Myth of Cool Judgment.* He served as an APSA Congressional Fellow in the offices of U.S. Senator Thad Cochran (R-Miss.) and U.S. Representative George P. Radanovich (R-Calif.).

DAVID RICHARDS is a doctoral candidate at American University. He is currently preparing a dissertation that examines the determinants of economic growth in post-colonial states, with an emphasis on the effects of ethnic divisions in African and Caribbean nations.

JOHN F. STACK, JR. is Professor of political science and law at Florida International University and Director of the Jack D. Gordon Institute for Public Policy and Citizenship and the Ethnic Studies Certificate Program. He is author of *International Conflict in an International City: Boston's Irish, Italians, and Jews, 1935–1944,* and coeditor of *Ethnic Identities in a Transnational World; Policy Choices: Critical Issues in American Foreign Policy; The Primordial Challenge: Ethnicity in the Modern World; The Ethnic Entanglement;* and *Congress Confronts the Court: The Struggle for Legitimacy and Authority in Lawmaking.*

1

THE WAR POWER

NO CHECKS, NO BALANCE

LOUIS FISHER

Presidential war power has expanded dramatically in the past half-century, driven by major shifts in institutional positions: ambitious interpretations (and executions) of presidential power, acquiescence by the judiciary, and abdication by Congress. As a result, the fundamental characteristic of American government—the framers' reliance on checks and balances—has been abandoned in this area. We now have presidential wars, set in motion unilaterally by our chief executives and unrestrained either by judicial or legislative checks.

THE FRAMERS' CONSTITUTION

There can be little question about the framers' determination to prevent war making by a single person. They were well aware that British theorists, including John Locke and William Blackstone, had placed foreign affairs and the war power exclusively in the executive.[1] The framers repudiated that monarchical model of government in every respect. They made the subject of foreign affairs a power shared between Congress and the president, and they placed the power to initiate war solely in the hands of Congress.

There should be little doubt about the framers' intent in this area. At the Philadelphia Convention, Charles Pinckney said he was for "a vigorous Executive but was afraid the Executive powers of <the existing> Congress might extend to peace & war &c which would render the Executive a Monarchy, of the worst kind, towit an elective one." James Wilson supported a single executive but "did not consider the Prerogatives of the British Monarch as a proper guide in defining the Executive powers. Some of these prerogatives were of a Legislative nature. Among others that of war & peace &c." Edmund Randolph rejected any "motive to be governed by the British Governmt. as our prototype."[2]

The framers recognized that in times of emergency the president needed to exercise war powers of a defensive nature ("to repel sudden attacks"), but the power to mount an offensive war—to take the country from a state of peace to a state of war—was reserved solely to Congress.[3] When Pierce Butler recommended that the president be given the power to make war, the other delegates strongly objected. Roger Sherman said that the president "shd. be able to repel and not to commence war." Elbridge Gerry remarked that he "never expected to hear in a republic a motion to empower the Executive alone to declare war." George Mason agreed, noting that he was "agst giving the power of war to the Executive, because not <safely> to be trusted with it; . . . He was for clogging rather than facilitating war; . . . ."[4]

These sentiments were echoed during the debates at the Pennsylvania ratifying convention. James Wilson assured his colleagues that the system of checks and balances "will not hurry us into war; it is calculated to guard against it. It will not be in the power of a single man, or a single body of men, to involve us in such distress; for the important power of declaring war is vested in the legislature at large."[5] The framers gave Congress the power to initiate war because they believed that presidents, in their search for fame and glory, would have an appetite for war.[6] In *Federalist No. 4*, John Jay issued this warning:

> . . . absolute monarchs will often make war when their nations are to get nothing by it, but for purposes and objects merely personal, such as a thirst for military glory, revenge for personal affronts, ambition, or private compacts to aggrandize or support their particular families or partisans. These and a variety of other motives, which affect only the mind of the sovereign, often lead him to engage in wars not sanctified by justice or the voice and interests of his people.[7]

Writing in 1793, James Madison expressed similar concerns. War, he said, was "the true nurse of executive aggrandizement." War multiplies the honors and emoluments of executive office: "The strongest passions and most dangerous weakness of the human breast; ambition, avarice, vanity, the honourable or venial love of fame, are all in conspiracy against the desire and duty of peace."[8] In a letter to Thomas Jefferson in 1798, Madison said that the Constitution "supposes, what the History of all Govts demonstrates, that the Ex. is the branch of power most interested in war, & most prone to it. It has accordingly with studied care, vested the question of war in the Legisl."[9]

The framers did not depend on good intentions or virtuous behavior within a single branch. Nor did they rely on abstract formulations of separation of powers. By the late 1780s, the concept of checks and balances had replaced separation of powers, which one contemporary pamphleteer called a "hackneyed principle" and a "trite maxim."[10] Instead of trying to artificially separate the powers of government, the framers looked to a sharing and partial intermixture of powers. Checks and balances required some overlapping. The framers knew that the "danger of tyranny or injustice lurks in unchecked power, not in blended power."[11]

In *Federalist No. 51*, Madison argued that "the great security against a gradual concentration of the several powers in the same department, consists in giving to those who administer each department the necessary constitutional means and personal motives to resist encroachments of the others." Madison drove home his point with this axiom: "Ambition must be made to counteract ambition." Each branch would have to protect its own prerogatives. "The interest of the man must be connected to the constitutional rights of the place."[12]

IMPLEMENTING THE FRAMERS' DESIGN

For years, the framers' concept of the war power held sway. Presidents were entitled to use military force for defensive purposes. However, anything of an offensive nature—taking the country from a state of peace to a state of war—was reserved solely to Congress. That distinction was clearly understood by presidents and their executive officers. President George Washington restricted his military actions to defensive operations. His Secretary of War, Henry Knox, told territorial governors that military actions against hostile Indian forces were to be confined to "defensive measures" until Congress decided otherwise. Knox cautioned that Congress was "alone . . . competent to decide upon an offensive war."[13]

When President John Adams decided it was necessary to use military force against France in the Quasi-War of 1798, he never argued that he could do that singlehandedly. Instead, he came to Congress to seek authority by statute to increase the size of the military and reinforce the defense of ports and harbors. Under its exclusive power to "grant letters of Marque and Reprisal," Congress also authorized private citizens to provide vessels and other military assistance in the war against France. Alexander Hamilton, one of the strongest proponents of executive power, recognized that the Constitution vested in Congress the sole decision to make reprisals. Whatever power the president possessed to take defensive actions, any measure beyond that "must fall under the idea of *reprisals* & requires the sanction of that Department which is to declare or make war."[14]

President Thomas Jefferson acted unilaterally in 1801 when he dispatched a small squadron of frigates to the Mediterranean to protect against attacks by the Barbary pirates. Yet when Congress returned, he explained that he took no further action because he was "unauthorized by the Constitution, without the sanction of Congress, to go beyond the line of defense." It was up to Congress to authorize "measures of offense also."[15] Congress subsequently passed at least ten statutes authorizing Presidents Jefferson and Madison to take military actions against the Barbary pirates.[16] In 1805, when conflicts arose between the United States and Spain, Jefferson advised Congress about the situation and clearly identified the constitutional principles: "Congress alone is constitutionally invested with the power of changing our condition from peace to war."[17]

The actions of President James Polk illustrate that executive power can expand when the President moves troops into likely hostilities. Determined to gain from Mexico the territories known as Upper California and New Mexico, he moved U.S. troops into a disputed area and provoked a clash between American and Mexican troops. A bold move, but Polk never claimed that he could unilaterally take the country from a state of peace to a state of war. He knew that he had to come to Congress, explain the situation, and ask Congress to declare war, which it did.

President Abraham Lincoln is often described as a "military dictator." That is a misnomer. Although he took a number of extraordinary measures in the early months of the Civil War while Congress was in recess, he never argued that he possessed plenary power over war. Instead, he conceded that he might have exercised power that belonged to Congress, particularly when he suspended the writ of habeas corpus. For constitutional legitimacy, he looked to Congress. He notified the legislators that his actions, "whether strictly legal or not, were ventured upon under what appeared to be a popular demand and a public necessity, trusting then, as now, that Congress would readily ratify them."[18] The legislative debate on granting Lincoln retroactive authority for his actions rested on the assumption that his actions were illegal.[19] Congress subsequently passed legislation to legitimate what Lincoln had done.[20]

When one of Lincoln's actions was taken to the Supreme Court (seizing ships and their goods), the executive branch conceded the limits of presidential authority. Richard Henry Dana, Jr., representing the administration, told the Supreme Court that Lincoln's actions in responding to the Civil War had nothing to do with "the right *to initiate a war, as a voluntary act of sovereignty.* That is vested only in Congress."[21] Even in the midst of a national crisis unmatched in American experience, the executive branch understood the difference between a president's duty to take certain defensive actions and the constitutional authority reserved to Congress to mount an offensive war against other nations.

In addition to declaring war against England in 1812 and against Mexico in 1846, Congress also declared war against Spain in 1898 and issued declarations for World War I and World War II. Of course there were other presidential military actions that did not involve declared wars. On some occasions the president used military force after Congress had passed *authorizations*, as with the Quasi-War against France and the actions against the Barbary pirates. There were also other military actions by presidents when Congress had neither declared nor authorized the use of force. However, these so-called life-and-property actions were relatively modest in scope and limited in duration. Edward S. Corwin accurately summed up these presidential initiatives as consisting largely of "fights with pirates, landings of small naval contingents on barbarous or semi-barbarous coasts, the dispatch of small bodies of troops to chase bandits or cattle rustlers across the Mexican border, and the like."[22] However one might describe these presidential actions, they cannot be considered legitimate precedents for President Truman's decision to involve the nation in war against North Korea or President Bill Clinton's actions in mounting an air war against Yugoslavia.

THE ROLE OF THE JUDICIARY

In describing judicial precedents before World War I, Christopher N. May asserted that the Supreme Court, "with one short-lived exception—refused to pass on the validity of laws adopted under the war powers of the Constitution."[23] He spoke of the "long-standing position that war powers legislation is not subject to judicial review," and claimed that the "notion that the war powers were exempt from judicial scrutiny had a long and distinguished lineage."[24] A more recent study, by Martin S. Sheffer, offers a similar view: "One must constantly remember that executive–legislative conflicts regarding questions of emergency, war, and peace, although raising many constitutional controversies, rarely find their way to the judiciary and, when they do, are rarely decided according to proper constitutional interpretation. For the most part, they are resolved . . . through political settlements agreed to by Congress and the President."[25] The courts, says Sheffer, "lie back, seeking to avoid having to rule on questions of the conduct of commander-in-chief [and war] powers, and when they are forced to rule, they usually uphold presidential action."[26]

In fact, the record is quite the opposite. Until recent decades, federal courts regularly took war power cases and decided them like other legal matters: analyzing the dispute in terms of statutory and constitutional authority and balancing governmental powers against individual rights. Courts did not lie back or shy away from war power disputes. A number of private citizens and private corporations took war power issues to the courts to have their case adjudicated, and the courts often decided against the president. Many of the early decisions were written by justices who had been members of the Constitutional Convention or participated in state ratifying conventions. Their opinions reflected the prevailing view that taking the country to war was a matter for Congress, not the president.

As a result of French interference with American shipping in the late eighteenth century, Congress suspended commercial intercourse with France and enacted a number of statutes to prepare for military operations. The Supreme

Court decided three cases resulting from the Quasi-War, which lasted from 1798 to 1800. In *Bas v. Tingy* (1800), the Court decided a case involving a claim by Captain Tingy for compensation regarding the recapture from the French of a U.S. merchant ship belonging to Bas. Was Tingy entitled to compensation based on a 1798 act of Congress or a higher compensation based on a 1799 statute governing the recapture of ships from the "enemy"? In Justice Chase's language, "the whole controversy turns on . . . whether *France* was at that time an *enemy*? If *France* was an enemy, then the law [entitles Tingy] to one half of the value of the ship and cargo for salvage; but if *France* was not an enemy, then no more than one-eighth can be allowed."[27]

The Court did not flinch from this "war power" issue. It was asked to decide whether, in the absence of a formal declaration of war by Congress, the state of hostilities between the United States and France amounted to a war and entitled Tingy to a higher compensation. The Court ruled that the conflict amounted to war whether Congress decided to make a formal declaration or simply authorize military action, as it had done. War could be either declared ("perfect") or undeclared ("imperfect"). Thus, the Court fully addressed the legal and constitutional issues.

In 1801, the Court again analyzed the question of undeclared but authorized wars. In *Talbot v. Seeman*, Chief Justice John Marshall had his first opportunity to address a war-related case. Talbot, captain of a U.S. ship of war, captured a merchant ship flying a French flag. The owner of the ship sued the captain in libel for the value of the ship. Deciding that the seizure had been legal, the Court ruled in favor of Talbot. To decide his rights, it was necessary to examine the relative situation between the United States and France at the time of the capture. Notice Marshall's language:

> The whole powers of war being, by the constitution of the United States, vested in congress, the acts of that body can alone be resorted to as our guides in this inquiry. It is not denied, nor, in the course of the argument, has it been denied, that congress may authorize general hostilities, in which case the general laws of war apply to our situation; or partial hostilities, in which case the laws of war, so far as they actually apply to our situation, must be noticed. To determine the real situation of America in regard to France, the acts of congress are to be inspected.[28]

A third case from the Quasi-War involved a proclamation by President John Adams to seize ships sailing to and from French ports. Congress had only provided authority to seize ships sailing *to* a French port. Could a president, in time of war, exceed statutory authority and could such disputes be litigated in court? Not only did the Court take the case, it decided against the president. Chief Justice Marshall ruled that when national policy is defined by statute, presidential "instructions cannot change the nature of the transaction, or legalize an act which without those instructions would have been a plain trespass."[29]

The preeminence of congressional policy, once it has been expressed in a statute, appears again in an 1806 decision by a federal circuit court. Colonel William S. Smith, indicted under the Neutrality Act of 1794 for engaging in military action against Spain, claimed that his action "was begun, prepared, and set in foot with the knowledge and the approbation of the executive department of our government." The circuit court forcefully rejected his argument: "The president of the United States cannot control the statute, nor dispense with its execution, and still less can he authorize to do what the law forbids."[30] The court clearly understood the difference between the president's "defensive" power to resist invasion and the "the exclusive province" of Congress to undertake "offensive" military actions against foreign countries:

> If, indeed, a foreign nation should invade the territories of the United States, it would I apprehend, be not only lawful for the president to resist such invasion, but also to carry hostilities into the enemy's own country; and for this plain reason, that a state of complete and absolute war actually exists between the two nations. In the case of invasion hostilities, there cannot be war on the one side and peace on the other. . . . There is a manifest distinction between our going to war with a nation at peace, and a war being made against us by an actual invasion, or a formal declaration. In the former case, it is the exclusive province of congress to change a state of peace into a state of war.[31]

The president, then, had no constitutional authority to initiate war. Does the president, the court asked, "possess the power of making war? That power is exclusively vested in congress."[32]

For the next 140 years—up to the Korean War decisions of the 1950s—federal courts accepted and decided a range of other war power issues. In 1814, the Supreme Court was faced with the question of whether property found on land at the commencement of hostilities against England in 1812 could be considered "enemy property" as a result of the declaration of war by Congress. To decide that issue, the Court found it necessary to look for any other legislative act that authorized the seizure. Concluding that the declaration of war did not contain authority for the seizure, the Court ruled that the seizure required a supplementary instruction from Congress.[33] When Congress by law delegates to the president power to "call forth the militia" to suppress insurrections and repel invasions, the Court recognizes that the judgment as to how to deal most effectively with such situations rests with the president, for he is carrying out discretionary authority committed to him by Congress.[34]

In several cases arising from the Mexican War, the Court emphasized that the president's power as commander in chief is exercised to carry out congressional policy and cannot go beyond it. For example, the president had no authority to annex territory to the United States by virtue of military conquest. The president had no independent authority to enlarge the boundaries of the United States, for that could be done "only by the treaty-making power or the legislative authority, and is not a part of the power conferred upon the President by the declaration of war."[35] In a separate ruling, the Court granted a U.S. civilian trader damages for the seizure of his property by an officer of the U.S. army. Orders of a superior officer could not justify an unlawful seizure.[36] In yet another lawsuit, the Court decided that neither the president nor any military officer had authority to establish a court in a conquered country to decide questions about the rights of the United States or of individuals in prize cases.[37]

In a controversial decision in 1860, a circuit court upheld presidential authority to bombard Greytown (San Juan del Norte), Nicaragua, in retaliation for an affront to an American diplomat.[38] The U.S. military response would be considered disproportionate today for several reasons. In 1868, Congress passed legislation stating that it shall be the duty of the president to use such means "not amounting to war" in obtaining the release of U.S. citizens deprived of liberty by a foreign government. That legislative policy remains as part of current law.[39] Moreover, most of the "life-and-property" actions of the nineteenth and early twentieth centuries would be condemned today, both under the nonintervention policy of the Organization of American States (OAS) and the UN Charter. The OAS Charter provides that the territory of a nation is inviolable and it "may not be the object, even temporarily, of military occupation or of other measures of force taken by another State, directly or indirectly, or any grounds whatsoever." Article 2(4) of the UN Charter proscribes "the threat or use of force against the territorial integrity or political independence of any state."

The Civil War ushered in a number of lawsuits, most of them accepted and decided by the federal courts. Regarding the president's authority to suspend the writ of habeas corpus, Chief Justice Taney sitting on circuit ruled that such authority belonged to Congress, not the president.[40] President Lincoln rebuffed this judicial limitation, but other cases involving suspension of the writ were decided, some in favor of the president and some against.[41] In 1863, the Court upheld President Lincoln's blockade of Southern ports and the seizing of neutral vessels in response to the rebellion of the South. In upholding Lincoln's action in this matter, the Court also regarded the power to initiate war as the exclusive province of the legislature. The president has "no power to initiate or declare a war either against a foreign nation or a domestic State."[42] During this period, the Court decided a number of cases concerning the authority of the president and the executive branch to operate military courts that infringed upon the responsibilities of civil courts.[43]

One of the few cases ducked by the Supreme Court is *Mississippi v. Johnson* (1867), which involved Mississippi's effort to enjoin President Andrew Johnson from using the military to implement two Reconstruction Acts. Writing for the Court, Chief Justice Chase held that the Court lacked jurisdiction to issue the injunction. The president's duties were "purely executive and political" and lay outside the scope of "judicial interference with the exercise of Executive discretion."[44] The Court saw it as a no-win situation. First, Johnson might refuse to comply with a court order. Second, if he complied with the injunction, he might face impeachment by Congress. Would the Court then step in to support the president in opposition to the legislature?[45]

Courts have had to decide a number of cases to determine when war begins and when it ends,[46] the authority of U.S. military commanders to impose duties on goods coming from the United States into an occupied territory,[47] the right to damages to the owner of a vessel seized as enemy's property,[48] and the actions of military authorities in making arrests without a warrant.[49] In the famous *Curtiss-Wright* decision of 1936, the Court decided whether Congress could delegate to the president authority to declare an arms embargo in South America.[50] In none of these cases did the courts draw back and refuse to decide a dispute because it involved some aspect of the war power.

During and after World War II, the Court decided a number of cases on whether Congress had too broadly delegated wartime economic power to the president, including mobilization of the resources of the business community, price-fixing authority, rent control, and determination and recovery of "excess profits."[51] The Court decided the cases involving military judgments to place a curfew on Japanese Americans and put them in detention centers.[52] In 1946, the Court reviewed—and rejected—the government's claim that the continuation of military rule in Hawaii was made necessary by prevailing circumstances.[53] In 1952, in a stunning 6 to 3 opinion, the Court decided that President Truman lacked constitutional authority to seize most of the nation's steel mills for prosecuting the war in Korea.[54] Although Truman consistently denied that the nation was at war, preferring to call the hostilities in Korea a "police action,"[55] federal judges had no problem in selecting the word "war" to decide clauses in life insurance cases. As one district judge noted: "We doubt very much if there is any question in the minds of the majority of the people of this country that the conflict now raging in Korea can be anything but war."[56] Prior to the Korean War, courts had also decided whether war exists within the meaning of life insurance claims.[57]

It was only with the Vietnam War cases that federal courts began to regularly duck war power cases. These cases were dismissed on the grounds that the issue was a political question, an unconsented suit against the United States, or that the plaintiffs lacked standing. For the first time in the nation's history, the courts were using the political question doctrine to avoid constitutional challenges regarding the war power.[58] From the administrations of Ronald Reagan to Bill Clinton, members of Congress brought war power cases to court, but they were routinely denied relief under doctrines that included nonjusticiability, mootness, ripeness, and standing. The most recent example is the suit brought by Representative Tom Campbell (R-Calif.) and twenty-five other members of the House against the war in Yugoslavia.

The judicial message in these cases has been consistent: If members want to challenge presidential war power, they must first use the institutional powers available to Congress as a whole, acting through a majority of its members rather than having a few legislators bring their dispute to the judiciary. Only after Congress acted against a president to create a true constitutional impasse would there be a basis for legislative standing.[59] Clearly the ball is in Congress's court, but legislators have muffed the opportunity for the past half century.

THE ROLE OF CONGRESS

In 1945, while the Senate debated the UN Charter, President Harry Truman sent a cable to Senator Kenneth D. McKellar (D-Tenn.) defining executive power over war. At issue was a procedure that allowed the UN to use military force to deal with threats to peace, breaches of the peace, and acts of aggression. All UN members would make available to the Security Council, "on its call and in accordance with a special agreement," armed forces and other assistance for the purpose of maintaining international peace and security. Aware of this provision, Truman pledged that all agreements involving U.S. troop commitments to the UN would first have to be approved by both Houses of Congress: "When any such agreement or agreements are negotiated it will be my purpose to ask the Congress for appropriate legislation to approve them."[60]

After the Senate approved the UN Charter, Congress passed legislation spelling out the conditions for U.S. participation in military actions authorized by the Security Council. Section 6 of the UN Participation Act of 1945 provides that agreements "shall be subject to the approval of the Congress by appropriate Act or joint resolution."[61] Truman's pledge and the unambiguous statutory language seemed to nail down a key principle: Any U.S. military action pursuant to a Security Council directive would require joint action by the president and Congress.

Nevertheless, five years later Truman took the country to war in Korea without ever seeking authority from Congress, and legislators offered few objections. How could Truman act militarily in Korea under the UN umbrella without obtaining congressional approval? The short answer is that he did not use the "special agreement" procedure that was the mechanism for assuring congressional control. In fact, no special agreement has ever been entered into by any country.

Truman met with congressional leaders at 11:30 A.M. on June 27, after the administration had already issued the orders for military intervention. In later meetings with congressional leaders, designed to give them briefings on developments in Korea, he never asked for congressional authority. Members of Congress seemed to have no recollection of, or regard for, the legislative history of the UN Charter and the specific language in the UN

Participation Act. One of the few Senators to challenge Truman's initiative was Arthur V. Watkins, Republican of Utah, who reminded his colleagues that during debate on the UN Charter "we were told time and time again . . . that nothing would take us into war under that pact without action by the Congress. The President could not do it."[62] No other Senator developed that point. Instead, Senators deferred to presidential leadership and decisiveness. Typical was the remark by Senator Estes Kefauver (D-Tenn.), who advised that "this is a time to close our ranks, to forget political considerations, and to stand behind the President in the vital decision he has made."[63] He might have added that it was time to forget constitutional, treaty, and statutory considerations. In the House, Representative Vito Marcantonio, a member of the American Labor Party from New York, offered one of the few constitutional critiques of Truman's action.[64]

Senate Majority Leader Scott W. Lucas (D-Ill.) saw no need for a congressional role. When Truman asked congressional leaders on July 3 whether he should present to Congress a joint resolution expressing approval of his action in Korea, Lucas counseled against it. He said that Truman "had very properly done what he had to without consulting the Congress." He told Truman that many legislators had suggested that the president "keep away from Congress and avoid debate." Lucas added that "if there should be a row in Congress that would not help abroad."[65] The fear of speaking with a divided voice meant that Congress would have no voice at all. However, whatever Lucas wanted to say in private or in public could not change the language and intent of the Constitution, the UN Charter, or the UN Participation Act. Lucas had no authority to alter those documents and neither did Truman.

The next step in congressional acquiescence was the Vietnam War. Based on sketchy and inconclusive information about two "attacks" by North Vietnam, Congress passed the Tonkin Gulf Resolution in August 1964. There was not a single dissenting voice in the House, and only two Senators voted against the resolution, which carelessly transferred legislative power to the president by authorizing Lyndon Johnson to take "all necessary measures to repel any armed attack against the forces of the United States and to prevent further aggression." Neither House bothered to conduct independent investigations to verify Johnson's report of the two attacks. It is now well established that the second attack probably never occurred.[66]

Senator Frank F. Church (D-Idaho) acknowledged that independent legislative oversight was often necessary, but not here. He said there is a time "to question the route of the flag, and there is a time to rally around it, lest it be routed. This is the time for the latter course, and in our pursuit of it, a time for all of us to unify."[67] If lawmakers conclude there is no time to debate going to war, Congress becomes a cipher and the president an autocrat. Senator George D. Aiken (R-Vt.) did not believe that a legislator could afford to oppose the president for exercising the power "which we, under our form of government and through our legislative bodies, have delegated to his office."[68]

And yet no statute, and certainly no constitutional provision, had "delegated" the war power to the president. What was at stake was legislative abdication, not delegation.

On the House side, House Majority Leader Carl B. Albert (D-Okla.) urged legislators to set aside party differences and unite behind the president. House Minority Leader Charles Halleck (R-Ind.) offered similar reasons for supporting Johnson.[69] Representative Edwin R. Adair (R-Ind.) dismissed the concern that the Tonkin Gulf Resolution signaled an abdication by Congress of its constitutional duties over war and foreign affairs. Such issues were raised in committee "and we were given assurance that it was the attitude of the Executive that such was not the case, that we are not impairing our congressional prerogatives."[70]

Isn't that remarkable? Members of Congress, concerned that they might be abdicating their constitutional duties, are assured by executive officials that there is no problem. The framers expected the three branches to make independent judgments about their institutional prerogatives. They are not supposed to accept self-serving statements from officials who are in the process of encroaching upon the responsibilities of another branch.

That precise point was made in the National Commitments Resolution, which the Senate passed in 1969 (and has since ignored). In reporting this measure, the Senate Foreign Relations Committee stated that the Tonkin Gulf Resolution represented "the extreme point in the process of constitutional erosion that began in the first years of this century." In adopting the sweeping language of the Tonkin Gulf Resolution, Congress committed the error of "making a *personal* judgment as to how President Johnson would implement the resolution when it had a responsibility to make an *institutional* judgment, first, as to what any President would do with so great an acknowledgment of power, and, second, as to whether, under the Constitution, Congress had the right to grant or concede the authority in question."[71]

The National Commitments Resolution, which passed the Senate by a vote of 70 to 16, stated that a national commitment of U.S. armed forces results "only from affirmative action taken by the executive and legislative branches of the U.S. Government by means of a treaty, statute, or concurrent resolution of both Houses of Congress specifically providing for such commitment."[72] Of course a Senate resolution is not legally binding, but it is binding on the Senate as an institution. Nevertheless, senators have never complied with the language in this resolution. They have repeatedly accepted unilateral presidential military actions that are not sanctioned by treaties, statutes, or concurrent resolutions. The latter form of legislative action has never been legally binding, because they are not presented to the president for his signature or veto, and have little use as a result of the Supreme Court's decision in the legislative veto case of *INS v. Chadha* (1983).

The War Powers Resolution of 1973, enacted over President Nixon's veto, is generally treated as an effort at congressional "reassertion." In fact, by recognizing that the president may use armed force for up to ninety days without seeking or obtaining legislative authority, the resolution sanctions a scope of independent presidential power that would have astonished the framers. According to Section 2(a) of the resolution, the measure is intended to "fulfill the intent of the framers" and to "insure that the collective judgment of both the Congress and the President" will apply to the introduction of U.S. forces to foreign hostilities. The resolution has had no such effect. Instead, it violates the intent of the framers and does not in any sense insure collective judgment. Presidents Reagan, Bush, and Clinton have made repeated use of military force without either seeking or obtaining authority from Congress. The resolution compromised basic institutional and constitutional prerogatives. A few legislators, led by Senator Thomas F. Eagleton (D-Mo.) recognized that the resolution—despite the hype surrounding it—was in fact a legislative sell-out and a surrender to presidential power.[73]

There were only five military operations under Presidents Gerald Ford and Jimmy Carter, and three of those actions were efforts by Ford to evacuate American citizens and foreign nationals from Southeast Asia. The other two uses of military force involved the rescue effort of the *Mayaguez* crew in 1975 and Carter's attempt to rescue American hostages in Iran in 1980. However, military activity accelerated during the Reagan, Bush, and Clinton administrations, and Congress did little to assert its supposedly coequal status.

President Reagan used military force against other countries a number of times: sending troops to Lebanon, invading Grenada, ordering air strikes against Libya, involving the nation in the Iran-Contra affair, and committing U.S. warships to the Persian Gulf in 1987. Not once did Reagan ask Congress for authority, either in advance or afterwards. With regard to Lebanon, Congress called on Reagan to trigger the sixty-to-ninety-day clock of the War Powers Resolution, but he refused. Congress then passed legislation on October 12, 1983, to activate the clock, but instead of limiting military force to ninety days it authorized a period of eighteen months, obviously pushing the Lebanon issue beyond public debate in the 1984 elections. After the death of 241 U.S. Marines in a suicide bombing, Reagan pulled U.S. forces offshore and by March 30, 1984, terminated U.S. involvement. In response to the Grenada invasion, the House passed legislation to trigger the sixty-day clock and the Senate was poised to pass the same legislation. However, the administration's announcement that the operation would be concluded within sixty days prevented final enactment of the legislation.[74]

President George Bush invaded Panama in December 1989. A month later, in an address to Congress, he announced that American troops would be out of Panama by the end of February. Whether consciously or not, he appeared to be restricting himself to the sixty-to-ninety-day clock of the War Powers Resolution.[75] In August 1990, Bush made a larger commitment of U.S. troops, this time to Saudi Arabia after Iraq had invaded Kuwait. By November, Bush had increased the commitment to more than 500,000 troops, changing a defensive maneuver to an offensive capability. At no time did he or any other administration official acknowledge the need to come to Congress for authority to wage war against Iraq. The House Democratic Caucus, voting 177 to 37, adopted a resolution stating that the Constitution required Bush to first seek authorization from Congress.[76]

On January 8, 1991, with military action scheduled for a week away, Bush asked Congress to pass legislation "supporting" the use of American troops against Iraq. The next day he told reporters that he did not need a resolution from Congress. On January 12, Congress authorized Bush to take offensive actions against Iraq. In a separate vote on a nonbinding resolution, the House voted 302 to 131 for this language: "The Congress finds that the Constitution of the United States vests all power to declare war in the Congress of the United States. Any offensive action taken against Iraq must be explicitly approved by the Congress of the United States before such action may be initiated."[77]

In signing the bill, Bush continued to insist that he could have acted without congressional authority, explaining that his request for "congressional support did not, and my signing this resolution does not, constitute any change in the long-standing positions of the executive branch on either the President's constitutional authority to use the Armed Forces to defend vital U.S. interests or the constitutionality of the War Powers Resolution." Regardless of what he said in the signing statement, what governs legally is the language in the bill, not in his signing statement. Congress provided authority, not support.

Compared to military initiatives by Reagan and Bush, Clinton's eight years marked an extraordinary increase in the use of U.S. force against other countries. Clinton launched cruise missiles at Iraq in 1993 and 1996, ordered a four-day bombing in December 1998, and continued air strikes throughout 1999 and 2000. Under Clinton's term, the humanitarian venture started by Bush in Somalia turned into a military effort to remove the Somalia political figure, Mohamed Farah Aideed. Congress used its power of the purse to bring the military operation to a halt. Legislation in 1993 prohibited the use of any funds after March 31, 1994 for the operations of U.S. armed forces in Somalia unless the president requested an extension and received authority from Congress. The legislation permitted the use of funds after the cutoff date to protect American diplomatic facilities and American citizens.[78]

In 1994, Clinton was prepared to invade Haiti until a negotiating team led by former President Jimmy Carter settled the dispute peacefully. During 1993 and 1994, Congress considered a number of measures to restrict Clinton, but none was enacted into law. The legislative language ranged from binding limitations to nonbinding "sense of Congress" expressions. The latter typically gave Clinton total discretion to deploy American troops if he determined that military action was "vital" to U.S. national interests and there was insufficient time to seek and obtain congressional authorization. Legislators announced that Clinton, through his commander-in-chief powers, had full constitutional authority to order the invasion.[79] These legislators evidently interpreted presidential war authority as plenary and subject to no restrictions by the War Powers Resolution.

Clinton repeatedly intervened in the Balkans, using air strikes in 1994 against the Serbs, introducing 20,000 U.S. troops into Bosnia in 1995, and ordering an air war against Yugoslavia in 1999. At no time did he request authority from Congress. Initially he suggested that he would need "authority" from Congress for those operations, but that language was quickly replaced by the need for legislative "support."[80] Members of Congress debated a number of legislative provisions, but most of them were watered down to sense-of-Congress language. On October 20, 1993, the Senate voted 99 to 1 for these words: "It is the sense of Congress that none of the funds appropriated or otherwise made available by this Act should be available for the purposes of deploying U.S. Armed Forces to participate in the implementation of a peace settlement in Bosnia-Herzegovina, unless previously authorized by Congress." That language was later enacted into law, but it had no legally binding effect.[81] It was merely the "sense" of Congress.

In adopting that language, members of Congress demonstrated their awareness and support for constitutional principles, but they were never willing to enforce those principles. Instead, they regularly adopted statutory provisions that left the door totally open to presidential war initiatives. Clinton was satisfied in seeking authority not from Congress but from outside bodies such as the United Nations and NATO. In ordering air strikes against the Serbs in 1994, he announced that he was operating through UN Security Council resolutions and NATO's military command: "The authority under which air strikes can proceed, NATO acting out of area pursuant to UN authority, requires the common agreement of our NATO allies."[82] In other words, Clinton would have to obtain approval from England, France, Italy, and other NATO allies, but not from Congress. Legislators did not challenge his authority to conduct air strikes in Bosnia.

Clinton's decision in 1995 to introduce ground forces into Bosnia provoked legislative action, but once again Congress was unable or unwilling to place checks on presidential power. The Senate debated "sense of the Senate" language to prohibit the use of funds to deploy U.S. troops to Bosnia and Herzegovina unless "Congress approves in advance the deployment of such forces." Not only did this language have no binding effect, but exceptions were made to allow Clinton to deploy U.S. ground forces if needed to evacuate U.S. peacekeeping forces from a "situation of imminent danger, to undertake emergency air rescue operations, or to provide for the airborne delivery of humanitarian supplies."[83] Several senators agreed to support the provision only because it had no force of law.[84]

Senator Paul M. Simon (D-Ill.) explained that he would vote against the amendment, even though it was a sense of the Senate, "because foreign policy cannot be effective if Congress micromanages it." Sending 25,000 ground troops to Bosnia was micromanagement? What could have been a more fundamental issue for Congress, both in wielding the war power and in committing the power of the purse? Senator William S. Cohen (R-Maine) rejected Simon's position, noting that Clinton planned to deploy ground troops "to one of the most hostile regions in the world" and "without having any sort of defined plan presented to us."[85]

The House entered into a prolonged debate on the president's authority to commit ground troops to Bosnia. By a vote of 315 to 103, lawmakers passed a nonbinding resolution that U.S. troops should not be deployed without congressional approval. Ninety-three Democrats—nearly half of those in the House—joined 222 Republicans to support the resolution. As the months rolled by and the language shifted from nonbinding to legally binding, the margin of support declined to 242 to 171. Twelve Republicans voted against the second version. James B. Longley, Jr., a Republican from Maine, said he opposed sending American ground troops to Bosnia but deferred to presidential decisions: "I have to respect the authority of the Commander in Chief to conduct foreign policy. . . . I think there is no greater threat to American lives than a Congress that attempts to micromanage foreign policy. I have told the President that I would respect his authority as Commander in Chief."[86] First, the president's constitutional authority to "conduct foreign policy" does not include taking the nation to war. Second, respect for presidential authority should not be given a higher value than respect for constitutional limits. Third, presidential deployment of ground troops to Bosnia is not an issue of "micromanagement." Fourth, American lives are not threatened when Congress exercises its constitutional war power; they are threatened when presidents put American lives in harm's way.

Senate Majority Leader Robert J. Dole (R-Kans.) announced that Clinton had "the authority and the power under the Constitution to do what he feels should be done regardless of what Congress does."[87] Under this theory, no matter what Congress did in exercising its constitutional powers over war and peace, those legislative actions would be subordinated to what the president "felt" should be done. Congress would have no coequal (much less superior) power. There would be no checks and balance system, no tussling for power. In this substitution of autocracy for constitutional government, congressional challenges to presidential war initiatives became futile and useless. No matter how much lawmakers objected to presidential plans, they would have to swallow their reservations and stand to the side. A handful of senators spoke out in defense of congressional war prerogatives: Robert C. Byrd (D-W.Va.), Russell D. Feingold (D-Wis.), Kay Bailey Hutchison (R-Tex.), James M. Inhofe (R-Okla.), and Jon L. Kyl (R-Ariz.).[88]

What the Senate finally did was to pass a bill providing "support" for American troops in Bosnia but expressing "reservations" about sending them there.[89] If senators thought it was a bad idea sending troops to Bosnia, it would have been consistent to block the deployment. But consistency was not a high value. More important was having it both ways. If things went well, Congress had not stood in the way. If things went poorly, it would be Clinton's fault. Either way there would be no congressional accountability. On the same day as these Senate votes, the House failed by a vote of 210 to 218 to prohibit funds from being used to deploy troops to Bosnia. Clinton was able to send 20,000 troops to Bosnia without any legislative authority.

The next escalation of war was Clinton's decision in 1999 to bomb Yugoslavia. Although Congress was to be given no formal role in the use of force against the Serbs, legislatures in other NATO countries took votes to authorize military action in Yugoslavia. The Italian Parliament had to vote approval for the air strikes. The German Supreme Court ruled that the Bundestag, which had been dissolved with the election that ousted Chancellor Kohl, had to be recalled to approve deployment of German aircraft and troops to Kosovo. The U.S. Congress, supposedly the strongest legislature in the world, was content to watch from the back seat.

On March 11, 1999, the House voted to support U.S. armed forces as part of a NATO *peacekeeping* operation. That vote supported a peace agreement between Serbs and Kosovars, not military action. The Senate's vote on March 23 did support military air operations and missile strikes against Yugoslavia. However, that vote was on a concurrent resolution (S. Con. Res. 21), which passes both chambers but is not presented to the president. It therefore had no legal meaning.

On April 28, after the first month of bombing, the House took a series of votes on the war in Yugoslavia. It voted 249 to 180 to prohibit the use of appropriated funds for the deployment of U.S. ground forces unless first authorized by Congress. A motion to direct the removal of U.S. armed forces from Yugoslavia failed, 139 to 290. A resolution to declare a state of war between the United States and Yugoslavia fell, 2 to 427. A fourth vote, to authorize the air operations and missile strikes, lost on a tie vote, 213 to 213. Newspaper editorials and commentators derided the House of Representatives for taking multiple and supposedly conflicting votes. Nevertheless, the House articulated some basic values. It insisted that Congress authorize the introduction of ground troops and it refused to grant authority for the air strikes.

In contrast to the House, the Senate decided to duck the issue. Senator John S. McCain (R-Ariz.) offered a joint resolution to authorize Clinton to use "all necessary force and other means, in concert with U.S. allies, to accomplish U.S. and North Atlantic Treaty Organization objectives in the Federal Republic of Yugoslavia (Serbia and Montenegro)." That measure was tabled, 78 to 22. A few weeks later the Senate tabled another amendment, this one by Senator Arlen Specter (R-Pa.) to direct the president to seek approval from Congress before introducing ground troops in Yugoslavia. Failure to obtain approval would deny the president funds to conduct the operation. His amendment was tabled, 52 to 48. An amendment by Senator Robert C. Smith

(R-N.H.), to prohibit funding for military operations in Yugoslavia unless Congress enacted specific authorization, was tabled 77 to 21.[90] The Senate might just as well have considered one final motion: "Do we want to exercise our constitutional powers and participate in matters of war?" Tabled, 63 to 37.

OPTIONS FOR GEORGE W. BUSH

George W. Bush faces a number of key choices in the White House. He can accept and implement the big-presidency model adopted by most presidents over the past half century. Certainly he will be surrounded by aides who will urge him to press presidential power to the limit and not concede any territory or authority to Congress. It will be tempting to repeat one of the great constitutional clichés: "I didn't enter office to reduce the constitutional power of the presidency." No doubt presidential machismo—the display of virility—is the dominant model.[91]

Another model, faithful to constitutional principles, is available. It provides a sounder and healthier foundation for the presidency, the country, and world peace. After Truman had taken the nation to war against North Korea, Dwight D. Eisenhower concluded that his action was a serious mistake, both politically and constitutionally. Eisenhower thought that national commitments would be stronger if entered into jointly by both branches. Toward that end he asked Congress for specific authority to deal with national security crises. He stressed the importance of *collective* action by Congress and the president: "I deem it necessary to seek the cooperation of Congress. Only with that cooperation can we give the reassurance needed to deter aggression."[92]

In 1954, when Eisenhower was under pressure to intervene in Indochina to save beleaguered French troops, he refused to act unilaterally. He told reporters at a news conference: "There is going to be no involvement of America in war unless it is a result of the constitutional process that is placed upon Congress to declare it. Now, let us have that clear; and that is the answer."[93] Eisenhower told Secretary of State John Foster Dulles that in "the absence of some kind of arrangement getting support of Congress," it "would be completely unconstitutional & indefensible" to give any assistance to the French.[94]

Eisenhower's respect for constitutional principles is also evident in his handling of the Formosa crisis with China in 1954. A memorandum from Secretary Dulles stated that "it is doubtful that the issue can be exploited without Congressional approval."[95] Eisenhower said that any attack on airfields in China would require "Congressional authorization, since it would be war. If Congressional authorization were not obtained there would be logical grounds for impeachment. Whatever we do must be in a

Constitutional manner."[96] When the situation in the Formosa Straits grew worse in 1955, Eisenhower did not turn for authority to the UN Security Council, as Truman had done. He urged Congress to pass appropriate legislation to authorize presidential action. That legislation, with strong majorities in each House, was enacted.[97]

In his memoirs, Eisenhower explained the choice between invoking executive prerogatives or seeking congressional authorization. On New Year's Day in 1957, he met with Secretary Dulles and congressional leaders of both parties to consider legislation leading to possible military action in the Middle East. House Majority Leader John W. McCormack (D-Mass.) asked Eisenhower whether he, as commander in chief, already possessed authority to carry out actions in the Middle East without waiting for congressional authorization. Eisenhower's reply demonstrates a profound understanding of the constitutional system. He told the congressional leaders that

> greater effect could be had from a consensus of Executive and Legislative opinion, and I spoke earnestly of the desire of the Middle East countries to have reassurance now that the United States would stand ready to help. . . . Near the end of this meeting I reminded the legislators that the Constitution assumes that our two branches of government should get along together.[98]

Eisenhower's understanding of the war power was extremely perceptive. He knew that lawyers and policy advisers in the executive branch could always cite a multitude of precedents to justify unilateral presidential action. It was his seasoned judgment, however, that a commitment by the United States would have much greater impact on allies and enemies alike when it represented the collective judgment of the president and Congress. Singlehanded actions taken by the president, without the support of Congress and the people, can threaten national prestige and undermine the presidency. Eisenhower's position was sound then and it is sound now.

NOTES

1. Louis Fisher, *Congressional Abdication on War and Spending* (College Station, TX: Texas A&M University Press, 2000), p. 8.
2. Max Farrand, ed., *The Records of the Federal Convention of 1787*, vol. 1 (New Haven, CT: Yale University Press, 1937), 64–66.
3. Ibid., vol. 2, p. 318.
4. Ibid., pp. 318–319.
5. Jonathan Elliot, ed., *The Debates in the Several State Conventions on the Adoption of the Federal Convention*, vol. 2 (Washington, D.C.: J. B. Lippincott Co., 1836–1845), p. 528. Similar comments were made by delegates to the North Carolina and South Carolina ratifying conventions. Ibid., vol. 4, pp. 107, 287 (statements by James Iredell and Charles Pinckney).
6. William Michael Treanor, "Fame, the Founding, and the Power to Declare War," *Cornell Law Review* 82 (1997), p. 695.
7. Benjamin Fletcher Wright, ed., *The Federalist* (Cambridge, MA: Harvard University Press, 1961), p. 101.

8. Gaillard Hunt, ed., *The Writings of James Madison*, vol. 6 (New York: G. P. Putnam & Sons, 1900–1910), p. 174.
9. Ibid., p. 312.
10. M. J. Vile, *Constitutionalism and the Separation of Powers* (Oxford: Clarendon Press, 1967), p. 153.
11. Kenneth Culp Davis, *Administrative Law and Government* (St. Paul, MN: West, 1960), p. 54.
12. Wright, ed., *The Federalist*, p. 356.
13. Fisher, *Congressional Abdication of War and Spending*, pp. 15–16.
14. Harold C. Syrett, ed., *The Papers of Alexander Hamilton*, vol. 21 (New York: Columbia University Press, 1974), pp. 461–462 (emphasis in original).
15. James D. Richardson, ed., *A Compilation of the Messages and Papers of the Presidents*, vol. 1 (New York: Bureau of National Literature, 1897–1925), p. 315.
16. Louis Fisher, *Presidential War Power* (Lawrence, KS: University of Kansas Press, 1995), p. 26.
17. *Annals of Congress*, 9th Cong., 1st sess., 1805, p. 19.
18. Richardson, *A Compilation of the Messages and Papers of the Presidents*, vol. 7, p. 3225.
19. *Congressional Globe*, 37th Cong., 1st sess., 1861, p. 393 (Senator Howe).
20. 12 Stat. 326 (1861).
21. *The Prize Cases*, 67 U.S. 635, 660 (1863) (emphasis in original).
22. Edward S. Corwin, "The President's Power," *The New Republic*, 29 January 1951, p. 16.
23. Christopher N. May, *In the Name of War: Judicial Review and the War Powers since 1918* (Cambridge, MA: Harvard University Press, 1989), p. vii.
24. Ibid., pp. 1, 16.
25. Martin S. Sheffer, *The Judicial Development of Presidential War Powers* (Westport, CT: Praeger, 1999), p. ix.
26. Ibid., p. x.
27. 4 Dall. (4 U.S.) 37, 43 (1800) (emphasis in original).
28. 5 U.S. (1 Cranch) 1, 28 (1801) (emphasis added).
29. *Little v. Barreme*, 2 Cr. (6 U.S.) 170, 179 (1804).
30. *United States v. Smith*, 27 Fed. Cas. 1192, 1230 (C.C.N.Y. 1806) (No. 16,342).
31. Ibid.
32. Ibid.
33. *United States v. Brown*, 12 U.S. (8 Cr.) 110 (1814).
34. *Martin v. Mott*, 25 U.S. (12 Wheat.) 19, 28, 30 (1827).
35. *Fleming v. Page*, 50 U.S. (9 How.) 603, 614-15 (1850).
36. *Mitchell v. Harmony*, 54 U.S. (13 How.) 115 (1851).
37. *Jecker v. Montgomery*, 54 U.S. (13 How.) 498, 515 (1852).
38. *Durand v. Hollins*, 8 Fed. Cas. 111 (S.D.N.Y. 1860) (No. 4,186). See also *Perrin v. United States*, 4 Ct. Cl. 543 (1868).
39. 15 Stat. 224, sec. 3 (1868); 22 U.S.C. 1732 (1994).
40. *Ex parte Merryman*, 17 Fed. Cas. 144, 148 (C.C. Md. 1861) (No. 9,487).
41. *Ex parte Benedict*, 3 Fed. Cas. 159 (D.N.Y. 1862) (No. 1,292) (against the President); *Ex parte Field*, 9 Fed. Cas. 1 (C.C. Vt. 1862) (No. 4,761) (for presidential suspensions but against suspensions by the Department of War); *In re Dunn*, 8 Fed. Cas. 93 (S.D.N.Y. 1863) (No. 4,171) (upholding presidential suspensions); *In re Fagan*, 8 Fed. Cas. 947, 949 (D. Mass. 1863) (No. 4,604) (upholding President because of statutory authority).
42. *The Prize Cases*, 67 U.S. (2 Black) 635, 668 (1863).
43. *Dynes v. Hoover*, 61 U.S. (20 How.) 65 (1858); *Ex parte Vallandigham*, 68 U.S. (1 Wall.) 243. (1864); *Ex parte Milligan*, 71 U.S. (4 Wall.) 2 (1966); *Raymond v. Thomas*, 91 U.S. 712 (1876).
44. 71 U.S. (4 Wall.) 475, 499 (1867).
45. Ibid., 485.
46. For example, *United States v. Anderson* 76 U.S. (9 Wall.) 56 (1870); *United States v. Russel* (13 Wall.) 623 (1871); The Protector (12 Wall.) 700 (1872); *Hamilton v. Kentucky Distilleries Co.*, 251 U.S. 146 (1919); *Rupert v. Caffey*, 251 U.S. 264 (1920); *United States v. Standard Brewery*, 251 U.S. 210 (1920); *United States v. Cohen Grocery Co.*, 255 U.S. 81 (1921); *Commercial Trust Co. v. Miller*, 262 U.S. 51 (1923); *U.S. Trust Co. v. Miller*, 262 U.S. 58 (1923); *Ahrenfeldt v. Miller*, 262 U.S. 60 (1923); *Chastleton Corp. v. Sinclair*, 264 U.S. 543 (1924).
47. *Dooley v. United States*, 182 U.S. 222 (1901).
48. *Hijo v. United States*, 194 U.S. 315 (1904).
49. *Ex parte Orozco*, 201 F. 106 (W.D. Tex. 1912), dismissed, 229 U.S. 633 (1913).
50. *United States v. Curtiss-Wright Export Corp.*, 299 U.S. 304 (1936).

51. *United States v. Bethlehem Steel Corp.*, 315 U.S. 289 (1942); *Yakus v. United States*, 321 U.S. 414 (1944); *Bowles v. Willingham*, 321 U.S. 503 (1944); *Lichter v. United States*, 334 U.S. 742 (1948); *Woods v. Miller Co.*, 333 U.S. 138 (1948).

52. *Hirabayashi v. United States*, 320 U.S. 81 (1943); *Yasui v. United States*, 320 U.S. 115 (1943); and *Korematsu v. United States*, 323 U.S. 214 (1944).

53. *Duncan v. Kahanamoku*, 327 U.S. 304 (1946).

54. *Youngstown Co. v. Sawyer*, 343 U.S. 579 (1952).

55. *Public Papers of the Presidents*, 1950, pp. 504, 522.

56. *Weissman v. Metropolitan Life Ins. Co.*, 112 F.Supp. 420, 425 (D. Cal. 1953). See also *Gagliormella v. Metropolitan Life Ins. Co.*, 122 F.Supp. 246, 250 (D. Mass. 1954); *Carius v. New York Life Insurance Co.*, 124 F.Supp. 388, 390 (D. Ill. 1954).

57. *New York Life Ins. Co. v. Durham*, 166 F.2d 874 (10th Cir. 1948); *New York Life Ins. Co. v. Bennion*, 158 F.2d 260, 264 (10th Cir. 1946).

58. Louis Fisher, "Litigating the War Power with *Campbell v. Clinton*," *Presidential Studies Quarterly* 30 (September 2000), pp. 564, 567–569.

59. Ibid., pp. 569–574.

60. 91 *Congressional Record*, 8185 (1945).

61. 59 Stat. 621, sec. 6 (1945).

62. 96 *Congressional Record*, 9233 (1950).

63. Ibid.

64. Ibid., 9268.

65. *Foreign Relations of the United States*, 1950, vol. 7, Korea, H. Doc. No. 82-264, vol. 7, 82d Cong., 1st Sess. (1976), pp. 287–288, 289–290, 291.

66. Fisher, *Congressional Abdication on War and Spending*, p. 54.

67. 110 *Congressional Record* 18421 (1964).

68. Ibid., 18457.

69. Ibid., 18542.

70. Ibid., 18543.

71. S. Rept. No. 129, 91st Cong., 1st (1969), 22–23 (emphasis in original).

72. 115 *Congressional Record*, 17245 (1969).

73. Fisher, *Congressional Abdication on War and Spending*, pp. 65–67; Louis Fisher and David Gray Adler, "The War Powers Resolution: Time to Say Goodbye," *Political Science Quarterly* 113 (1998), pp. 1–20.

74. Fisher, *Congressional Abdication on War and Spending*, p. 69.

75. Ibid., p. 74.

76. *Congressional Quarterly Almanac*, 1990, p. 742.

77. 137 *Congressional Record* 1034, 1049 (1991).

78. 107 Stat. 1476, sec. 8161(b)(B) (1993).

79. Fisher, *Congressional Abdication on War and Spending*, pp. 84–88.

80. Ibid., pp. 89–90.

81. 139 *Congressional Record* 25479, 25485 (1993); 107 Stat. 1474, sec. 8146 (1993).

82. *Public Papers of the Presidents*, 1994, vol. I, p. 186.

83. 141 *Congressional Record* S14634 (daily ed. September 29, 1995).

84. Fisher, *Congressional Abdication on War and Spending*, p. 93.

85. 141 *Congressional Record* S14640 (daily ed. September 29, 1995).

86. Ibid., H13239.

87. Ibid., S17529.

88. Fisher, *Congressional Abdication on War and Spending*, p. 97.

89. 141 *Congressional Record* S18552 (daily ed. December 13, 1995).

90. Fisher, *Congressional Abdication on War and Spending*, pp. 102–103.

91. Alexander DeConde, *Presidential Machismo: Executive Authority, Military Intervention, and Foreign Relations* (Boston: Northeastern University Press, 2000).

92. *Public Papers of the Presidents*, 1957, p. 11.

93. *Public Papers of the Presidents*, 1954, p. 306.

94. *Foreign Relations of the United States* (FRUS), 1952–1954, vol. 13, part 1, p. 1242.

95. Ibid., vol. 14, part 1, p. 611.

96. Ibid., p. 618.

97. 69 Stat. 7 (1955).

98. Dwight D. Eisenhower, *Waging Peace* (Garden City, NY: Doubleday, 1965), p. 179.

2

CONGRESS

HOW SILENT A PARTNER?

JOHN F. STACK, JR. AND COLTON C. CAMPBELL

With the collapse of the Soviet Union and the demise of Cold War anti-communism, U.S. foreign policy now confronts a number of uncertainties in the world at large and in the halls and committee rooms of Congress. The harsh realities of twenty-first-century world politics intruded on American consciousness on September 11, 2001, with the terrorist attacks on the World Trade Center and the Pentagon. The vulnerability of the United States to terrorism opens a new chapter in American foreign policy. Terrorism is not a new phenomenon confronting democratic societies, but the explicitly transnational character of terrorism raises new challenges to the conduct of U.S. foreign policy and the workings of our governing institutions. For many Americans, foreign policy begins at the water's edge. September 11, 2001 forever changes America's perceptions that foreign affairs is a somewhat distant, even abstract, endeavor.

For nearly the past sixty years, presidential dominance was axiomatic in the design and execution of American foreign relations. Congress was cognizant of such unfettered presidential dominance in light of its obligation to control the purse strings and to provide advice and consent.[1] However, increasing legislative concern with the excesses of an imperial presidency, particularly notable during the Johnson and Nixon administrations, culminated in the passage of the War Powers Act (1974) that sought to constrain presidential initiatives in the area of undeclared wars.[2] Congressional action has attempted to chip away at presidential dominance in U.S. foreign affairs. The era of undisputed presidential leadership has evolved into a more complex and fragmented process in which both Congress and the judiciary have weighed into the foreign policy making process. Increasing levels of transnational relations, and unprecedented levels of interdependence, as expressed in reliance on multinational institutions, such as NAFTA and the World Trade Organization, increase Congress's ability to participate in foreign policy at the expense of the presidency.[3]

Lawmakers' preoccupation with domestic affairs, especially constituency concerns and business, has traditionally been the cause for episodic, at times highly selective, congressional intervention in foreign policy, often precipitated by some crisis abroad or by a widely publicized foreign policy debacle.[4] Subsequently, Congress's attention span in foreign affairs was often brief, lacking an overall strategy, and mirroring the decentralized role contemplated by James Madison.[5] With the emergence of the United States as the only full-service superpower, however, new challenges confront the conduct of foreign relations at both institutional and constitutional levels. Legislators increasingly challenge presidential proposals in every area of foreign policy. According to Lee Hamilton, former chair of the House Foreign Affairs Committee, members of Congress "speak out frequently in a cacophony of conflicting voices."[6]

In this chapter we explore the changing parameters of congressional action in foreign policy. The Constitution implicitly requires both competition and cooperation between the legislative and executive branches in this area. Historical patterns and individual attitudes have deviated between conflict and compromise. Congress and the presidency at times work as tandem institutions that need each other's support and active acquiescence to succeed.[7] At other times they compete fiercely, such as when legislators see the executive as contemptuous and arbitrary, if Congress perceives American sovereignty threatened, or when executive officials view Congress as inefficient and intrusive.[8] While the dominant reality is that the president has emerged as the ultimate decider, especially during armed conflict, lawmakers are finding new and creative ways to contribute to, and influence, foreign policy. The classic congressional method for exercising foreign policy prerogatives through legislation is being supplemented by an array of alternative techniques,[9] such as Senate confirmation of ambassadorial nominees, treaty ratification, and the mobilization of ethnic interest groups in pursuit of parochial objectives. At various points, the Supreme Court has affirmed Congress's part in foreign policy making. And, greater congressional activism over the past decade is due to an increase in the number of actors attempting to influence American foreign policy, among them the rise of ethnic lobbies.

FOREIGN POLICY UNDER THE CONSTITUTION

Congress has an arsenal of explicit constitutional duties, such as the power to declare war, to regulate foreign commerce, and to raise and support military forces. The president's explicit international powers are to serve as commander in chief, to negotiate treaties and appoint ambassadors, provided two-thirds of the Senate concurs, and to receive other nations' representatives. In short, the Constitution invites both ends of Pennsylvania Avenue to participate in the foreign policy making process.[10] Members' constituency interests, policy preferences, and ideological or institutional dispositions, as well as the impact of public opinion and partisan politics are also important variables that define the contours of the struggle between Congress and the presidency in foreign policy.

Contemporary presidential power in foreign affairs is often seen as near limitless, in part because of the rise of the modern, post–World War II administrative state with its emphasis on national security bureaucracies, which has propelled the executive branch to the forefront of foreign policy making. But such development of the modern presidency would likely surprise our founders. As James Madison observed in *Federalist No. 51*, "In republican government, the legislative authority necessarily predominates."[11]

THE ROOTS OF PRESIDENTIAL POWER IN FOREIGN POLICY

The story of American foreign policy in modern times is how presidents have sought to enhance their ability to make foreign policy, with Congress attempting to curb such presidential prerogatives, and with the Supreme Court frequently being asked to arbitrate the differences. For President Theodore Roosevelt this extended to "anything not expressly forbidden, so long as it serves the public interest and does not conflict with existing legislation."[12] His oft-quoted maxim, "speak softly but carry a big stick," illustrated a growing concern about America's role in foreign policy. Alternatively, Chief Justice William Howard Taft (himself the twenty-seventh U.S. president) maintained that the president's inherent powers must be linked and traceable to constitutional powers or legislation.[13]

Beginning in *Missouri v. Holland* (1920) the court considered a Tenth Amendment claim by the state of Missouri to halt enforcement of a treaty between the United States and Great Britain (1916) protecting migrating birds between Canada and the United States.[14] In striking down Missouri's claim, Justice Oliver Wendell Holmes conceptualized the treaty-making power in the following terms: "Here a national interest of very nearly the first magnitude is involved. It can be protected only by national action in concert with that of another power."

Executive agreements are entered into by the president without the advice and consent of the Senate. The court examined the constitutionality of unilateral executive agreements in foreign relations in *United States v. Belmont* (1937).[15] As part of the president's recognition of the Soviet Union in 1933 (the United States had terminated diplomatic relations following the Soviet revolution in 1917, confiscating the assets of the Russian state), it was agreed that frozen assets of the United States and the former Russian state would be transferred. A private New York bank contended that the location (*situs*) of its assets within New York state defeated the ability of the president to assign those assets to another party via an executive agreement. The court held that President Franklin D. Roosevelt possessed the ability to transfer Russian assets to the newly recognized Soviet state under the Constitution. "Governmental power over internal affairs," stated Justice Sutherland, "is distributed between the national government and the several states. Governmental power over external affairs is not distributed, but is *vested exclusively in the national government . . . the executive had the authority to speak as the sole organ of that government.*" (italics added for emphasis)

Perhaps the most expansive reading of presidential power in foreign affairs was decided in *United States v. Curtiss-Wright Export Corp.* (1936).[16] In an effort to halt a war between Paraguay and Bolivia over the disputed Chaco region, Congress passed a joint resolution in 1934 empowering the president to stop the sale of armaments by American manufacturers to these countries. President Roosevelt issued an order that prohibited the sale of arms and charged the Secretary of State with its enforcement. The embargo was then rescinded by the president eighteen months later. Following a federal indictment, Curtiss-Wright Corporation was charged with conspiracy to sell fifteen machine guns to Bolivia during the embargo. Curtiss-Wright maintained that Congress illegally delegated its lawmaking authority to the president. The court dismissed the separation of powers claim upholding the powers of the presidency in the area of foreign policy. "The powers to declare and wage war, to conclude peace, to make treaties, to maintain diplomatic relations with other sovereignties, if they had never been mentioned in the Constitution, would have vested in the federal government as necessary concomitants of nationality," declared Justice Sutherland. "In the vast external realm with its important, complicated, delicate and manifold problems, the President alone has the power to speak or listen as a representative of the nation. He *makes* treaties with the advice and consent of the Senate; but he alone negotiates. Into the field of negotiation the Senate cannot intrude; and Congress itself is powerless to invade. . . ."

THE PARAMETERS OF PRESIDENTIAL POWER

Notwithstanding a number of landmark decisions and presidential claims to either inherent or express power in foreign affairs, the Supreme Court has balked at ceding limitless lawmaking power to the executive even during a crisis that seemingly posed a fundamental threat to U.S. national security. There is, perhaps, no better illustration of the collision between asserted presidential primacy in foreign affairs and the ability of Congress to legislate during a period of crisis than in the 1952 case of *Youngstown Sheet & Tube Co. v. Sawyer.*[17] In 1946, Congress, over President Harry S Truman's veto, enacted the Taft-Hartley Act, authorizing the president to impose a cooling-off period of eighty days to avert a strike that seriously threatened the public interest. *Youngstown Sheet & Tube* (the *Steel Seizure Case*) came about six years later, during the Korean conflict, after Truman disregarded Taft-Hartley and ordered his secretary of commerce to seize the nation's steel mills in order to guarantee the continuing production of steel, an essential component of all weapons and other war materials. President Truman asserted his right to take such emergency action based on his inherent powers as chief executive and commander in chief. He claimed that the nation could ill afford any disruption to the flow of military supplies to Korea.[18] By this time, Truman had sent American ground troops to Korea as part of a United Nations effort to contain the North Korean invasion. The steel-seizure directive was the latest in a line of executive orders by the president that drew their justification from his earlier declaration that the Korean conflict had created a national state of emergency and therefore supported bold presidential action.[19]

Mill owners were furious. Although they went along with the order, they filed suit in federal court contesting the president's action. Charging that the seizure was unauthorized by Congress or any other provision of the Constitution, the steel companies asked the court to invalidate the seizure and to prevent enforcement of the executive branch's orders in this matter. Voting 6 to 3 the Supreme Court drew a firm line on the exercise of executive prerogative in the domestic sphere.[20] Rejecting the contention that the president's power could be implied from the "aggregate of his powers under the Constitution," the high bench held that "the order cannot properly be sustained as an exercise of the President's military power as Commander in Chief of the Armed Forces."[21] Despite the administration's reliance on the concept that broad powers flow to military commanders engaged in an ongoing theater of war (the American steel industry was construed as part of that theater of war), the court concluded: "We cannot with faithfulness to our constitutional system hold that the Commander in Chief of the Armed Forces has the ultimate power as such to take possession of private property in order to keep labor disputes from stopping production. This is a job for the Nation's lawmakers, not for its military authorities."[22] The Supreme Court also stated that constitutional provisions granting the president executive power could not sustain his order to seize steel mills. In short, a president's power to see that laws are faithfully executed disputes the idea that he is a lawmaker; that is, he is to execute the law not make it.[23] "The President might act in external affairs without congressional authority," remarked Associate Justice Robert Jackson, "but not that he might act contrary to an act of Congress."[24]

Justice Jackson best characterized the fluctuating nature of presidential and legislative power under the Constitution in the area of foreign affairs in his concurring opinion. Recognizing how the Constitution purposefully diffuses power between the two branches, Jackson noted: "It enjoins upon its branches separateness but interdependence, autonomy but reciprocity. Presidential powers are not fixed but fluctuate depending upon their disjunction or conjunction with those of Congress."[25] Jackson then articulated three situations in which presidential authority in foreign affairs could be analyzed, beginning with the president's maximum authority. In the first instance, presidential authority is at its highest point when the president "acts pursuant to an expressed or implied authorization of Congress." Presidential action combines the authority that the chief executive possesses under the Constitution and all the authority that Congress can delegate. For Jackson, in this case and only in this case, the president or presidential action personifies "federal sovereignty."[26]

In the second case, should the president act without "either a congressional grant or denial of authority," he relies only upon his independent powers. Jackson described this situation as "a zone of twilight" where the president and lawmakers may have "concurrent authority" or when the distribution of authority between the two branches is uncertain. Here congressional "inertia, indifference or quiescence may . . . enable, if not invite, measures on independent presidential responsibilities."[27] For Jackson an assessment of presidential or congressional power in this scenario relies upon the force of events rather than on legal theories.

In the third example, assertions of presidential power absent the "expressed or implied will of Congress" find themselves at their weakest because the president must only depend upon "his own constitutional powers minus any constitutional powers of Congress over the matter."[28] The judiciary can buttress such presidential powers only at the expense of congressional will. In this last situation, Justice Jackson argued that presidential power must be carefully reviewed because the constitutional "equilibrium" of the system is at stake.

This was precisely the situation that the court confronted in President Truman's decision to seize the steel industry. Even the assertion of inherent presidential powers in the area of foreign affairs could not stand in the face of constitutionally enacted legislation (the Taft-Hartley Act). Here the claim of presidential prerogative in an emergency situation characterized by the commander in chief as an "extended theater of war" could not pass constitutional muster.

In later years, other Supreme Court decisions reaffirmed that presidential power in foreign affairs is not unlimited. At the height of the Watergate crisis, President Richard M. Nixon refused to forward tape recordings subpoenaed by the Special Watergate Prosecutor. A unanimous Supreme Court in *United States v. Nixon* (1974) ordered the president to turn over the tape recordings. Presidential claims to executive privilege could not stand when the president of the United States was an unindicted coconspirator in an ongoing criminal investigation, notwithstanding the claim that a lack of confidentially of presidential discussions or conversations would weaken the chief executive's ability to conduct foreign affairs. The court concluded that since the transcripts of the tapes were to be reviewed *in camera* (i.e., in secret within the judge's chambers with only counsel present) national security would not be compromised.[29] To do otherwise would elevate the president's status, based on claims of executive privilege, above the constitutionally mandated separation of powers doctrine. Moreover, it would enable the president to stand outside of the legal process.

Presidential power in foreign affairs has been defined negatively, not in terms of the doctrine articulated by the court but how history has treated the application of two infamous decisions. During the Second World War, the court permitted curfews to be applied to Japanese Americans, and later, allowed military authorities to relocate Japanese Americans to detention centers. In 1942 Congress approved President Roosevelt's Executive Order 9066, authorizing the Secretary of War or any designated commander to establish curfews and "relocation centers" as central to the prosecution of America's war effort with Japan. In *Hirabayashi v. United States* (1943), a unanimous court held that the 1942 executive order was not an unconstitutional delegation of legislative power to the chief executive and relied upon the president's war powers.[30] A year later, the court in a 6 to 3 opinion upheld the conviction of a Japanese-American man who refused to relocate to a detention center in *Korematsu v. United States*.[31] Justice Robert Jackson's passionate dissent became famous with time in part because of his belief that the court validated a ". . . principle of racial discrimination in criminal procedure and of transplanting American citizens." Jackson predicted that, "The principle then lies about like a loaded weapon ready for the hand of any authority that can bring forward a plausible claim of an urgent need." During the high point of anticommunist fever in 1950, Congress enacted the Emergency Detention Act, 64 Stat. 1019, of Title II of the Internal Security Act of 1950, empowering the president in a self-proclaimed internal security emergency to detain persons where there are reasonable grounds to believe that such persons would engage in espionage or sabotage.[32] In 1967, the House Un-American Affairs Committee called for the establishment of camps for "certain" persons arrested in urban riots.[33] Congress repealed the Emergency Detention Act in 1971.[34]

The precedential value of both *Hirabayashi* and *Korematsu* have been compromised by time and history. In 1988, President Ronald Reagan signed legislation that offered a formal apology to Japanese Americans who had been held in detention camps during the Second World War as well as providing for limited financial reparations.[35] The overt race-based determinism of these cases has been repudiated by the passage of time.

CHALLENGING THE POWER OF APPOINTMENT

Although the court, in *Marbury v. Madison* (1803), held that the power to appoint executive officials resides solely with the president, the exercise of this power has evolved through a combination of informal custom, constitutional mandates, and laws passed by Congress.[36] Presidents have historically claimed not only their explicit powers but those not spelled out in the Constitution to expand presidential leverage in matters abroad. Whether they are called implied, inherent, or emergency powers, presidents have used them to conduct foreign policy in part because of the innate advantages of the executive office. As John Jay wrote in *Federalist No. 64*, the office's unity, its superior information sources, and its capacity for secrecy and dispatch give the president daily charge of foreign intercourse.[37] And before he became chief justice, John Marshall commented: "The president is the sole organ of the nation in its external relations, and its sole representative with foreign nations."[38] But in the expectation that Congress would be a deliberative body, the founders gave the legislative branch a set of special policy prerogatives in foreign policy, granting senators the power to ratify treaties and to confirm the appointment of ambassadors. A wise and stable Senate, the founders believed, would guard the nation's reputation in foreign affairs. Along with other provisions, these powers placed the Senate in a unique position to "exercise an extra increment of influence over the executive branch."[39]

In recent years, the area of presidential appointments to ambassadorial positions has been a contentious battleground between Congress and the presidency over foreign policy making. No ambassador can represent the United States abroad without having been confirmed by a majority vote of the Senate. Before 1994 congressional cooperation in appointments was more the rule than the exception.[40] Rising partisanship has shaped the appointment process, however. Some senators routinely take advantage of their leverage to foil presidential nominations if they consider the nominees are out of step with existing congressional majorities.[41] Others regard advice and consent not as a mere formality but as an important constitutional weapon guarding the independence of Congress from the executive branch.[42]

A high level of confirmation success can be found with presidential nominations for ambassadorial positions. Table 2.1 (on page 30) indicates that between 1987 to 1996, 91 percent of the persons named to ambassadorial positions were confirmed by the Senate. Of the fifty-four not confirmed (about 9 percent of the total), thirty-seven had no hearings on their nominations. Many of these were instances in which the nomination was submitted late in the session or in which consideration was delayed for other reasons.[43]

In the uncommon tactic of "hostage taking," however, senators may place all designees on hold in order to extract concessions from the president. For example, in 1995, Senator Jesse Helms (R-N.C.), then chairman of the Senate Foreign Relations Committee, sponsored legislation to consolidate three foreign policy agencies—the Agency for International Development (AID), the Arms Control and Disarmament Agency (ACDA), and the U.S. Information Agency (USIA)—within the State Department in order to downsize their operations. The Clinton administration was internally divided over the reorganization proposal. Although certain key figures in the White House and State Department favored consolidation, the affected agencies and their allies fiercely opposed the idea. Particularly vocal was AID administrator J. Brian Atwood, a close friend of President Clinton.

Ambassadorial nominations were bottled up during much of the first session of the 104th Congress (1995–1997) by the standoff, as Senator Helms placed holds on nominations (and on other actions, such as the START II treaty

TABLE 2.1   SENATE ACTION ON AMBASSADORIAL NOMINEES, 1987–1997

	100TH CONGRESS 1987–1989	101ST CONGRESS 1989–1991	102ND CONGRESS 1991–1993	103RD CONGRESS 1993–1995	104TH CONGRESS 1995–1997	TOTAL
Total Nominations	91	145	124	152	106	618
Those Confirmed	82	137	102	148	95	564
With Hearings	73	133	100	148	93	547
Without Hearings	9	4	2	0	2	17
Those Not Confirmed	9	8	22	4	11	54
With Hearings	3	3	3	2	6	17
Without Hearings	3	1	10	1	1	16
Submitted in Last Months of Session	2					
Without Hearings, Submitted Earlier	3	4	9	1	4	21
Those Not Confirmed Who Were Confirmed in Next Congress	4	2	11	1	7	25
Hearings in Prior Congress	0	2	1	0	6	9
No Hearings in Prior Congress	4	0	10	1	1	16
Those Not Confirmed Who Were Not Confirmed Later	5	6	11	3	4	29
With Hearings	3	1	2	2	0	8
Without Hearings	2	5	9	1	4	21

Source: Adapted from Jonathan Sanford, *Senate Disposition of Ambassadorial Nominations, 1987–1996*, Congressional Research Service Report No. 97-864 F, September 19, 1997.

and the Chemical Weapons Convention) to sidetrack them from being considered on the Senate floor. At one point 15 percent of all U.S. embassies worldwide were left without new ambassadors.[44] The deadlock ended in 1997 when the administration, apparently in capitulation, offered its own foreign agencies reorganization scheme. Atwood himself was denied an ambassadorial position for his spirited defense of AID. After announcing his resignation from AID and being nominated by Clinton as ambassador to Brazil, he asked in May 1999 that his name be withdrawn after it became apparent Chairman Helms and the Foreign Relations Committee would not act on it.

In 1997 Helms defied a majority of the committee and a majority of Senate members by exercising his prerogative as chair to scuttle the nomination of William F. Weld to be ambassador to Mexico. Helms indicated that he denied a hearing on Weld's nomination so that his power as chairman would not be violated. Some senators suggested that he was acting out of both a bruised ego and a belief that Weld would be an unfit envoy, especially to any country with a substantial drug problem. Helms maintained there was adequate precedent to justify his refusal to allow a hearing on Weld's nomination.

Chairman Helms and the Clinton administration clashed again over the October 1997 nomination of James Hormel as ambassador to Luxembourg. Hormel's status—heir to a meatpacking fortune, prominent philanthropist, and political contributor—might have made him an obvious choice for such an honorific noncareer posting. But Hormel was also an openly gay man who had contributed an important collection of gay and lesbian literature to the San Francisco Public Library. Several conservative senators placed holds on Hormel's nomination on the pretext that his lifestyle would be offensive to Luxembourg's overwhelmingly Catholic populace.

The conflict escalated when Clinton appointed Hormel to the Luxembourg post during Congress's 1999 Memorial Day recess. "President Clinton has shown contempt for the Congress and the Constitution," fumed Senator James M. Inhofe (R-Okla.), leader of the opponents. "He has treated the Senate confirmation process as little more than a nuisance which he can circumvent whenever he wants to impose his will on the country."[45] To back up his words, Inhofe placed holds on seven judicial and foreign affairs nominations awaiting floor action. There was even a possibility that the high-priority nomination of Lawrence Summers as Treasury Secretary could be held up.

Responding to Inhofe's actions, Democratic leader Tom Daschle (S.D.) threatened to block committee hearings and slow down the GOP legislative agenda until the nominations were allowed to move forward. Daschle warned that his reprisal would include "all of the options available to us, including refusing to allow committees to meet, including stopping legislation."[46] He termed the blanket holds unprecedented and dismissed Republicans' suggestion that Inhofe was merely repeating a tactic used by then–Majority Leader Robert C. Byrd (D-W.Va.) during a 1995 impasse over judicial nominations.

Clearly the war over nominations had gotten out of hand. The Hormel fracas came at the same time as a long-running battle over such foreign policy nominees as Atwood and UN ambassador–designee Richard Holbrooke. Then–Majority Leader Trent C. Lott (R-Miss.) signaled his displeasure with the situation by suggesting that blanket holds might not be sustained. Under pressure from several quarters, Inhofe then claimed his actions were not due so much to Hormel's sexuality as to Clinton's precipitous action. The full episode seemed to be resolved by an exchange of letters between the White House and Senator Lott. President Clinton reportedly promised to reinstate the custom of giving the Senate prior warning of his intention to make a recess appointment, thus presumably providing senators the chance to act on the nomination in question.

ADVICE AND CONSENT AND THE TREATY-MAKING PROCESS

Legislators provide the president and other executive officials with informal advice, and this advice sometimes proves decisive.[47] The precise meaning of Congress's duty to advise and consent in the making of foreign treaties is imprecise.[48] Practically, however, the Senate unambiguously defined its role in the summer of 1789 when President George Washington appeared at the doorway of the Senate seeking the members' advice in person concerning a treaty with southern Indians. The episode was recounted by Anti-Administration Senator William Maclay of Pennsylvania in his celebrated *Journal*. Not too dissimilar from today, there was a great deal of discussion, after which someone proposed that the matter be referred to a committee. In Maclay's words:

> As I sat down the President of the United States started up in a Violent fret. This defeats every purpose of my coming here, were the first words he said, he then went on that he had brought his Secretary at War with him to give every necessary information, that the Secretary knew all about the Business— and yet he was delayed and could not go on with the Matter—he cooled however by degrees. . . . We waited for him to withdraw, he did so with a discontented Air. . . . the President wishes to tread on the Necks of the Senate. He wishes Us to see with the Eyes and hear with the ears of his Secretary only, the Secretary to advance the Premises the President to draw Conclusion. and to bear down our deliberations with his personal Authority & Presence, form only will be left for Us—This will not do with Americans. but let the Matter Work it will soon cure itself.[49]

Washington got the answers he sought when he returned the following week, at which time, as Maclay noted, his disposition was deferential: "The President wore a different aspect from What he did Saturday he was placid and Serene. and manifested a Spirit of Accomodation, declared his consent."[50]

Senators routinely advise the president on treaties, which provide a history of U.S. foreign policy.[51] The Treaty of Ghent with Great Britain in 1814, for example, arranged for settlement of issues after the War of 1812. In the Treaty of Paris of 1898, Spain ceded Puerto Rico, Guam, and the Philippines to the United States. The Hay-Pauncefote Treaty of 1901 gave the United States the right to build a canal across the Isthmus of Panama, and the Panama Canal Treaty of 1977 returned total control of the canal to Panama after December 31, 1999.

Rarely does the Senate reject a treaty outright. Since 1789, it has turned down only nineteen treaties. More often the Senate attaches reservations (qualifications that change obligations under the treaty), understandings (an interpretation or elaboration clarifying the treaty), and declarations, provisos, or other statements (statements of policy relating to the subject of a treaty but not necessarily affecting its provisions); amends it (changes in the text of a treaty); or simply allows it to languish.[52] Generally, scores of treaties negotiated by various presidents languish without Senate approval.[53]

On a few occasions the Senate has rejected major treaties to force changes in international agreements brokered by presidents. The most notable example was the 1919 Treaty of Versailles. President Woodrow Wilson departed for the Paris peace conference without seeking the advice of senators from either party; once there he insisted that his proposal for a League of Nations be incorporated into the peace settlement. This tactic was to prevent the inevitable outcry that would go up in Allied nations if the original draft was softened in response to German complaints.[54] For Wilson it seemed ridiculous to communicate a draft to senators only to present another draft a month later with the request that the Senate disremember the first one.[55] Criticism surfaced immediately, however. Many senators warned the president against including the League provision in the treaty. During floor deliberation several senators voiced opposition to weakening the Monroe Doctrine, taking away from Congress its constitutional power to declare war, or to permit international control over such matters as immigration.

When Wilson submitted the treaty to the Senate he announced that he was ready to confer with the members and provide them such information as he had. But when nearly a week went by with no response to the invitation, he reluctantly summoned individual senators to the White House for conferences.[56] Thirty-nine Republican senators, more than the one-third necessary to defeat the treaty, declared that the League was unacceptable. Although some opponents would have preferred to defeat the treaty outright, a majority pressed for a series of reservations aimed at protecting U.S. sovereignty.

Compounding the problem was the Foreign Relations Committee, a traditional graveyard of many presidential hopes. The committee's newly anointed chair, Republican Senator Henry Cabot Lodge of Massachusetts, went to great lengths to seat new members of his committee who were not too kindly disposed toward the League. Four appointed Republican lawmakers were all at least strong reservationists, with two of them among the most active opponents. Lodge held a series of public hearings ostensibly for the edification of senators, but primarily to consume time and delay the treaty unduly.

The Senate eventually added several "reservations" that were strongly opposed by the president. Spurning compromise, Wilson set out on an extensive speaking tour to mobilize popular support for the treaty. Not to be outdone, senators opposed to the pact organized a "truth squad" that trailed the president and rebutted his arguments.[57] As it turned out, Wilson's tour was a disastrous blunder. He suffered a stroke from which he never fully recovered. In the end Wilson requested his supporters in the Senate to vote against the final resolution of ratification, believing the reservations nullified rather than ratified the Covenant.[58] The treaty finally failed along party lines by voice vote, 49 in favor to 35 opposed, falling short of the required two-thirds majority.

As with previous presidents, Wilson experienced the unique conditions that the Senate's constitutional powers impose upon treaty making, and senators did not hesitate to inform him. The hostile attitude toward the advances made by Wilson was not so much displeasure at his failure to keep the Senate informed with the negotiations, nor disapproval of the treaty that had been negotiated. Rather, it was a reflection of the Senate's traditional stiffness and jealousy in insisting upon exercising an entirely independent judgment upon foreign relations and placing its individual stamp upon every important treaty that is negotiated.[59]

An even more abrupt rejection came in 1997 when President Clinton submitted the Comprehensive Test Ban Treaty (CTBT). Following two years of sparring between the White House and treaty opponents, Senate GOP leaders suddenly scheduled brief committee hearings and an equally short floor debate. In the October 1999 vote, CTBT failed to muster even a majority—48 to 51—much less the necessary two-thirds.

In the twilight of his presidency, President Clinton signed a treaty not yet ratified by the Senate that would create the first permanent international court designed to try people accused of genocide, war crimes, and other offenses against humanity. Several Republican lawmakers denounced the administration's action. "This decision will not stand," said then–Senate Foreign Relations Committee Chair Jesse Helms. "I will make reversing this decision, and protecting America's fighting men and women from the jurisdiction of this international kangaroo court, one of my highest priorities in the new Congress."[60] Helms and others opposed the creation of the permanent International Criminal Court under the auspices of the United Nations because they believed its powers were too extensive, and could subject American citizens to trial without allowing them the rights and protections normally guaranteed to them by the Constitution.

Modern chief executives must usually inform the Senate during the process of negotiating a major treaty, often appointing key senators as "observers" to monitor the process,[61] or Senate leaders provide presidents with informal advice.[62] Presidents have a variety of choices available to influence their effectiveness with the Senate. They find supporters on Capitol Hill even when they are opposed by a majority of either chamber. Both branches pursue support for their policy preferences from each other and from outside allies. Their relationship requires that the president engage in a continual process of legislative coalition building, a task made easier or harder, depending on the nature of the institutional environment, the contour of political forces, and the substantive character of the treaty on the nation's agenda.[63]

Although the personal legislative skills of presidents are relevant, many factors lead to variations in legislative success or failure with the Senate regarding treaties. Senators' constituency interests, policy preferences, and ideological or institutional dispositions, as well as public opinion and the number of partisan seats in the Senate, are important in shaping senatorial outcomes. As a result, White House liaison activities with the Senate, patronage services, and public appeals for support are some of the ways used by presidents to enhance their bargaining power with senators over treaty negotiations.

Somewhat less contentious and generally more productive than the recent conflicts over the president's appointment power and the Senate's power to approve treaties is congressional involvement in issues of foreign trade. The goal of trade liberalization, the process of lowering tariff barriers among countries, was a central tenet of post–World War II foreign policy involving both ends of Pennsylvania Avenue. As trade issues have become more complex under multinational negotiating frameworks and the stakes and number of "players" have increased domestically, the executive branch and Congress have generally worked out a way of doing business balancing domestic attempts to protect local industries with the needs to formulate long-term trade policies designed to benefit the United States and its principal trading partners. Central to such relations is the understanding of the importance of trade among overlapping political, military, and economic objectives.

The complexity and high stakes nature of trade policy reverberates throughout the halls of the Capitol as it does throughout the executive branch. The Cold War may well have increased the power of the modern presidency, but it did not truncate Congress's role as a full partner in setting trade policy. Indeed, with the end of the Cold War, the politics of trade has become all the more significant. Article 1, Section 8[3] of the Constitution gives Congress the power to regulate trade with foreign countries, the so-called Foreign Commerce Clause: "To regulate Commerce with Foreign Nations, and among the several States, and with the Indian Tribes."

Multiple constituencies involved in establishing American military and economic objectives converged, together setting America's post–World War II course. These included the Marshall Plan (1947), the establishment of the North Atlantic Treaty Organization (NATO) in 1949, the Bretton Woods Agreement (1946) setting up the global economic system through the International Monetary Fund (IMF), the World Bank (also known as the International Bank for Reconstruction and Development, IBRD), and the General Agreement on Tariff and Trade (GATT). Established in 1947, GATT is perhaps the least well known of the major postwar institutions, but it was central in designing a system to implement American trade policy throughout the world. Each of the postwar organizations advanced political, military, and economic goals simultaneously and sometimes in conflict with one another.

As the world's wealthiest country facing the Soviet Union as a fundamental ideological, military, and political adversary, the United States used economic incentives strategically as a way of rebuilding and strengthening allies in Western Europe and Japan against Communist upheaval. The Marshall Plan pumped in more than $17 billion to help stabilize Western European allies.[64] Initially, the United States protected European and Japanese economic sectors from direct competition with the United States, based on the belief that Europe and Japan would prove to be important markets for American goods. Cold War anticommunist policies in the United States also emphasized that only economically viable states could stave off internal Soviet-sponsored subversion. With the Bretton Woods economic system, the American dollar became the world's currency, providing American goods, companies, and economic activities with a huge global reach throughout the 1950s and 1960s.

The attempt to create a free-trade system based on membership in a multilateral organization (the General Agreement on Tariff and Trade) and through the systematic lowering of duties and tariff barriers across state lines was believed to be the most efficient way to expand American markets, strengthen the economies of dozens of countries, and marginalize the Soviet Union. Thus, GATT constituted "the cornerstone" of the U.S. attempt to establish a liberal trading framework in the postwar period.[65] The GATT treaty was successful in reducing trade barriers based on the "most favored nation" (MFN) principle. Most Favored Nation status held that "tariff preferences granted to one nation must be granted to all other nations exporting the same product."[66] Trade barriers were successfully lowered through GATT in a series of complex negotiations from the late 1940s through the 1980s.

Congress enacted three major laws that empowered the president to enter into successive negotiating session "rounds" under the GATT framework: The Trade Expansion Act of 1962 established the parameters for the Kennedy round of negotiations; the Trade Act of 1974 was followed by the Toyko round; and the Omnibus Trade and Competitiveness Act of 1988 permitted the United States to enter the Uruguay round.[67] The Trade Act of 1974 sought to recapture congressional control previously delegated to the president and trade representatives who negotiated trade reductions under the GATT framework. It mandated the presidents to ". . . actively consult, notify, and involve Congress as they negotiate trade agreements."[68] Congress also insisted that the negotiated agreements would come into force only after Congress passed an implementing bill based on Congress' expedited review including limits on debate and no amendments to the legislation.[69] The "Fast Track" procedure was a compromise between Congress's demand for greater accountability in trade policy making clearly affecting multiple congressional interests yet permitting complex multilateral trade negotiations to move forward—a clear recognition of the role of trade in the conduct of both U.S. domestic and foreign affairs. The Omnibus Trade and Competitiveness Act of 1998 heightened presidential accountability to Congress in this area.

The United States sought to modernize GATT during the Uruguay round resulting in the establishment of the World Trade Organization. The WTO seeks to extend GATT's reach to include "products, sectors, and conditions of trade" inadequately addressed by GATT.[70] A central dimension of the WTO is the binding character of its "dispute resolution system." The WTO judicial system that is binding on the legal systems of member countries raises additional issues of the nature of sovereignty. The Clinton administration launched a number of trade initiatives with Japan and the European Community (now the European Union, EU) to end discrimination against U.S. companies, underscoring the difficulty of pushing forward a trade agenda absent the enormous power of the United States during the height of the Cold War.[71] The administration embraced the establishment of the North American Free Trade Agreement (NAFTA) in 1993 between Canada, Mexico, and the United States, in part because of the need to create larger markets, illustrating the heightening power of the European Union and Japan as major trading blocs. The fight to establish NAFTA also illustrates the complex yet overlapping multiple agendas of the White House and members of Congress. A bipartisan effort resulted in NAFTA's approval by Congress with only 40 percent of Democratic lawmakers supporting the White House, although the legislation passed easily in the Senate.[72] Increasing tensions between Capitol Hill and the White House resulted in the refusal of Congress to grant the Clinton administration fast-track provisions in 1998, underscoring lawmakers' increasing oversight in the area of trade policy.

THE RISE OF ETHNIC LOBBIES

The formulation, implementation, and evaluation of foreign affairs are the product of national politics. When stripped to its essence, foreign policy is a mechanism to ensure the survival and success of a nation's goals and objectives. As such, the insertion of specific group interests based on culture, national origins, language, history, or race was viewed as illegitimate throughout much of the nineteenth and twentieth centuries. American national culture tolerated ethnicity because immigrants provided the human capital necessary to build the nation's industrial economy. During times of economic crises, anti-immigrant and anti-ethnic sentiments surged forward. In times of economic growth and international stability, acceptance of ethnic diversity tended to rise. Under the very best circumstances, however, the predominantly Anglo-Saxon American leaders were ambivalent about America's increasing ethnic diversity.

National concerns with the increasing diversity of the ethnic composition of newcomers culminated in the immigrant restriction legislation of the nineteenth century, leading to the passage of the 1924 Johnson Act, ending unrestricted European immigration into the United States. The United States demanded loyalty from its citizens in order to survive as a viable nation, and "hyphenated Americans"—representing Americans of Jewish, Italian, German, Arab, Greek, Irish, and Armenian descent, and those with ancestry of the so-called Captive European Nations—represented disloyalty and danger to the national interest.[73] This "Americanization" movement forced schoolchildren to learn English and forsake foreign ways in culture, appearance, and demeanor. Despite the pressures to conform to American values and forsake the cultures, languages, and religions of the homeland, ethnic identity continued to persist in the United States for the descendants of immigrants. American culture thus transformed immigrants into Americans, but the form and content of Americanism—at home and abroad—was also defined by ethnicity.

In the immediate period following the Second World War, ethnic groups exercised limited influence in American foreign policy. For an ethnic group's interest to be advanced, the agenda had to coincide with American foreign policy, a nearly impossible burden for most groups during the Cold War.[74] More politically active, contemporary ethnic groups have grown in number, especially influential because of concentrated populations within the electoral districts of various members of Congress.[75] Such concentration can translate into electoral clout, prompting incentives to promote the foreign policies advocated by these constituencies.

Today's ethnic groups have honed their political skills. They influence foreign policy using tactics normally associated with domestic interest group activity, such as writing letters to members of Congress, testifying before congressional committees, tracking legislation, publicizing the voting records of candidates for office, working in electoral campaigns, raising large sums of money, and mobilizing grassroots support within congressional districts.[76]

The end of the Cold War boosted this newfound influence. "The relatively benign international environment and the focus of most Americans on domestic concerns," writes former Foreign Affairs chair Lee Hamilton (D-Ind.), "have produced a political vacuum that can frequently be filled by special interests."[77] The absence of a single, coherent foreign policy doctrine, such as opposition to the former Soviet Union (Cold War anticommunism), leaves greater room for ethnic groups to argue that their positions are part of the American national interest. The breadth of American foreign policy interests and its complexity permit ethnic groups to attempt to influence American foreign policy in a number of areas. Both Capitol Hill and the White House are central players in the battle to advance ethnic agendas.

The success of a variety of ethnically based lobbies in recent congresses is rooted in committee chairmen's shifting views. For example, a decade ago, Senator Mitch A. McConnell (R-Ky.) was a leading critic of U.S. foreign aid. Similar to Senator Helms, he advocated either abolishing the U.S. Agency for International Development (USAID) or folding it into the State Department. This view significantly changed after Republicans took control of Congress in 1994, and McConnell became chairman of the Senate Appropriations' Foreign Operations Subcommittee, the panel that funds foreign aid programs. During his chairmanship, McConnell reshaped U.S. foreign aid allocation, such as cutting assistance to Africa and Russia while earmarking aid packages to the Ukraine, Georgia and Armenia.[78] His public rationale was that these three nations were fledgling democracies on the fringes of the old Russian empire in need of help.[79]

Jewish Americans are particularly successful in advocating pro-Israeli foreign policy positions. The effectiveness of the pro-Israeli lobbying effort has long been viewed as the textbook example of how an ethnic group successfully influences American foreign policy. First, Jewish Americans have made the case that the survival of the state of Israel remains a fundamental goal of American foreign policy given the geopolitical significance of the Middle East and the significance of Israel's status as the only viable democracy in the region. Second, despite the ferocious opposition of most of the Arab states in the region, Jewish-American groups have steadfastly maintained that the United States needs a country that it can rely on in good times and bad. Third, pro-Israeli groups underscore the impact that the United States has had in developing a coherent foreign policy agenda in the Middle East and assisting in stabilizing peace and security in the region, serving the interests of Israelis and their neighboring states. Israel's support for American objectives during the Persian Gulf War is just one example of continuing American–Israeli cooperation for more than fifty years.

The America–Israel Public Affairs Committee (AIPAC)—an organized, legislatively effective, well-financed umbrella organization—coordinates Jewish lobbying activities on Capitol Hill. Since the recognition of Israel by President Truman in 1947, and in virtually all other issues, such as financial aid, sales of military weapons, and political support, members of Congress have been confronted by its power.[80] AIPAC vigorously supports sympathetic legislators as well as backs challengers of unfriendly incumbents. Senator Jesse Helms' (R-N.C.) opponent in 1984 received strong support from pro-Israeli organizations. Following his reelection, Senator Helms changed course to endorse American foreign policy for Israel.[81] In 1986, for example, AIPAC mobilized over seventy pro-Israeli political action committees to contribute nearly $7 million to various congressional candidates. Senator Charles C. Percy (R-Ill.) was defeated, in part, based on AIPAC's opposition.

Whereas ten years ago Armenia was of little concern to most members, today the Armenian-American lobby is one of the most active ethnic lobbies on Capitol Hill, a power that stems from the heavy concentration of Armenian Americans in states like California, Massachusetts, New Jersey, and New York. Lobbying groups representing Armenian Americans have used their wealth, influence, and votes to sharply increase U.S. economic assistance to their compatriots overseas. With the help of key members of Congress, they have turned Armenia into one of the largest recipients in recent years of U.S. aid on a per-person basis after Israel.[82] Armenia's good fortune counters overall shrinking foreign aid trends. In the last three congresses, lawmakers voted to increase aid for the nation of three million beyond levels requested by the Clinton administration, earmarking aid to universities, earthquake victims, and improvements for nuclear reactors. Such lobbying demonstrates how, in an era when Congress stresses investment and trade as the best ways to raise living standards, political connections are important.

Hispanics and African Americans have been far less successful than their Jewish counterparts, largely because of the lack of prominence of Latin-American and African foreign policy concerns. African-American attempts to change U.S. foreign policy toward South Africa in the mid-1980s generated some congressional attention. This was based on the activities of the Congressional Black Caucus (CBC), the creation in 1977 of TransAfrica, the key advocacy group for African-related issues, and the unsuccessful presidential campaign of Jesse Jackson in 1984.[83] Cuban Americans are by far the most effective Hispanic ethnic lobby on Capitol Hill. Unlike Mexican Americans and Puerto Ricans who form a core constituency for Democrats, Cuban-American Republicans work both sides of the partisan divide. For example, the Cuban American National Foundation (CANF), through its Free Cuba political action committee (PAC), donated $114,000 in the 1990 midterm elections.[84] Again, in 1992 CANF and its PAC contributed money to more than twenty-six congressional candidates, including then–Representative Robert Torricelli (D-N.J.), author of the 1992 Cuban Democracy Act, prohibiting American companies from conducting business with Cuba. CANF again flexed its muscles in American foreign policy toward Cuba in 1994 by getting the Clinton administration to change its policy and bar Cuban Americans from wiring money to relatives still in Cuba and ending family reunification flights.

Although not a traditional ethnic lobby, Irish-American influence in the legislative arena stems from the seniority and clout of a number of Irish-American lawmakers. Senator Edward M. Kennedy (D-Mass.), former Senator Daniel P. Moynihan (D-N.Y.), former House Speaker Thomas P. (Tip) O'Neill (D-Mass.), and former Representative Hugh L. Carey (D-N.Y.) initiated congressional efforts and pressured presidents to define American foreign policy toward Great Britain, with special reference to Northern Ireland. Throughout the 1970s and 1990s, these Irish-American legislators were sensitive to the role of ethnicity. They coalesced in support of the Irish-Catholic minority in Northern Ireland, condemning the violence and demanding unification of the island nation-state. Senator Kennedy was the most vocal in the 1970s, repeatedly analyzing British involvement in Northern Ireland based on historic patterns of British colonialism, analogized to U.S. involvement during the Vietnam War.[85] These lawmakers sponsored congressional resolutions calling for the withdrawal of British forces from Northern Ireland as well as gathered and sent 100 lawmakers' signatures to the White House protesting discrimination faced by Catholics in Northern Ireland and denounced the British Army as "thugs."[86] By the 1980s, Irish-American legislators led efforts to reduce Irish-American contributions to the Irish Republican Army (IRA) and supporting the Republic of Ireland's peace efforts with Great Britain. In 1981 The Friends of Ireland was formed by Speaker O'Neill. The Reagan administration repeatedly responded to the policy initiatives of this group of lawmakers resulting in a reversal of policy by the Thatcher government.

CONCLUSION

The Second World War, fear of Soviet-dominated communism, and the alarm over bipolar nuclear balance long provided the executive branch with unprecedented agenda-setting prerogatives. But the emergence of mid-level issues involving economics, trade, immigration, and transportation policies has set the stage for substantial changes in the conduct of U.S. foreign policy. This new context includes the demise of the Soviet Union and the continued weakening of the military threat of Russia and China, the commercial assertiveness of developing economic markets around the world, and the struggle for greater popular participation and government accountability around the globe.[87] Such change has provided lawmakers the means to address and formulate foreign policy concerns. Newly fashioned techniques include articulating American ethical (human rights) principles and insisting they be reflected in U.S. foreign policy;[88] providing a congressional "yellow light" function, in which Congress prevails on the White House to reexamine its policies, to make certain that the nation is on the right diplomatic course;[89] and compelling changes in established policies through budgeting procedures and legislative norms.[90] Such increased legislative assertiveness has made American foreign policy representative of the diverse views of the general public.

NOTES

1. James M. Lindsay and Randall B. Ripley, "Foreign and Defense Policy in Congress: A Research Agenda for the 1990s," *Legislative Studies Quarterly* 27 (1992), pp. 417–449; James M. Lindsay, *Congress and Nuclear Weapons* (Baltimore: Johns Hopkins University Press, 1991); Bruce W. Jentleson, "American Diplomacy: Around the World and Along Pennsylvania Avenue," in *A Question of Balance: The President, the Congress, and Foreign Policy*, ed. Thomas E. Mann (Washington, D.C.: Brookings Institution, 1990); and Kenneth E. Sharpe, "The Post-Vietnam Formula under Siege: The Imperial Presidency and Central America," *Political Science Quarterly* 102 (1987–1988), pp. 549–569.
2. Louis Fisher, *Constitutional Conflicts between Congress and the President*, 4th ed. (Lawrence, KS: University Press of Kansas, 1997) and Louis Fisher, *Presidential War Powers* (Lawrence, KS: University Press of Kansas, 1995).
3. Lee Hamilton, "The Making of U.S. Foreign Policy: The Roles of the President and Congress Over Four Decades" (presented at the conference "Rivals for Power: Comity or Partisanship in Presidential–Congressional Relations?" Washington, D.C., November 17, 2000).
4. Eileen K. Burgin, "Representatives' Decisions on Participation in Foreign Policy Issues," *Legislative Studies Quarterly* 16 (1991), pp. 521–546; Darrell M. West, "Activists and Economic Policymaking in Congress," *American Journal of Political Science* 32 (1988), pp. 662–680; and Aage R. Clausen, *How Congressmen Decide* (New York: St. Martin's, 1973).
5. Cecil V. Crabb, Jr., "Foreign Policy," in *The Encyclopedia of the United States Congress*, vol. 2., ed. Donald C. Bacon, Roger H. Davidson, and Morton Keller (New York: Simon & Schuster, 1995).
6. Hamilton, "The Making of U.S. Foreign Policy: The Roles of the President and Congress Over Four Decades," p. 1.
7. Mark A. Peterson, "The President and Congress," in *The Presidency and the Political System*, 5th ed., ed. Michael Nelson (Washington, D.C.: CQ Press, 1998).
8. Roger H. Davidson and Colton C. Campbell, "The Senate and the Executive," in *Esteemed Colleagues: Civility and Deliberation in the U.S. Senate*, ed. Burdett A. Loomis (Washington, D.C.: Brookings Institution, 2000).
9. Eileen K. Burgin, "Congress and Foreign Policy: The Misperceptions," in *Congress Reconsidered*, ed. Lawrence C. Dodd and Bruce I. Oppenheimer (Washington, D.C.: CQ Press, 1993).
10. Edward S. Corwin, *The President: Office and Powers, 1787–1957*, 4th ed. (New York: New York University Press, 1957); and Cecil V. Crabb, Jr., and Pat M. Holt, *Invitation to Struggle: Congress, the President, and Foreign Policy* 4th ed. (Washington, D.C.: CQ Press, 1992).
11. See David M. O'Brien, *Constitutional Law and Politics: Struggles for Power and Governmental Accountability*, 4th ed. (New York: W. W. Norton and Co., 2000).
12. Ibid., p. 221.
13. Ibid.
14. *Missouri v. Holland*, 252 U.S. 416 (1920).

15. *United States v. Belmont*, 301 U.S. 324 (1937).
16. *United States v. Curtiss-Wright Export Corp.*, 299 U.S. 304 (1936).
17. *Youngstown Sheet & Tube Co. v. Sawyer*, 343 U.S. 579 (1952).
18. Gregg D. Ivers, *American Constitutional Law: Power and Politics*, vol. 1 (Boston: Houghton Mifflin, 2001).
19. Ibid, p. 256.
20. Ibid., p. 242.
21. *Youngstown Sheet & Tube Co. v. Sawyer*, 863 S.Ct. (1952).
22. Ibid.
23. Ibid.
24. Ibid.
25. Ibid.
26. Ibid.
27. Ibid.
28. Ibid.
29. *United States v. Nixon*, 418 U.S. 683 (1974).
30. *Hirabayashi v. United States*, 320 U.S. 81 (1943) and Craig R. Ducat, *Constitutional Interpretation*, 7th ed. (Belmont, CA: West Publishers, 2000), p. 187.
31. *Korematsu v. United States*, 323 U.S. 214 (1944).
32. Ducat, *Constitutional Interpretation*, p. 193.
33. Ibid.
34. Ibid.
35. Ibid.
36. Ivers, *American Constitutional Law: Power and Politics*.
37. John Jay, *The Federalist No. 64*, *The Federalist Papers*, with introduction by Garry Wills (New York: Bantam Books, 1982).
38. *Annals of Congress*, 6th Cong., 1800, p. 613.
39. Richard F. Fenno, Jr., "Senate," in *The Encyclopedia of the United States Congress*, vol. 4., ed. Donald C. Bacon, Roger H. Davidson, and Morton Keller (New York: Simon & Schuster, 1995), p. 1786.
40. Fisher, *Constitutional Conflicts between Congress and the President*.
41. Peterson, "The President and Congress" and Neil A. Lewis, "Clinton Has a Chance to Shape the Courts," *New York Times*, 9 February 1997, p. 16.
42. Raymond Smock, ed., *Landmark Documents on the U.S. Congress* (Washington, D.C.: Congressional Quarterly, 1999).
43. Jonathan Sanford, *Senate Disposition of Ambassadorial Nominations, 1987–1996*, Congressional Research Service Report No. 97-864 F, September 19, 1997.
44. Davidson and Campbell, "The Senate and the Executive."
45. John Bresnahan, "Holds Threaten Senate Agenda," *Roll Call*, 10 June 1999, p. 30.
46. Ibid.
47. Roger H. Davidson and Walter J. Oleszek, *Congress and Its Members*, 7th ed. (Washington, D.C.: CQ Press, 2000).
48. See Joseph P. Harris, *The Advice and Consent of the Senate* (Berkeley: University of California Press, 1953); and G. Calvin Mackenzie, *The Politics of Presidential Appointments* (New York: Free Press, 1981).
49. Kenneth R. Bowling and Helen E. Veit, eds., *Documentary History of the First Federal Congress of the United States of America*, vol. 9, *The Diary of William Maclay and Other Notes on Senate Debates*, 4 March 1789–3 March 1791 (Baltimore: Johns Hopkins University Press, 1989), pp. 128–131.
50. Ibid.
51. Ellen C. Collier, "Treaties," in *The Encyclopedia of the United States Congress*, vol. 4., ed. Donald C. Bacon, Roger H. Davidson, and Morton Keller (New York: Simon & Schuster, 1993).
52. Ibid.
53. Davidson and Campbell, "The Senate and the Executive."
54. Thomas A. Bailey, *Woodrow Wilson and the Great Betrayal* (Chicago: Quadrangle Books, 1945), p. 3.
55. Ibid.
56. Thomas A. Bailey, "Woodrow Wilson and the Lost Peace," in *Wilson at Versailles*, ed. Theodore P. Greene (Boston: D.C. Heath and Company, 1957), p. 56.

57. Davidson and Oleszek, *Congress and Its Members*, 7th ed.
58. Collier, "Treaties."
59. George H. Haynes, "The Executive–Legislative Conflict," in *Wilson and the League of Nations*, ed. Ralph A. Stone (New York: Holt, Rinehart and Winston, 1967), p. 17.
60. Quoted in Thomas E. Ricks, "U.S. Signs Treaty on War Crimes Tribunal: Pentagon, Republicans Object to Clinton Move," *Washington Post*, 1 January 2000, pp. A-1, A-16.
61. Davidson and Oleszek, *Congress and Its Members*, 7th ed.
62. Byron C. Hulsey, *Everett Dirksen and His Presidents: How a Senate Giant Shaped American Politics* (Lawrence, KS: University Press of Kansas, 2000).
63. Peterson, "The President and Congress," p. 494.
64. Charles W. Kegley, Jr., and Eugene R. Wittkopf, *American Foreign Policy: Pattern and Process*, 4th ed. (New York: St. Martin's Press), p. 188.
65. Thomas A. Bailey, *The Hyphenate in Recent American Politics*; and Charles W. Kegley, Jr., and Eugene R. Wittkopf, *American Foreign Policy*, 5th ed. (New York: St. Martin's Press, 1996).
66. Kegley and Wittkopf, *American Foreign Policy*, 5th ed., p. 260.
67. Ibid.
68. Ibid., p. 226.
69. Davidson and Oleszek, *Congress and Its Members*, 7th ed., p. 386.
70. Ibid.
71. Kegley and Wittkopf, *American Foreign Policy*, 5th ed., p. 240.
72. Ibid., p. 240.
73. Davidson and Oleszek, *Congress and Its Members*, 5th ed., p. 387.
74. This may help to explain the success of Cuban Americans following the revolution that brought Fidel Castro to power and the aborted American-sponsored invasion of Cuba by Cuban exiles at the Bay of Pigs in 1962.
75. Hamilton, "The Making of U.S. Foreign Policy: The Roles of the President and Congress Over Four Decades," p. 6; and John F. Stack, Jr., "Ethnic Groups as Emerging Transnational Actors," in *Ethnic Identities in a Transnational World*, ed. John F. Stack, Jr. (Westport, CT: Greenwood Press, 1981).
76. Glenn P. Hastedt, *American Foreign Policy: Past, Present, Future*, 3rd ed. (Upper Saddle River, NJ: Prentice Hall, 1997).
77. Ibid., p. 5.
78. Michael Dobbs, "Foreign Aid Shrinks, but Not for All: With Clout in Congress, Armenia's Share Grows," *Washington Post*, 24 January 2001, p. A-1.
79. Ibid.
80. Hastedt, *American Foreign Policy: Past, Present, Future*.
81. Ibid.
82. Dobbs, "Foreign Aid Shrinks, but Not for All: With Clout in Congress, Armenia's Share Grows."
83. Hastedt, *American Foreign Policy: Past, Present, Future*, p. 143.
84. Ibid., p. 144.
85. Richard B. Finnegan, "Northern Ireland: Transnational Ethnic Pressures and Institutional Responses," in *The Ethnic Entanglement: Conflict and Intervention in World Politics*, ed. John F. Stack, Jr., and Lui Hebron (Westport, CT: Praeger Publishers, 1999).
86. Ibid., p. 65.
87. Ernest J. Wilson, III, "Interest Groups and Foreign Policymaking: A View from the White House," in *The Interest Group Connection: Electioneering, Lobbying, and Policymaking in Washington*, ed. Paul S. Herrnson, Ronald G. Shaiko, and Clyde Wilcox (Chatham, NJ: Chatham House, 1998).
88. William P. Avery and David P. Forsythe, "Human Rights, National Security, and the U.S. Senate: Who Votes for What, and Why?" *International Studies Quarterly* 23 (1979), pp. 303–320; David P. Forsythe, *Human Rights and U.S. Foreign Policy: Congress Reconsidered* (Gainesville, FL: University of Florida Press, 1988); David P. Forsythe, "Congress and Human Rights Legislation in U.S. Foreign Policy: The Fate of General Legislation," *Human Rights Quarterly* 9 (1987), pp. 382–404; and David P. Forsythe and Susan Welch, "Human Rights Voting in Congress," *Policy Studies Journal* 15 (1986), pp. 173–188.
89. Crabb, "Foreign Policy."
90. Ellen C. Collier, "Foreign Policy by Reporting Requirement," *Washington Quarterly* 11 (1988), pp. 75–84.

ADVICE AND CONSENT

THE FORGOTTEN POWER

DAVID P. AUERSWALD[1]

Politics is fundamentally about the exercise of public authority and the struggle to gain control over it.[2]

The policy process in Washington rarely produces ideal results. One reason for this is future uncertainty over policymaking authority. In essence, who controls policy today may not tomorrow. Current winners therefore have an incentive to alter the policymaking process to guard against the day when someone else takes power; that is, to insulate their preferred policies from future attack.[3] Not surprisingly, this yields suboptimal policy from the perspective of other policymakers with dissimilar preferences. A second reason is that the realities of policymaking make realizing one's ideal policies unlikely even for those on the winning side. Policymaking in a separation-of-powers system necessitates compromise—within congressional chambers, between chambers, and between branches of government.[4] And compromise by definition means agreeing to policies that from any particular perspective are less than perfect.[5]

The legislative process is particularly susceptible to problems of political uncertainty and the necessity for compromise, making it difficult for any one part of government to impose its preferences on other domestic policymakers. An exception to the rule, and the subject of this chapter, is the Senate's use of the treaty advice and consent process to affect U.S. foreign policy. Policymaking through the advice and consent process allows the Senate to avoid the pitfalls associated with normal foreign affairs legislation. Ratification documents generated during the advice and consent process are attractive tools for Senate policymaking because they allow the Senate to enact initiatives without substantial compromises with the House or president, their provisions have the force of law, and they are resistant to short-term changes in executive or congressional preferences. In short, they allow the Senate to bypass many of the compromises inherent in the normal policymaking process while at the same time insulating preferred policies from future uncertainty.

This chapter's first section reviews the reasons why the normal legislative process makes translating Senate preferences into foreign policy difficult. In the second section, I discuss how a ratification document represents a fundamentally different policy process. I argue that the treaty advice and consent process, when available, gives the Senate a tremendous opportunity to shape long-term U.S. foreign policy by including substantive policy initiatives in ratification documents. This is particularly true when a Senate majority disagrees with a president's foreign policy initiatives, but legislation is not a viable option, such as during periods of divided government or intrabranch polarization. In the final section, I apply this argument to the case of NATO enlargement.

THE LIMITS OF LEGISLATION

The Constitution gives the president significant powers over U.S. foreign policy. Congress's powers over foreign affairs seem to pale in comparison. Congressional initiatives are slow, cumbersome, difficult to enforce, or rarely available to influence the content of foreign policy. This constellation of powers has led many to conclude that U.S. international behavior, particularly on national security issues, is to a large degree dependent on presidential preferences.[6]

The general problem facing Congress is that its institutional powers are often rendered useless because of collective action problems.[7] This is particularly true when Congress attempts to pass legislation. Indeed, recent literature has pointed to significant collective action problems associated with achieving interbranch agreement on policy initiatives in the modern era of divided government, or achieving intrabranch agreement when polarized politics and ideologically heterogeneous parties lead to differences between House and Senate preferences.[8]

Consider the problems of passing legislation that might alter U.S. foreign policy. From the Senate's perspective, any such attempts are beholden to the preferences of the House, because Senate bills do not reach the president without House concurrence. The greater the difference between House and Senate preferences, the harder it becomes to pass a bill that contains a Senate initiative, to say nothing of passing a bill with the Senate initiative unaltered.[9] Passing legislation is even more difficult if the House is internally polarized or ideologically heterogeneous—making it difficult for the House to reach a compromise position among its own members, much less reaching a compromise with the Senate.

Differences between House and Senate preferences become even more important as presidential opposition increases to a Senate initiative. The Senate leadership's bargaining position becomes weaker vis-à-vis the president due to the difficulties associated with overriding a veto. The two-thirds majorities of each chamber required to override a veto is a significant hurdle to overcome when the two chambers differ in ideology. Senate leaders could try to forestall a veto by giving the president something in the bill that he wants badly enough to sign the overall legislation. This option, however, requires agreement on issue linkages by bicameral majorities. Of course, Senate leaders could drop their desired initiative, but that obviously is not a preferred option. Intrabranch agreement is crucial—and difficult—under the first two alternatives. Both require either agreement among supermajorities in each chamber or very complex issue linkages. Widely diverging inter- or intrachamber congressional preferences make either option difficult.[10]

An example of the difficulties associated with passing legislation is provided by the domestic debate over U.S. troop deployments at the beginning of the Cold War. On July 21, 1949, the United States formally committed to defending Western Europe from external attack by ratifying the North Atlantic (Washington) Treaty, creating NATO. The United States initially maintained two Army divisions in Germany and pushed the European allies to "maintain and develop their individual and collective capacity to resist armed attack" (North Atlantic Treaty, Article 3). With the outbreak of the Korean conflict, the Truman administration announced that it was sending four additional Army divisions to Europe to bolster NATO forces. The additional deployments were deemed necessary to shore up inadequate European contributions to alliance defense. In response, Senate foreign policy leaders, already concerned over U.S. involvement in Korea, began a three-month deliberation over the roles of Congress and the president in troop deployments. The press dubbed these deliberations "the Great Debate."

The Senate eventually passed two identical resolutions (S. Res. 99 and S. Con. Res. 18) approving Truman's deployments but questioning the process by which they had been decided. Senators attempted to prohibit further deployments without prior congressional authorization, noting in section six of both resolutions that "congressional approval should be obtained of any policy requiring the assignment of American troops abroad when such assignment is in implementation of article 3 of the North Atlantic Treaty." The resolutions also stated: "It is the sense of the Senate that no ground troops in addition to such four divisions should be sent to Western Europe . . . without further congressional approval."[11]

Both measures passed the Senate (S. Res. 99 by a 69–21 vote and S. Con. Res. 18 by a 45–41 vote) but had little effect on administration behavior because each suffered from the limitations inherent in the normal legislative process. Specifically, Senate leaders knew that Truman had the support of Democratic leaders in the House.[12] As a result, Senators attempted to pass only nonbinding resolutions. For instance, S. Res. 99 was merely a sense-of-the-Senate resolution. Its companion concurrent resolution was referred to the House Foreign Affairs Committee but was never considered by the full House. And even if passed by the House, it, too, would not have legally bound future presidential actions. Thus, even though Truman's actions sparked considerable Senate opposition, the Senate was unable to limit future presidential behavior. Indeed, Truman's disdain for the Senate's actions was apparent when he publicly stated that S. Res. 99 did not legally constrain his future behavior.[13]

Even had the Senate succeeded in restricting Truman's behavior, it then would have been faced with a second problem of insulating the resulting policy from future political changes. Generally speaking, engineering long-term policy change via normal legislation holds open the possibility of repeated future challenges to its provisions. A challenge need only be successful once to overturn a legislative initiative. In the worst case, the Congress could even rescind the legislation in the next session. Alternatively, successfully engineering a long-term change in U.S. behavior via the appropriations process requires that the Senate perform the juggling act of reaching an intrabranch compromise on an annual basis for the foreseeable future, with all the complications, possible issue linkages, and legislative bundling that go into the appropriations cycle. Frequent divided government and intrabranch policy disagreements make such a sustained effort unlikely. A future Congress could easily deadlock and fail to include (or fund) the Senate initiative in a future authorization or appropriations bill.[14] Thus, the two most important congressional powers—the power over budgets and legislation—lose some of their luster when we factor in the difficulties associated with the passage and long-term stability of congressional policy.

THE POWER OF ADVICE AND CONSENT

The Senate has a much better chance of affecting long-term U.S. foreign policy in a consistent manner when it has the opportunity to exercise its treaty advice and consent power. This may come as a surprise. After all, we normally think of the advice and consent process as a yes or no vote, with the Senate either accepting or rejecting a treaty. The Senate's 1999 rejection of the Comprehensive Test Ban Treaty reinforces that impression.

There is more to the advice and consent process, however, than an either-or result. An intermediate outcome is also possible. Rather than simply accepting or rejecting a treaty, the Senate can accept a treaty but attach amendments, reservations, understandings, and policy declarations to that treaty's document of ratification.[15] Amendments to the treaty itself require renegotiating the treaty with U.S. treaty partners. Reservations, understandings, and declarations often do not require a new round of diplomacy. Instead, these latter three qualifiers demarcate future U.S. behavior, intent, or policy positions as a result of the treaty. Nor are these qualifiers necessarily limited to the particular issues of the treaty. They can also specify U.S. policy on unrelated issues, in that no constitutional requirement or Senate rule specifies that provisions in a ratification document be germane to a treaty's subject matter.[16]

Policymaking through the advice and consent process has significant advantages over the power of the purse or normal legislation should a Senate majority want to affect presidential foreign policy initiatives. The contents of ratification documents supercede existing legislation, in essence changing law without the normal legislative process. Using a ratification document allows the Senate to bypass the House when making policy, decreasing the need for compromise. It also protects that policy from subsequent House or presidential challenges and has the support of the courts, minimizing the effects of future political uncertainty. Given these advantages, there is every reason to expect the Senate to advance policy initiatives through the treaty advice and consent process, when available, particularly when a Senate majority has concerns regarding a president's foreign policy initiatives and Senate legislative initiatives might be hindered by the House or the president.[17]

PASSAGE

Passing a ratification document is relatively easy compared to passing legislation. Article 2, Section 2 of the Constitution states that passage of a ratification document requires a two-thirds majority of all senators present and voting (rather than of the full Senate). In many cases achieving that milestone requires less governmental consensus than does passage of normal legislation or an appropriations bill (hereafter collectively referred to as legislation). Moreover, ratification documents require that the Senate make few compromises to enact Senate initiatives. Indeed, passage of a document of ratification usually ensures presidential concurrence and the advice and consent process leaves the House of Representatives largely out of the process.

To demonstrate these points, Table 3.1 summarizes four scenarios involving the treaty advice and consent process. There are three groups of actors in each scenario: senators, members of the House of Representatives, and the president. For simplicity's sake, assume that each of these actors behaves myopically, that is, as if it were engaged in a single iteration without concern for future interactions. Also assume that each actor is relatively unsophisticated, in the sense of not anticipating the likely behavior of the other actors.[18]

In any of the four scenarios, the requirements to pass legislation through the Senate alone (to say nothing of getting House and presidential concurrence) may in fact be more stringent than those required to pass a document of ratification. This may not seem an obvious conclusion when we consider that from 1975 to the present day, sixty senators must vote to invoke cloture if they are to prevent a filibuster. Advice and consent requires a two-thirds vote of those senators present and voting, making advice and consent a higher standard than cloture, at least on well-attended votes.[19] Yet

TABLE 3.1   REQUIRED SUPPORT FOR A SENATE INITIATIVE

Parties in Agreement on Policy Initiative	Legislation/Appropriations Containing Senate Initiative	Document of Ratification
(1) President, Senate and House Leadership	Senate: 3/5 majority (1975–on) 2/3 of Senators present and voting (1959–1975) 2/3 majority (1949–1959) House: simple majority President: agreement	Senate: 2/3 of Senators present and voting
(2) Senate and House Leadership	Senate: 2/3 majority House: 2/3 majority OR Significant compromise with the President, then see (1) above.	Senate: 2/3 of Senators present and voting
(3) Senate Leadership and President	Senate initiative requires significant compromise with House, then see (1) above.	Senate: 2/3 of Senators present and voting
(4) Senate Leadership	Senate initiative requires significant compromise with House (then see (2) above), or with House and President (then see (1) above).	Senate: 2/3 of Senators present and voting

in some cases, and in some historic periods, it has been at least as hard, if not harder, to invoke cloture and debate legislation in the Senate than it has been to pass a document of ratification. From 1959–1975, cloture required the support of two-thirds of senators present and voting, the same requirement as providing Senate advice and consent. Between 1949–1959, cloture required two-thirds of *all* senators, making it more difficult to invoke cloture than to pass a ratification document.[20] In sum, it has not always been the case that providing advice and consent is more difficult than is passing legislation through the Senate. As Table 3.1's four scenarios suggest, it is easier to pass a document of ratification than it is to pass legislation when one factors in the president and the House of Representatives.

The first row of Table 3.1 depicts a scenario where Senate and House majorities and the president all agree on policy. These are issues with broad consensus support. Given the preceding discussion, the question here is whether passing a ratification document in the Senate is any harder than *enacting* legislation by the Congress and the president (given the Senate's current cloture rules). Before a bill can be debated in the Senate, cloture must be invoked or sixty senators must be committed to the bill's passage—enough to forestall a filibuster attempt. In those circumstances, there is every reason for nonideologue senators to support a bill rather than appear on the losing side, at least if the bill is assured passage by the House and the president's signature. Support of sixty senators therefore should produce a bandwagoning effect and lopsided votes in favor of the legislation. For example, the fiercely contended 1999 National

Missile Defense Act passed by a surprising 97–3 vote, in large part because the minority Senate Democrats realized they could not prevent cloture and President Clinton withdrew his veto threat. If legislation reflecting bicameral and inter-branch consensus can garner the support of two-thirds of the Senate (as did the 1999 missile defense bill) it seems likely that a ratification document reflecting a consensus position could receive equivalent support. On issues with broad consensus, then, passing a document of ratification should not be appreciably more difficult than enacting similar legislation, even in the current era.

The second row displays a scenario in which the president and Senate disagree on policy. Here the Senate leadership will have to muster a two-thirds majority to pass legislation, roughly the same requirement as passing a document of ratification.[21] Although the Senate could always make concessions to the president and avoid a veto of legislation, such concessions would compromise the integrity of its initiative. A ratification document requires little compromise with the president. It also has the added benefit of bypassing the House of Representatives when the Senate and president disagree. This is an attractive option if the president would likely veto the Senate's policy were that policy included in legislation and a strong-enough minority of House members voted to sustain the veto and curtail the Senate initiative.[22] By contrast, the Senate supermajority required to pass a treaty ratification document is a significantly lower threshold than the two-chamber supermajority necessary to override a presidential veto of legislation.

The third reason a ratification document is an attractive option compared to legislation is that the advice and consent process bypasses the House when the president and Senate agree on policy but a House majority does not. This is portrayed in the third row. From senators' perspective, a document of ratification is very attractive if House and Senate majorities disagree, because legislation containing a Senate initiative goes nowhere if House and Senate majorities become deadlocked. When the Senate has only the option of legislation but not treaty advice and consent, Senate leaders must either abandon their initiative or engage in significant compromises with the House. The latter course of action will result in a substantially altered Senate initiative. From the Senate's perspective, then, a ratification document is preferable to legislation because the advice and consent process bypasses the House of Representatives.[23]

Finally, using ratification documents for policymaking has obvious advantages when both the president and the House oppose the Senate's initiative. Under this scenario, shown in row four, passing legislation to alter or constrain foreign policy requires the Senate to compromise significantly in one of two ways. It could compromise enough to win the support of two-thirds of the House, enough to pass the Senate's altered initiative through Congress and override a presidential veto. Alternately, it could compromise enough to win the president's support and that of a simple House majority. In either case, going the legislative route forces the Senate to compromise significantly or abandon its initiative.

In short, when both congressional chambers and the president agree on policy, the requirements for passing a document of ratification in the Senate are effectively identical to or even easier than those needed to pass legislation. Such broad consensus is likely to make passage of a ratification document no more difficult than achieving the sixty votes currently necessary to invoke cloture on legislation. Passing a document of ratification is significantly easier than enacting legislation when Senate preferences differ from those of the president, from those of a majority of House members, or from both the president and a House majority. Any of these latter three scenarios is a likely occurrence in the modern era of divided government and heterogeneous political parties. In each case, a ratification document requires few if any compromises with the House or the president. In each, the Senate is significantly better off making policy via a ratification document than it would be by using normal legislation.[24]

Passage with Strategic Behavior

The Senate is not completely unconstrained when passing ratification documents. On the contrary, managers of the ratification debate must garner the support of two-thirds of senators voting, a task that may be impossible given the issues involved, the specific terms of the treaty, or the domestic and international political dynamics at the time.[25] Allowing for more sophisticated behavior among the three actors also introduces two other constraints on Senate actions.

The first constraint comes from the House of Representatives when treaties require implementing legislation to bring the United States into compliance with the terms of the treaty. For those treaties, the Senate could be constrained when crafting ratification documents by the need for House support for that implementing legislation. Senate leaders would have to know that very extreme policy initiatives might be overturned by the House. Or the need for implementing legislation might allow the House to pressure the Senate for *additional* provisions in a ratification document, rather than *constraining* the Senate's use of reservations, understandings, and declarations. In either case, the standards for passing a ratification document would be roughly equivalent to those necessary for passing legislation.[26]

A number of reasons explain why House preferences might not seriously influence the content of Senate treaty ratification documents.[27] Most treaties are considered self-executing unless they affect private behavior. When a treaty does require implementing legislation, that legislation may sometimes predate Senate consideration of the treaty itself. There are even instances when the Senate has prohibited the president from depositing the U.S. instruments of ratification until implementing legislation is passed.[28] It is doubtful that the Senate would take such a step if it anticipated a challenge from the House. Finally, a treaty can still enter into force even if the necessary implementing legislation is held hostage by an irate House of Representatives. The United

States would be in violation of whatever treaty provisions required implementing legislation, but that violation would not invalidate Senate ratification provisions unless the U.S. violation were serious enough to void the underlying treaty. That very fact might blunt some House demands because treaty compliance is in the interests of U.S. credibility.

Second, the discussion associated with Table 3.1 should not be construed to imply that the president cannot act strategically, or that the Senate always gets its way vis-à-vis the president. Presidents can delay submitting a treaty to the Senate if they believe there is a high probability that the Senate might defeat the treaty outright or consent to the treaty but only subject to unacceptable conditions.[29] Conversely, there is little reason to expect the Senate to put forward a ratification document laden with initiatives that might scuttle the underlying treaty.

The president *could* refuse to deposit the ratification document with the appropriate international body if that document constrained or altered presidential policy, making the document subject to a final presidential veto of sorts. However, exercising that option would kill the underlying treaty and killing treaties is not something presidents take lightly. Indeed, they almost never do so unless the treaty in question was negotiated by an earlier president.[30] Instead, presidents are likely to accept most stipulations included in documents of ratification because the administration has invested significant time, effort, and prestige in negotiating the treaty. Most presidents are loath to abandon that investment except in the most extreme circumstances.[31]

A more effective constraint on Senate behavior is the likely reaction of international treaty partners. In recent Senate debates during the advice and consent process, senators have anticipated the ratification provisions that might undermine the treaty in the eyes of treaty partners. If two-thirds of the Senate supports the underlying treaty, then senators are unlikely to include such treaty-killing provisions in a ratification document. Treaty proponents frequently refrain from offering such killer provisions and try to defeat them when they are offered on the Senate floor. If instead there is widespread Senate support for such extreme provisions—provisions that senators know would kill the treaty—then the treaty itself probably does not receive Senate advice and consent in the first place. This helps explains why so few Senate reservations are rejected by treaty partners, why presidents hesitate before sending extremely controversial treaties to the Senate, and why the Senate occasionally rejects controversial treaties—usually when the president miscalculates the degree of Senate support for a treaty.[32]

ENFORCEMENT

Ratification documents must be enforceable if they are to have long-term effects on policy. A crucial question, then, is what recourse the Senate has if the president ignores the provisions of a ratification document. The short answer is that the Senate can turn to the courts. With precedents dating back to 1869, the Supreme Court has ruled that the contents of treaty ratification documents, combined with the record from the Senate advice and consent process, are binding on future presidential behavior.[33] In other words, Senate reservations and understandings regarding the purpose of the underlying treaty or Senate definitions or declarations of what U.S. behavior is or is not consistent with that purpose bind the United States to the Senate's interpretation until the treaty is amended to reflect a new purpose or is voided.

In normal legislation, such Senate understandings do not have the force of law. In a ratification document, however, they do.[34] Most recently, the Supreme Court has declared in *U.S. v. Stuart* (1983) that treaty interpretation depends on looking "beyond the text of the treaty itself [to] the accompanying resolution of ratification to determine what the Senate intended."[35] Nor has the Court been reluctant to reinforce its 1869 precedent when given the opportunity. In addition to *Stuart*, the Supreme Court has based its rulings on the Senate's expressed intent in the advice and consent process at least seven times since 1949, as demonstrated by references to the texts of formal ratification documents and material from relevant Senate hearings and reports when deciding on a case.[36]

The modern Senate also has demonstrated an interest and ability in itself enforcing presidential compliance with the contents of a ratification document. Perhaps the watershed example of this was in response to the Reagan administration's reinterpretation of the Anti-Ballistic Missile Treaty (ABM). The administration had announced on October 6, 1985, that it understood the ABM Treaty to allow for the testing and development of space-based ABM weapons. Witnesses in subsequent House and Senate hearings during late October opined that that reinterpretation, if allowed, spelled the death of the ABM Treaty, prompting Senate Democrats to warn the administration against reinterpreting the treaty without Senate consultation.[37] Senator Sam A. Nunn (D-Ga.), then–chairman of the Senate Armed Services Committee, said that the administration risked a "constitutional confrontation of profound dimensions" if it did not abide by the original treaty interpretation. The Democratic leadership in both chambers then introduced appropriation bills linking Strategic Defense Initiative (SDI) funding to the administration's continued adherence to the traditional interpretation of the ABM Treaty. When thirty-four Republican senators urged a Reagan veto—enough senators to sustain such a veto—the Democrats responded that a veto would force them to withhold all SDI funds from the fiscal year 1988 budget. The administration subsequently agreed that there would be no deployment in violation of the ABM Treaty, a concession that essentially spelled the demise of the SDI program as a deployable system.[38]

The practice of using appropriation bills to enforce presidential compliance has obvious shortcomings in terms of the bills' timing vis-à-vis presidential action, the collective action problems confronting Congress when passing legislation, and presidential brinksmanship should he veto the defense budget. As a solution, the binding nature of Senate understandings and reservations is now made explicit in ratification documents by the so-called Biden condition. Named after its author, Senator Joseph R. Biden (D-Del.), the Biden condition states that by depositing ratification documents with this condition attached, current and future presidents agree to be bound by the Senate's understanding of a treaty's intent as it was understood by the Senate during the treaty's advice and consent proceedings. The Senate first used the Biden condition in the 1987 Intermediate Nuclear Force Treaty, and has included or referred to the condition in most lengthy, subsequent, ratification documents.[39] So although it was already difficult for presidents to ignore these provisions, the Biden condition made it even harder for post-1987 presidents to successfully argue such a case. Senate staffers believe that this is why there has not been a single instance where a president has successfully reinterpreted a treaty since then.[40]

DURABILITY

Crafting a document of ratification has an additional advantage over normal legislation. Policies included in ratification documents are resistant to change once enacted. There is every reason to expect that the Senate would take advantage of the opportunity provided by a ratification document to embed its preferences into policy for the long term, particularly if it is uncertain as to the future partisan composition of the House, the Senate, or the presidency.[41]

Ratification documents minimize senatorial uncertainty over the future direction of U.S. policy because they are difficult to change after being enacted. There are two types of ratification document provisions, each with a specific procedure associated with its amendment or rescission. Senate reservations or understandings as to the purpose of the underlying treaty, the parties to the treaty, or declarations as to how the United States will comply with and enforce the treaty can be thought of as *crucial* ratification document provisions.[42] Crucial provisions define for America's international treaty partners the behavior they can expect from the United States under the terms of the treaty. *Mundane* provisions deal with purely domestic interactions between the branches of government (i.e., executive branch reports or certifications to Congress, etc.) and have little effect on international understandings of the underlying treaty.

Both crucial and mundane provisions can be rescinded through legislation. Indeed, the Supreme Court has ruled that subsequent legislation supercedes an existing treaty, regardless of a ratification document's content.[43] Yet because crucial provisions establish international expectations, changing or rescinding those provisions requires either amending the underlying treaty or voiding it altogether. Mundane provisions, on the other hand, can be changed solely through the legislative process without changing the U.S. relationship with its international treaty partners. In either instance, legislative attempts to amend or rescind a ratification document can be blocked if forty-one senators simply vote no. Achieving the same durable policy result using the appropriations process would require annual action by at least three-fifths of the Senate.

Additional difficulties are involved in rescinding or amending either crucial or mundane provisions, making such provisions at least as durable as normal legislation. For instance, the House or Senate can introduce legislation to alter or rescind a crucial provision in a ratification document. The requirements for passage are the same as for any legislation, either a sixty-seat Senate majority, a majority in the House and presidential concurrence, or two-thirds supermajorities in the House and Senate if the president objects. These numbers, however, belie the fact that such action not only changes the offending provision but places the United States in violation of the treaty itself, for all practical purpose voiding it.[44] Unilaterally voiding a treaty can have detrimental international ramifications for U.S. credibility, which presumably the president and one-third of either congressional chamber, or forty-one senators or a House majority, would like to avoid. So although the numeric requirements are the same as for normal legislation, there is every reason to believe that government officials would hesitate before unilaterally voiding an international treaty.

If Congress amends or rescinds a crucial provision without voiding the underlying treaty, additional procedural requirements come into play, far beyond anything associated with normal legislation. Most importantly, the president must amend the treaty itself and repeat the advice and consent process, allowing a minority of thirty-four senators to block such major rescissions, to say nothing of getting the requisite concurrence of the president and the international parties to the treaty. These are significant procedural hurdles. Thus, changing or rescinding crucial provisions to ratification documents is often significantly more difficult than altering normal legislation, in large part because of the international ramifications and prerequisites of that change.

Rescinding a ratification document's mundane provisions can be accomplished through legislation that waives or rescinds that provision, but only as long as the legislation specifically refers to the provision being rescinded.[45] And like any bill, the legislation must be supported by a House majority and at least sixty senators (to invoke cloture), and must meet with the president's approval, or it must receive two-thirds supermajorities in both chambers when lacking presidential concurrence. As noted earlier, this is difficult and requires significant compromises when inter- and intrachamber preferences diverge. And again, forty-one senators can block any such effort. Table 3.2 (on page 56) illustrates changing ratification provisions through legislation.

There is a second and equally important reason why documents of ratification make it possible for the Senate to enact long-term changes to U.S. foreign policy. In any scenario for changing ratification provisions through legislation, convincing sixty senators (or sixty-seven senators if the president

TABLE 3.2   CHANGING RATIFICATION PROVISIONS THROUGH LEGISLATION

	REQUIREMENTS	RESULT
Crucial Provision	Senate: 3/5 majority House: simple majority President: concurrence OR Senate: 2/3 majority House: 2/3 majority	Violates treaty, with possibility of international repercussions
Crucial Provision	Requirements listed above, plus: President: concurrence on amending the treaty Concurrence of international partners to the treaty Senate: 2/3 majority	Amends treaty consistent with congressional wishes
Mundane Provision	Legislation specifically noting the provision, passed with: Senate: 3/5 majority House: simple majority President: concurrence OR Senate: 2/3 majority House: 2/3 majority	Deletes or amends the offending provision without altering the underlying treaty

objects) to change their preferences in the short term is extremely difficult. Because only a third of the Senate stands for reelection every two years and many Senators serve multiple terms, a high Senate turnover is unlikely in any particular election, making it improbable that there will be a dramatic change in near-term Senate preferences.

Consider a scenario in which a ratification document passes with sixty-seven votes. On average, roughly twelve Senate seats turn over at each election.[46] If all twelve departing senators favor the ratification document, and they are all replaced by new senators opposed to the ratification document's provisions, it would take six years for a sixty-seven-vote supermajority of the Senate to gather sufficient numbers to overturn the offending provisions through legislation (assuming that the preferences of continuing senators stay relatively constant over time). If all the departing senators at the end of each Congress support the treaty but only half of their replacements oppose the ratification provisions, then it will take a full twelve years to marshal sufficient Senate votes to overturn the ratification provision. If one quarter of entering senators oppose the ratification document's provisions, on average, then it takes a full eighteen years before opponents have the sixty votes necessary to invoke cloture, and twenty-four years before they could pass a veto-proof measure to overturn the offending provision. Of course, these estimates grow even longer if we relax our assumptions about the preferences of the departing senators.[47] Moreover, all this assumes that a House majority (or supermajority, if necessary) shares the Senate's opposition to the provisions at the time when the Senate musters the necessary votes against the ratification provisions. By this logic, the stipulations contained in Senate documents of ratification should influence U.S. foreign policy well into the future.

Determining NATO Relations by Advice and Consent

The Senate ratification debate over NATO enlargement is an instructive example of the Senate's use of the advice and consent power and the theoretic implications for future U.S. security policy of policymaking by advice and consent. From a practitioner's perspective, consideration of NATO enlargement holds clues as to how the United States might respond to the creation of the European Security and Defense Identity (ESDI). The ESDI aims to provide members of the Western European Union with a military capability independent of the United States.[48] The worry in Washington is that without a significant increase in European defense spending, the ESDI will be created at the expense of NATO.[49] This is particularly troublesome at a time when NATO members agree that the Europeans must do more to close the widening technological gap between U.S. and European military forces. As a result, Europe may field an ineffective ESDI rapid reaction force while sacrificing the capabilities of what many have called the single most successful military alliance in history.[50]

Most commentary in 1998 focused on the Senate's overwhelming approval of NATO membership for Poland, Hungary, and the Czech Republic.[51] Ignored was the fact that the Senate also produced an extensive document of ratification (Treaty Doc. No. 105-36) that detailed America's role in European security.[52] The use of a ratification document was attractive because it kept the House out of the policy process at a time when there were significant ideological differences between the House and the Senate. The ratification document also ensured that Senate policy initiatives would be accepted by the Clinton administration, something that had not always occurred between the Republican-controlled Senate and the Democratic president. Finally, policymaking through advice and consent assured that Senate preferences will continue to affect U.S. alliance policy into the foreseeable future. This last point was particularly important because the Clinton administration's acceptance of the Senate's ratification document does not mean that some future president might not want to violate the Senate's 1998 intent.[53] Use of a ratification document prevents such changes.

The Senate fundamentally altered the policy process on the issue of transatlantic security when it crafted that ratification document, enacting three broad policy initiatives focusing on the U.S. costs of NATO membership, Senate input into NATO's future purpose, and the prerequisites for future U.S. security commitments. The Senate also included provisions providing them with the information necessary to ensure future compliance with these terms. Increased information, in the form of presidential certifications and executive reports, would help the legislature monitor and prevent drastic changes to the transatlantic security relationship.[54]

COSTS OF NATO MEMBERSHIP

The Foreign Relations Committee changed the process of estimating the U.S. share of NATO costs, in large part due to worries that an ever-expanding NATO might translate into an increasingly costly alliance for the United States. Throughout 1997 and into the winter of 1998, estimates for NATO expansion ranged widely, with ten-year cost estimates varying from a Congressional Budget Office (CBO) figure of $21–$125 billion to a final administration figure of $1.5 billion.[55] As a result of this confusion, the Committee made clear that equitable burden-sharing was one of its top priorities for the future. In the words of Senate Foreign Relations Committee Chairman Jesse Helms (R-N.C.):

> The majority of the costs of making and keeping NATO militarily effective will be the responsibilities of our allies, a point that this committee will empha-size in the Resolution of Ratification. It is assumed, of course, that the ad-ministration will continue its insistence that all NATO members must meet their commitments to the common defense. If not, the expansion of NATO this year may be followed shortly thereafter by NATO's collapse, and nobody wants that to happen.[56]

The Foreign Relations Committee made good on Helms' word, including language in the ratification document to prevent the United States from shoul-dering an increased defense burden, either as a result of an ally's outdated ca-pabilities or through an increase to the U.S. share of the NATO budget. Specifically, the Committee required the president to certify that the United States was under no obligation to subsidize the military upgrades required of the three new NATO members, that enlargement did not detract from the U.S. ability to meet its other security requirements, and that the three new allies would not increase the U.S. contribution to the NATO common budget (Section 3.2A). The committee also demanded annual reports on allied burden-sharing, the adequacy of that allied contribution to meeting NATO security obligations, and U.S. costs associated with the first round of enlargement (Section 3.2B).

Together, these reports and certifications established a baseline cost es-timate for U.S. membership in NATO, provided Congress with improved in-formation on allied burden-sharing, and required that future costs remain within congressionally accepted bounds. These provisions have important implications for future U.S. behavior. They signify that the United States is not willing to subsidize alliance partners (new or old) if they do not maintain the capabilities necessary for alliance security. Moreover, they give Congress the information to judge whether that has in fact occurred. Should an ally's behavior lead to a decrease in NATO capabilities or its contributions to the alliance, Congress will know about it and has made it harder for the United States to make up the difference.

When the ratification document was reported to the floor, Senator Ted Stevens (R-Alaska), chair of the Senate Appropriations Committee, weighed in on the issue of the U.S. share of the NATO common-fund budget. Stevens was frustrated by the administration's practice of paying for the NATO mission in Bosnia by skimming money from unrelated Department of Defense (DOD) accounts. He saw this as circumventing the congressional budget process and a threat to U.S. military readiness. Stevens introduced two amendments to prevent the U.S. contribution to NATO's common budget from increasing without explicit congressional approval while at the same time ensuring that the president had the freedom to respond to emerging threats. Executive Amendment 2066 stipulated that the U.S. share of the NATO common budget could never exceed 1998 levels unless specifically authorized by law. It further suggested that the U.S. attempt to decrease its share of the NATO common-fund budget by 1 percent each year over the subsequent five years, eventually taking the United States down to a 20 percent share. The first Stevens amendment effectively prohibits the United States from making up for shortfalls in an ally's contribution to the NATO budget, absent prior congressional approval. Steven's companion amendment (Ex. Amdt. 2065) said that no costs from NATO enlargement could be paid by the United States without those funds being specifically authorized by law for that purpose. In effect this prevented the administration from paying for hidden costs of NATO enlargement and signaled the administration of renewed congressional vigilance.[57] The amendment warned that the Senate will likely refuse to provide monetary support for new U.S. security commitments unless they had prior congressional approval. Both amendments passed by voice vote.[58]

NATO's Purpose

The Foreign Relations Committee established strict guidelines on the issue of NATO's future purpose.[59] The Committee went on record that it preferred NATO stay a defensive organization. In the declarations section of the ratification document (Section 2.6) the Committee affirmed that it understood NATO's purpose was "the collective defense of its members," rather than the promotion of democracy, crisis prevention, or a forum for the resolution of political disputes among European states (i.e., the OSCE), or an organization for the economic, political, and social integration of all Europe (i.e., the EU). The implication was that the Senate had unequivocally defined NATO as a defensively oriented alliance, at least as far as the United States was concerned. The United States therefore was not committed to any task other than collective NATO defense.

The committee then set out a series of binding conditions to limit presidential flexibility when negotiating changes to NATO's strategic concept. Section 3.1A stated that "the core purpose of NATO must continue to be the collective defense of the territory of all NATO members." The ratification document allowed other actions (like peacemaking) should they be necessary to respond to a threat, but only on a case-by-case basis and only when there was a consensus among all NATO members. Under these conditions the president could not support changes to NATO that would move the alliance away from collective defense. That in effect assured that any change to NATO's strategic concept would remain consistent with Senate preferences, since changing NATO's purpose requires the unanimous agreement of all NATO members.[60] Building on their earlier purpose-related provision (Section 2.6), the Committee was ensuring that NATO would not someday take on missions similar to those currently contemplated for the ESDI.

Finally, the Committee also required that NATO maintain the defense infrastructure to achieve its core defensive purpose (Section 3.1B). Individual peacemaking missions in Europe were permissible to committee members, but they could not come at the expense of that core defensive purpose. The implication was that the Senate saw NATO capabilities as the crucial milestone for assessing the viability of the alliance. Activities conducted by ESDI were fine, members said, so long as they would not degrade core alliance capabilities. If they did, Section 3.2 of the ratification document would imply that the Senate was unlikely to support increased U.S. contributions to European defense, either if the alliance itself took part in extra-European peacemaking duties or if alliance members expected the United States to subsidize their independent peacemaking activities. Rescinding these provisions was extremely difficult since each is crucial to NATO's underlying purpose.

The full Senate debate on NATO's primary purpose centered on worries that peacemaking missions like Bosnia would become NATO's rationale for existence. The successful Kyl amendment (Ex. Amdt. 2310), offered by Senator Jon L. Kyl (R-Ariz.), reaffirmed the Committee's interpretation of NATO's existing strategic concept, specifying that NATO was first and foremost a military alliance aimed at collectively responding to external threats. It also referred to ESDI by implication. It allowed for "ad hoc coalitions of willing partners" to project NATO power outside alliance territory, but only so long as that did not detract from NATO's core defensive mission. The Kyl amendment thus would seem to demonstrate U.S. conceptual support for ESDI, as long as the resulting organization did not come at the expense of NATO capabilities and the Senate's more traditional notion of European defense.[61] At the same time, however, it further specified NATO's purpose, making this provision difficult to waive or rescind. A vast majority of senators supported the Kyl amendment in a 90 to 9 vote.

FUTURE U.S. SECURITY COMMITMENTS

The Foreign Relations Committee ruled out implicit or explicit U.S. security commitments to non-NATO countries unless that commitment had the Senate's formal and prior consent.[62] This provision was motivated by Senate worries that the United States might repeat its implicit 1998 security commitment to the Baltic states contained in the January 1998 Baltic–U.S. Charter of Partnership.[63] The committee left little to chance on this score, declaring that the Senate would not recognize any statement that "constitutes a security commitment pursuant to NATO" without the consent of the U.S. Senate (Section 2.7B).[64] Lest such an informal security commitment lead to NATO membership, the document of ratification also specified that the United States would not support either the admission *or invitation for admission* of any other country without the Senate's advice and consent (Section 2.7A). With this clause, senators forestalled future invitations of NATO membership before they were made unless those invitations had broad-based support in both the executive and legislative branches.[65] Before such an invitation would be accepted by the Senate, the president would have to certify that a "prospective NATO member can fulfill the obligations and responsibilities of membership, and its inclusion would serve the overall political and strategic interests of NATO and the United States," (Section 2.7Aii).[66]

The full Senate also addressed the possibility of future implicit security commitments to non-NATO states that might lead to their formal acceptance into the alliance. The vehicle of choice was a bipartisan amendment (Ex. Amdt. 2319) introduced by Senators Helms and Biden. It stated that prior to any decisions by the North Atlantic Council to begin accession talks with prospective NATO members, the administration must evaluate for the Senate: each prospective member's contribution to NATO security; its military readiness; its effect on U.S. national security if admitted to NATO; its effect on the NATO common-fund budget and how much of that cost would be borne by the United States; and the effect of its admittance on the U.S. defense and foreign affairs budgets. The administration would be required to update this report prior to the signing of any formal invitation to that country, and would further be required to include an analysis of the prospective member's ability to pay the costs of NATO membership and that member's military effectiveness once in NATO. All reports would be subject to immediate review by the General Accounting Office (GAO), a nonpartisan support agency staffed with experts who provide Congress with analytical talent matching that in universities or specialized groups.

The leadership amendment had wide support, passing by voice vote after virtually no public deliberation.[67] It ensured that Congress was included in the commitment process very early on, and could veto such a commitment (given that any membership invitation had to have prior Senate approval, as specified in Section 2.7A of the ratification document). The amendment also corrected a number of deficiencies in the just-completed round of enlargement. In particular it strengthened the Committee language regarding how the future costs of NATO enlargement would be estimated and provided an independent evaluation of that report. With a new reporting process in effect, Congress would receive robust information on future alliance costs.[68] Moreover, combined with the second Stevens amendment (prohibiting the United States from absorbing future enlargement costs) the Senate would be well within its rights to refuse requests for additional support from NATO-ESDI members who might someday make security commitments to non-NATO countries.

Table 3.3 summarizes the results of the advice and consent process. Senators agreed to the Stevens amendments that required congressional approval for all NATO-related expenditures while curtailing the administration's practice of shifting money from one budget item to another. This complemented the Committee's requirements that Congress receive detailed information on the U.S. share of NATO common-fund costs. The Senate passed the Kyl amendment to ensure that the president would have the flexibility to meet emerging threats, but not at the expense of the alliance's defensive purpose. This complemented the Committee's prohibition on changing NATO's strategic purpose away from collective defense. Finally, the Senate strengthened the reporting requirements contained in the original Committee draft, especially with regard to prospective members and the costs of future enlargement. This complemented the Committee's desire to maintain a congressional check on future alliance decisions and U.S. security commitments.

The Senate's actions on these three issues—limiting the U.S. contribution to the alliance, preventing NATO from altering its core defensive purpose, and prohibiting either implicit or explicit U.S. security commitments beyond current NATO members—have direct implications for ESDI. The United States would seemingly welcome ESDI, but only if it did not add to the American burden (e.g., should U.S. allies fail to improve their military capabilities as a result), or increase U.S. security commitments due to ESDI activities beyond NATO territory. These provisions were included by design rather than by accident.[69] Table 3.3 summarizes the Senate ratification document.

Note that table entries with an asterisk represent provisions defining the alliance's underlying purpose. They cannot be waived or rescinded without amending the original treaty, a process that would require presidential concurrence and a two-third supermajority in the Senate to take effect. That is, when the Senate reaffirmed the primacy of NATO's collective defense mission, prohibited U.S. support of efforts to change that mission or degrade the alliance's ability to achieve that mission, and ruled out extending U.S. security commitments to non-NATO members without prior Senate consent, the language used in the ratification document made these understandings and prohibitions integral to the Senate's definition of the NATO alliance. Changing them would require further international amendments to the Washington Treaty and the subsequent consent of two-thirds of the Senate, an unlikely occurrence given that eighty-two senators supported the 1998 document of ratification and its stipulations on U.S. behavior. The Senate also put monetary limits on the U.S. contribution to the NATO budget and to expenses related to NATO enlargement, unless authorized by law. In theory, these monetary provisions could be rescinded by subsequent legislation, but there

TABLE 3.3   SENATE CONSIDERATION OF NATO ENLARGEMENT

ISSUE	SENATE UNDERSTANDINGS	EXECUTIVE CERTIFICATIONS AND REQUIRED REPORTS	PROHIBITED BEHAVIOR
Costs of NATO Membership	*Amendment*: The U.S. should attempt to decrease its contribution to the common budget by 1 percent each year over the following five years.	*Sec 3.2A*: Certification that new members will not increase U.S. costs. *Sec 3.2B*: Annual reports on burden-sharing, security obligations, and costs of expansion.	*Amendment*: Exceeding 1998 contributions to NATO's common fund unless authorized by law. *Amendment*: Funding NATO enlargement expenses unless authorized by law.
NATO's Purpose	*Sec 2.6*: NATO serves a different purpose than do other European organizations (e.g., the EU or OSCE). *Amendment*: NATO is a defensive alliance that is also capable of responding to common threats.		*Sec 3.1A*: Efforts to move NATO away from a defensive focus. *Sec 3.2B*: Efforts to degrade NATO's defense-oriented infrastructure and capabilities.
Future Security Commitments		*Sec 2.7Aii*: Certification that any prospective member meets NATO membership criteria and will serve U.S. political and security interests. *Amendment*: Executive reports on the effect of prospective members on alliance costs, subject to GAO review.	*Sec 2.7A*: An invitation to prospective members without prior Senate consent. *Sec 2.7B*: Commitments pursuant to NATO made without prior Senate consent

is little incentive for Congress to do so.[70] After all, they serve the interests of Congress by reaffirming the congressional role in the budgetary process. Moreover, these provisions have wide support in a body whose membership changes very slowly. For both reasons, then, we are unlikely to see them rescinded anytime soon.

CONCLUSION

The advice and consent process is an underappreciated form of policymaking. The Senate is significantly advantaged when it utilizes the advice and consent process rather than the normal legislative process. Policymaking through advice and consent dramatically reduces the necessity for intra- and interbranch policy compromise. Once enacted, ratification documents produced by the advice and consent process are extremely resistant to change, in effect reducing the political uncertainty associated with policymaking. Finally, using advice and consent for policymaking has the courts' support. In sum, advice and consent privileges Senate initiatives relative to those of either the president or the House in a manner not possible through the normal legislative process.

The NATO case suggests that practitioners should perhaps devote more attention to Senate policymaking by advice and consent. If ratification documents are at all durable, the 1998 document of ratification on NATO enlargement has far-reaching implications for the transatlantic defense relationship, particularly should the ESDI divert European resources earmarked for NATO, make security commitments outside NATO territory that involve the United States by extension, or intervene militarily in far-flung locations and then require U.S. assistance. How the United States will react to any and all of these scenarios will in large part be determined by the provisions of the 1998 ratification document. Should these scenarios develop, the Senate's 1998 actions portend a crisis in transatlantic security relations.

The broader discussion of the advice and consent process has implications for the study of Congress and foreign policy. Much of the literature on U.S. foreign policy notes the declining role of Congress in foreign policy from the 1930s until at least the 1970s. One factor contributing to that decline, and to the somewhat anemic resurgence since then, says this literature, is that the president forwards fewer and fewer international agreements to the Senate as treaties for its advice and consent. Instead, Presidents increasingly use executive agreements to bypass Congress altogether.[71]

Comparing the number of treaties versus executive agreements may be a misleading indicator of congressional influence in foreign policy. The fact that presidents have entered into an increasing number of executive agreements may not signify declining Senate influence.[72] The number of treaties considered annually by the Senate *has* declined relative to the total number of international agreements concluded by the executive branch each year. But the Senate can use the treaty advice and consent process to insert far-ranging guidance as to future U.S. foreign policy priorities, both on the issues addressed in the treaty and on nongermane subjects. So while the number of treaties considered by the Senate may not have kept pace with U.S. international commitments, the Senate can certainly still influence those commitments through the advice and consent process.

NOTES

1. The author thanks Debbi Avant, Sarah Binder, Larry Evans, Jim Goldgeier, Forrest Maltzman, Lee Sigelman, Jay Smith, and Paul Wahlbeck for useful suggestions, and numerous Senate and Administration officials who agreed to be interviewed on the condition of anonymity.

2. Terry M. Moe, "Political Institutions: The Neglected Side of the Story," *Journal of Law, Economics, and Organization* 6 (special issue 1990), p. 221.

3. Moe, "Political Institutions: The Neglected Side of the Story," p. 227; and Terry M. Moe, "The Politics of Structural Choice," in *Organization Theory*, ed. Oliver Williamson (New York: Oxford University Press, 1995).

4. Moe, "Political Institutions: The Neglected Side of the Story," pp. 229–230; and Moe, "The Politics of Structural Choice," pp. 125–127.

5. Compromise might also lead to issue linkages that produce suboptimal outcomes.

6. This argument is reviewed in James Lindsay, *Congress and the Politics of Foreign Policy* (Baltimore: Johns Hopkins University Press, 1994), pp. 90–93.

7. For a summary of institutional and electorally based collective action problems confronting Congress on foreign policy issues, see David P. Auerswald and Peter C. Cowhey, "Ballotbox Diplomacy: The War Powers Resolution and the Use of Force," *International Studies Quarterly* 41 (1997), pp. 510–512.

8. Sarah A. Binder, "The Dynamics of Legislative Gridlock, 1947–1996," *American Political Science Review* 93 (1999), pp. 527–528. For earlier work on divided government, see Gary Cox and Samuel Kernell, *The Politics of Divided Government* (Boulder: Westview Press, 1991); Gary C. Jacobson, *The Electoral Origins of Divided Government* (Boulder: Westview Press, 1990); and Susanne Lohmann and Sharyn O'Halloryn, "Divided Government and U.S. Trade Policy," *International Organization* 48 (1994), pp. 595–632.

9. Binder, "The Dynamics of Legislative Gridlock, 1947–1996," p. 530.

10. Passing major legislation is certainly possible, but only after significant compromises have been made or if the legislation was supported by a preexisting consensus. The resulting compromise is one explanation advanced by David R. Mayhew as to why most major laws were supported with large supermajorities in both congressional chambers. See David R. Mayhew, *Divided We Govern: Party Control, Lawmaking and Investigations, 1946–1990* (New Haven, CT: Yale University Press, 1991), pp. 119–124. Mayhew writes (pp. 131–132): "In this complicated setting, it seldom makes sense to aim for a 51 percent majority. What does make sense is to try to cut down the size and intensity of a bill's opposition. . . . Not surprisingly, many bills that make it through to final passage enjoy wide appeal, or at least assent."

11. For a text, see: *Congressional Record*, 82nd Cong., 1st sess., April 4, 1951, S3382.

12. For a legislative history, see *Congressional Quarterly Almanac*, 1951, VII, pp. 220–232; Senate, *Senate Report 175*, 82nd Congress, 1st Session (Washington, D.C.: U.S. Government Printing Office), pp. 2–3; and Louis Fisher, *Constitutional Conflicts between Congress and the President*, 4th ed. (Lawrence, KS: University of Kansas Press, 1997), pp. 97–101.

13. Privately, the administration saw the legislation as an attempt by congressional Republicans to opportunistically criticize Truman. See *Public Papers of the President, Harry S. Truman, 1951* (Washington, D.C.: U.S. Government Printing Office, 1965), pp. 18–22; State Department, *Foreign Relations of the United States, 1950*, VII (Washington, D.C.: U.S. Government Printing Office, 1975), pp. 200–202, 286–291; *Congressional Record*, 81st Cong., 2nd sess., June 1950, S9154-60, S9268-69, S9319-29, S9537-40; and Dean Acheson, *Struggle for a Free Europe* (New York: Norton, 1971), pp. 32–33.

14. Provisions that might provoke a presidential veto would necessitate the annual support of bicameral supermajorities.

15. *Congressional Quarterly, Guide to Congress*, 5th ed. (Washington D.C.: CQ Press, 2000), p. 204.

16. Louis Henkin, *Foreign Affairs and the Constitution* (New York: Foundation Press, Inc., 1972), p. 136. For example, the Senate conditioned ratification of the Flank Document to the Conventional Forces in Europe (CFE) Treaty on presidential actions related to the ABM Treaty (Section 2[9]). See *Congressional Record*, 105th Cong., 1st sess., May 14, 1997, S4477.

17. Moe, "Political Institutions: The Neglected Side of the Story." Moe (p. 225) notes: "Groups want to ensure that their favored policies and programs are carried out as effectively as possible. They evaluate their structural options accordingly, and this strongly influences the positions they take and the strategies they pursue in the political struggle."

18. The four scenarios therefore represent ideal types and are not meant to reflect every instance of Senate advice and consent. More sophisticated behavior is considered later.

19. The Senate regularly takes advantage of the two-thirds present and voting provision to pass ratification documents by voice vote or with less than sixty-seven votes.

20. Of course, proceeding to debate a ratification document might require invoking cloture. At the least that meant that a ratification document was no harder to pass than was legislation, all else being equal.

21. Passage of a ratification document is actually slightly easier, given that it requires two-thirds of Senators present and voting.

22. Legislation goes nowhere after a presidential veto should at least one-third of the House oppose the Senate initiative—a near certainty if one or both major parties are internally divided, as has been the case with House majority parties in recent decades, or if each chamber is controlled by different political parties, as occurred during portions of the Reagan administration and seems to be occurring in the 107th Congress (2001–2003).

23. Henkin, *Foreign Affairs and the Constitution*. Henkin (p. 149) writes: "The House of Representatives has frequently bristled, but its exclusion from the treaty process was the clear constitutional plan." Again, there are always exceptions to any rule, particularly when a treaty requires implementing legislation. These exceptions are discussed later.

24. This discussion assumes that a treaty is under consideration and the Senate *wants* to change U.S. policy.

25. This may be why a nontrivial number of treaties receive no consideration during each Congress. For examples of intra-Senate politics and its effect on treaty advice and consent, see Chapter 5 by Evans and Oleszek.

26. This is particularly true for Table 3.1, rows 3 and 4.

27. Author's interviews with Senate staff, 2000.

28. The ratification documents associated with the 1978 Panama Canal Treaty (Ex. N, 95-1) and a recent treaty on International Adoptions (Treaty Doc. 105-51) both contain such provisions.

29. President Clinton refused to submit for the Senate's advice and consent the so-called Demarcation Agreement and Memorandum of Understanding on State Succession to the ABM Treaty, knowing that both would fail in the Senate. Author's interviews with Senate staff, 1999.

30. Senate, *S. Prt. 103-53: Treaties and Other International Agreements; the Role of the United States Senate* (Washington D.C.: U.S. Government Printing Office, 1993), pp. 116–117.

31. Lisa Martin's recent work on treaties lends support to this intuition. She argues that a president's choice to conclude an executive agreement rather than a formal treaty is greatly affected by concerns regarding international credibility. Presidents are more likely to negotiate a formal treaty and forego an executive agreement when they care deeply about an issue and want to demonstrate a U.S. commitment to a particular course of action. Treaties are a more credible commitment device internationally, says Martin, because the U.S. advice and consent process is costly for a president—thereby demonstrating the president's commitment to the agreement—and the Congress has an opportunity to signal its support of the agreement through the ratification process—thereby demonstrating the country's commitment to the agreement. Martin's argument therefore reinforces the idea that a president is unlikely to abandon treaties except when they were negotiated by a previous president or if the Senate conditions ratification on truly onerous requirements. Martin's argument also suggests that the international nature of treaties may be a more effective constraint against extreme provisions in ratification documents than is a presidential "veto." That is, the Senate may feel prohibited from pursuing its ideal policy because including that policy in a ratification document would be unacceptable to international treaty partners. Including such provisions could lead treaty partners to withhold their own instruments of ratification, in effect killing the treaty. See Lisa Martin, *Democratic Commitments: Legislatures and International Cooperation* (Princeton: Princeton University Press, 2000), pp. 53–80.

32. Though the Senate has defeated only twenty-one treaties in its history, it has failed to act on or has returned to the president a much larger number. See *Congressional Quarterly, Guide to Congress*, p. 203.

33. Henkin, *Foreign Affairs and the Constitution*, p. 134, note 20.

34. Ibid., pp. 134–136, including examples in notes 30 and 31. Elsewhere, Henkin states that: "The Senate's understanding of the treaty to which it consents is binding on the President. He can make the treaty only as so understood. He cannot make the treaty and insist that it means something else." Quoted in Senate, *Senate Hearing 100–110, The ABM Treaty and the Constitution: Joint Hearings before the Committee on Foreign Relations and the Committee on the Judiciary*, 11, 26 March and 29 April 1987 (Washington D.C.: U.S. Government Printing Office, 1987), pp. 81–82, also see p. 87. Harold Koh notes: "Article III of the Constitution (not to mention

Marbury v. Madison) settled that the courts, not the President or the Senate, bear the final authority to decide cases and controversies arising under treaties made by the United States. Once the Supreme Court has ruled on a matter of treaty interpretation, its ruling is authoritative as United States law and binds the political branches of the federal government." See Harold Koh, "The President versus the Senate in Treaty Interpretation: What's all the Fuss About?" *Yale Journal of International Law* 15 (1990), p. 333.

35. Koh, "The President versus the Senate in Treaty Interpretation: What's All the Fuss About?" pp. 340, 342. See in particular the extended remarks at 109 S. Ct. 1191, note 7.
36. Ibid., p. 343, citing Detlev Vagts, "Senate Materials and Treaty Interpretation: Some Research Hints for the Supreme Court," *American Journal of International Law* 83 (1989), p. 547 note 5. For other precedents, see Henkin, *Foreign Affairs and the Constitution*, p. 134, note 20.
37. Senate, *Senate Hearing 100–110: The ABM Treaty and the Constitution: Joint Hearings before the Committee on Foreign Relations and the Committee on the Judiciary*, 11, 26 March and 29 April 1987; and S. Lakoff and H. York, *A Shield in Space? Technology, Politics, and the Strategic Defense Initiative* (Berkeley: University of California Press, 1989), pp. 188–189.
38. Lakoff and York, *A Shield in Space? Technology, Politics, and the Strategic Defense Initiative*, pp. 287–288.
39. For a review, see Senate, *S. Prt. 103-53: Treaties and Other International Agreements; the Role of the United States Senate*, pp. xxx–xxxi, 98–100; and Koh, "The President versus the Senate in Treaty Interpretation: What's All the Fuss About?" p. 334.
40. Author's interviews with Senate staff, 2000.
41. Studies of principal–agent relations have demonstrated that Congress tries to do just that when delegating to the federal bureaucracy. Congress does not simply abdicate all policy-making authority to bureaucratic agents and then hope for the best. Instead, Congress provides agents with selective incentives, enfranchises particular third parties into the policy process, and enacts specific reporting requirements, all in an effort to ensure that bureaucratic activities reflect the preferences of the congressional majorities who crafted the principal–agent relationship. For representative discussions of delegation to agents, see Barry R. Weingast and Mark Moran, "Bureaucratic Discretion or Congressional Control?" *Journal of Political Economy* 91 (1983), pp. 765–800; Mathew D. McCubbins and Thomas Schwartz, "Congressional Oversight Overlooked: Police-Patrols versus Fire-Alarms," *American Journal of Political Science* 2 (1984), pp. 65–179; Terry M. Moe, "The Economics of Organization," *American Journal of Political Science* 28 (1984), pp. 739–777; Barry R. Weingast, "The Congressional-Bureaucratic System: A Principal Agent Perspective," *Public Choice* 44 (1984), pp. 147–191; Mathew D. McCubbins and T. Page, "A Theory of Congressional Delegation," in *Congress: Structure and Process*, ed. Mathew D. McCubbins and Terry Sullivan (New York: Cambridge University Press, 1987); Mathew D. McCubbins, Roger G. Noll, and Barry R. Weingast, "Administrative Procedures as Instruments of Political Control," *Journal of Law, Economics and Organization* 3 (1987), pp. 243–277; and Terry M. Moe, "An Assessment of the Positive Theory of 'Congressional Dominance,'" *Legislative Studies Quarterly* 12 (1987), pp. 475–519.
42. Absent amending the treaty, changing these principles corresponds to some of the various ways of terminating a treaty as recognized by international law. See Senate, *S. Prt. 103-53: Treaties and Other International Agreements; the Role of the United States Senate*, pp. 153–158.
43. *Whitney v. Robertson*, 124 U.S. 581 (1888), p. 194.
44. Senate, *S. Prt. 103-53: Treaties and Other International Agreements; the Role of the United States Senate*, pp. xxxi, 50; Henkin, *Foreign Affairs and the Constitution*, pp. 163, 164 note 111; and author's interviews with Senate Staff, 2000.
45. Koh, "The President versus the Senate in Treaty Interpretation: What's All the Fuss About?" p. 333.
46. Gary C. Jacobson, *The Politics of Congressional Elections*, 5th ed. (New York: Longman, 2001), p. 23.
47. The estimates stay roughly as described if we allow some departing Senators to oppose the treaty and some continuing Senators to change their positions over time.
48. From the American perspective, ESDI holds great potential as well as peril. If successfully implemented, it could allow the European allies to engage in peacemaking without American troops, combat terrorism and the threat from weapons of mass destruction, and spur the Europeans to redress the imbalance between U.S. and European military capabilities in NATO (NATO, 1999B, "Development of the European Security and Defense Identity (ESDI) within NATO, April 1999," <http://www.nato.int/docu/facts/2000/dev-esdi.htm>; and Defense

Department "Press Conference by Secretary of Defense Cohen at NATO Headquarters, December 2, 1999," <http://www.nato.int/usa/dod/s991201b.htm>. But all this will take money—money the Europeans seem reluctant to spend. See General Accounting Office, *NATO: Implications of European Integration for Allies' Defense Spending*, Report GAO/NSIAD-99-185, June 1999 (Washington D.C.: General Accounting Office, 1999), pp. 6–8; NATO, "The European Security and Defense Identity within NATO—Luis Maria de Puig, Chairman of the WEU Assembly," in *NATO Review* 46 (1998), pp. 6–9, <http://www.nato.int/docu/review/1998/9802-03.htm>; J. Lepgold, "NATO's Post-Cold War Collective Action Problem," *International Security* 23 (1998), pp. 78–106; Charles Kupchan, "NATO and the Persian Gulf: Examining Intra-Alliance Behavior," *International Organization* 42 (1988), pp. 317–346. In that sense, the ESDI is emblematic of the larger issue of appropriate allied burden-sharing. See NATO, "ESDI: Berlin, St. Malo and Beyond—Speech delivered by Ambassador Vershbow, January 18, 1999," <http://www.nato.int/usa/ambassador/s990128a.htm> (NATO, 1999).

49. NATO, "ESDI: Berlin, St. Malo and Beyond—Speech delivered by Ambassador Vershbow, January 18, 1999"; and Defense Department, "Press Conference by Secretary of Defense Cohen at NATO Headquarters, December 2, 1999."

50. For a description of the rapid reaction force, see NATO, "The European Security and Defense Identity," <www.nato.int/docu/fact/esdi.htm>.

51. There was little opposition to NATO enlargement in either the Senate Foreign Relations Committee (where the vote was 18 to 2 in favor of enlargement) or on the Senate floor (where the final vote was 82 to 19).

52. For the text, see Senate, *Exec. Rpt. 105-14: Protocols to the North Atlantic Treaty of 1949 on Accession of Poland, Hungary, and the Czech Republic* (Washington D.C.: U.S. Government Printing Office, 1998).

53. Author's interviews with Executive Branch and Senate staff confirm that the Clinton administration did not object to the provisions contained in the 1998 ratification document.

54. Author's interviews with Senate staff, 1998. In essence, the Senate wrote into law the consultative process that characterized the 1998 round of NATO enlargement.

55. Estimates are summarized in General Accounting Office, *NATO Enlargement: Requirements and Costs for Commonly Funded Budgets*, GAO/NSIAD-98-113, March 1998 (Washington D.C.: General Accounting Office, 1998) and in Congressional Research Service, *NATO Expansion: Cost Issues*, 97-668F, February 26, 1998 (Washington D.C.: Government Printing Office, 1998A). For a discussion, see Senate, *S. Hrg. 105–285—The Debate on NATO Enlargement: Hearings by the Senate Committee on Foreign Relations* (Washington D.C.: U.S. Government Printing Office, 1998), pp. 123–182. For projections into the future, see General Accounting Office, *NATO History of Common Budget Cost Shares*, GAO/NSIAD-98-172, May (Washington D.C.: General Accounting Office, 1998); and Congressional Research Service, *NATO Common Funds Burdensharing: Background and Current Issues*, 98-239F, March 11 (Washington D.C.: Government Printing Office, 1998).

56. Senate, *S. Hrg. 105–285—The Debate on NATO Enlargement: Hearings by the Senate Committee on Foreign Relations*, p. 2.

57. Author's interview with Senate staff, 1998.

58. *Congressional Record*, 105th Cong., 2nd sess., April 30, 1998, S3859-60.

59. To some extent this was in response to the administration's ambiguous plans to revise NATO's so-called Strategic Concept before the April 1999 NATO summit. Hearings in 1997 by the House National Security Committee may have contributed to Senate unease over revising the 1991 strategic concept. See House, *HNSC No. 105–15, United States Policy Regarding NATO Expansion: Hearings by the House Committee on National Security* (Washington D.C.: U.S. Government Printing Office, 1997), pp. 30, and 22–23. When questioning administration witnesses, Committee members repeatedly asked for the administration's vision for NATO's future. For examples, see Senate, *Senate Hearing 105–285, The Debate on NATO Enlargement: Hearings by the Senate Committee on Foreign Relations*, pp. 22–25.

60. Author's interviews with Senate staff, 1998.

61. *Congressional Record*, 105th Cong., 2nd sess., April 28, 1998, S3695.

62. Congressional Research Service, *NATO Common Funds Burdensharing: Background and Current Issues*, pp. 20, 25, and 46.

63. *Public Papers of the Presidents, Administration of William J. Clinton, January 16, 1998* (Washington, D.C.: U.S. Government Printing Office, 1998), pp. 85–91.

64. Author's interviews with Senate staff, 1988.
65. Ibid.
66. With the exception of this last clause, these provisions are central to NATO's core purpose and thus are difficult to rescind. They also have direct implications for ESDI activities. If the ESDI were to make a security commitment to a non-NATO country, the Senate provisions make clear that such a commitment does not implicate the United States by extension. The provisions also anticipate a scenario where ESDI nations intervene outside NATO territory and then request U.S. assistance in the form of either direct U.S. military intervention or subsidies to NATO allies engaged in ESDI activities. Even were the U.S. to provide such assistance, the Senate provisions prevent that from evolving into de facto NATO membership for the beleaguered territory.
67. *Congressional Record*, 105th Cong., 2nd sess., April 29, 1998, S3767.
68. Author's interview with Senate staff, 1998.
69. Ibid.
70. Congress waived these monetary limits during the NATO air campaign in Kosovo.
71. Lawrence Margolis, *Executive Agreements and Presidential Power in Foreign Policy* (New York: Praeger, 1986). Chapter 4 by David O'Brien traces the rise of executive agreements to three Supreme Court cases (*U.S. v. Curtis-Wright* [1936], *U.S. v. Belmont* [1937], and *U.S. v. Pink* [1942]) that in combination granted executive agreements a status equivalent to treaties.
72. Martin, *Democratic Commitments: Legislatures and International Cooperation*. Martin's evidence suggests that presidents do not use executive agreements to evade Senate scrutiny.

4

Presidential and Congressional Relations in Foreign Affairs

THE TREATY-MAKING POWER AND THE RISE OF EXECUTIVE AGREEMENTS

David M. O'Brien

The battle over the respective roles of the Congress and the president in the conduct of foreign affairs centers on the treaty-making power and the rise of executive agreements. The first part of this chapter sets forth the classical understanding of foreign relations as a well-defined and constitutionally delineated practice. The treaty-making power was initially understood to play a central role, with Congress and the president sharing power, in foreign affairs. At the end of the nineteenth century, however, that understanding began to break down due, first, to increasing congressional delegation of power to the executive branch and, second, to growing presidential frustration in dealing with the Senate in securing ratification of treaties. But a third factor was the Supreme Court's abandonment of the classical understanding and replacing it with a revisionist theory of presidential predominance in foreign affairs, which is discussed in the chapter's second part. In other words, the Court's rulings in the first few decades of the twentieth century legitimated the rise of executive agreements and encouraged presidents to bypass the Senate and the treaty-making process. The third part, then, concludes by considering how, in the latter half of the twentieth century, the Court reinforced presidential predominance through greater judicial deference to the executive branch in recognition, or on the rationalization, of the need for political expediency in foreign affairs, thereby leaving it largely to Congress to check the president through its other, not inconsiderable, powers.

THE CLASSICAL UNDERSTANDING OF FOREIGN RELATIONS

It is easy to forget how long the classical understanding of foreign relations as a well-defined and constitutionally delineated practice persisted, largely unquestioned until the first decades of the twentieth century. The Constitution of 1787 was, of course, drafted in response to the defects of the Articles of Confederation.[1] More specifically, under the latter, Congress could only make treaties with the consent of nine of the thirteen states, and states exercised powers in both foreign and domestic affairs. That proved unworkable and resulted in Britain and France refusing to honor trade agreements. Hence, among the objectives of the Constitutional Convention was to centralize control in the national government over foreign affairs and commerce.

The constitutional convention's Committee of Detail's initial draft gave the Senate exclusive authority over treaty making.[2] After reaching the "Great Compromise," creating a bicameral legislature, debate focused on which house should exercise the power and whether representatives from large states might use their influence to their own advantage. Just eleven days before completion of the ultimate draft, the matter remained unresolved. And the Committee on Postponed Matters made a final amendment to Article II to provide: "The president by and with the advice and consent of the Senate, shall have power to make Treaties. . . . But no Treaty shall be made without the consent of two-thirds of the members present."[3]

While it remains uncertain why the delegates unanimously agreed to that change, clearly the framers did not aim to lodge the power primarily in the executive, but rather to establish a power shared by the president with the Senate.[4] Moreover, Article 1, Section 8, Clause 3, gives Congress the power to legislate tariffs and to "regulate Commerce with Foreign Nations." In addition, the framers remained concerned about matters of federalism. On the one hand, though states are precluded from entering into "any Treaty," Article 1, Section 10 allows them to enter into an "Agreement or Compact with another State, or with a foreign Power," subject to congressional approval. On the other hand, Article 6 establishes that treaties override conflicting state laws, and thus provides an additional inducement for state compliance with treaties approved by their representatives in the Senate.

From the experience under the Articles of Confederation and the careful drafting of the Constitution in distinguishing treaties from tariffs, compacts, and other international agreements, it seems fair to conclude that the framers contemplated both different procedures for approving documents establishing foreign affairs, and for those documents to possess different legal status. Treaties bound the nation in perpetuity, as it were; whereas, tariffs, compacts, and other international agreements were transitory exchanges, not interchangeable with treaties.

The aim here is not to advance a jurisprudence of "original intention," which admittedly is problematic on a number of grounds.[5] Neither is the aim to quarrel (however inviting) with the inconsistencies of supporters of that view in the administrations of Republican Presidents Ronald Reagan and George Bush, who nevertheless sharply criticized Congress for intruding on executive power in foreign affairs.[6] Nor, at this point, is the purpose to rebut claims that the president was made the "sole organ of foreign affairs."[7] Instead, the objective lies simply in recapturing the classical understanding of the treaty-making power in order to highlight the sharp contrast with the contemporary understanding of the theory and practice of treaty making and the respective roles of the president and Congress in foreign affairs.

The persistence from the founding period throughout the nineteenth century of the classical understanding of the central place of the treaty-making power in the conduct of foreign affairs is underscored by the fact that there were no executive agreements during the first quarter century of the new Republic. In 1803, for instance, when President Thomas Jefferson negotiated the Louisiana Purchase from France, he doubted his constitutional authority and promptly submitted the agreement to the Senate as a treaty, along with asking for enabling legislation from both houses of Congress.[8] Likewise, when President James Monroe made, strictly speaking, the first executive agreement, the 1817 Rush-Bagot Agreement with Britain, limiting the use of military on the Great Lakes, he, too, doubted its constitutionality and submitted it to the Senate, which ratified it as an Article 2 treaty.[9]

Without giving further examples, the point is reinforced by the fact that up to 1910 there were only 124 executive agreements, or an average of one per year since the founding. Moreover, President Theodore Roosevelt (from 1901 to 1909) concluded 52 (or 40 percent of that total) during his time in the Oval Office.[10] Perhaps not surprisingly, executive agreements received little scholarly attention until after the turn of the twentieth century.[11] Furthermore, throughout the nineteenth century the Supreme Court generally narrowly construed the president's power as commander in chief, even during the Civil War.[12]

The principal tenets of the classical understanding of foreign relations may be summarized as follows: First, the conduct of foreign affairs was a constitutionally defined practice, constrained and restrained by specifically enumerated powers and procedures. Second, the treaty-making power set forth in Article 2, Section 2, Clause 2, presumed that most (and, certainly, the most important) international agreements would be treaties submitted to and ratified by the Senate, which as an active participant would serve as a check on the presidency. The president was given the power to initiate and negotiate treaties, but they remained subject to "the Advice and Consent of the Senate" and, ultimately, ratification by a two-thirds, not a simple majority, vote of the Senate. Third, the framers recognized other kinds of legally enforceable international agreements, but they were basically deemed either to be transitory and not constitutionally binding, or to fall into the category of nonjusticiable "political questions" for Congress and the president, not the courts, to determine.[13] Finally, there remained the matter of federalism, the reserved powers of the states under the Tenth Amendment. The treaty power was considered largely unlimited except for restraints, in the words of Justice Stephen Field, "arising from the government itself and that of the States."[14] In short, for most of the nineteenth century, there persisted an understanding of rather clear, bright-line constitutional rules governing the conduct of foreign affairs and the respective roles of the president and Congress, tempered by concerns over federalism.

Under the pressures of the Industrial Revolution and the opening of overseas commercial markets in the late nineteenth century, however, the classical understanding began to allow for an expanded presidential role. Writing for the Court in *Field v. Clark* (1892), Justice John Marshall Harlan upheld a series of reciprocal commercial agreements authorized by Congress in the McKinley Tariff Act of 1890. That act, for the first time, delegated to the president the power to suspend free trade in certain products (sugar, molasses, coffee, tea, and hides) with countries imposing duties on U.S. products. When rebuffing the claim that the law was an unconstitutional delegation of power to the president, Justice Harlan cited as precedents prior legislation, such as the Non-Intercourse Acts of 1809 and 1810. But none squarely supported the delegation at issue. For prior acts authorized the president to proclaim that other nations were not living up to trade agreements and then, if nothing changed, take actions that Congress had prescribed. By contrast, the McKinley Tariff Act, as dissenting Chief Justice Melvin Fuller and Justice Lucius Q. C. Lamar pointed out, "vested in the President the power to regulate our commerce with all foreign nations which produce" goods covered by the act.[15]

Although the delegation of power to the president upheld in *Field v. Clark* was an exception to the prevailing understanding and practice, between the 1890s and World War I, reciprocal commercial agreements gave way to a more general category of "executive agreements," including military, postal, and "temporary arrangements."[16] Still, the treaty-making power and the constitutionally defined roles of the president and the Senate remained generally respected. Congress, and in particular the Senate, along with the president shared policymaking roles in foreign affairs.

Another indicator of the Senate's active participation, or at least of the prevailing concern with obtaining its consent, in the conduct of foreign relations is illustrated in Table 4.1 (on page 74). While the Senate has ratified over 1,500 treaties, it rejected twenty-one proposed treaties. Of those, fifteen were rejected between 1789 and 1920, when the Senate refused to ratify the Treaty of Versailles, which ended World War I. By comparison, after 1920 just six treaties have failed to receive Senate ratification.

Throughout the nineteenth century, the Court acknowledged that treaties were as binding as any other legislation and sustained treaty provisions over conflicting state laws.[17] But, the Court also frequently warned that treaties may not violate principles of federalism or abrogate sovereign state powers.[18] In *Prevost v. Greneaux* (1856) the Court under Chief Justice Roger B. Taney went so far as to uphold a state inheritance tax despite a 1853 treaty with France establishing reciprocal rights of inheritance.[19] Most other matters of foreign affairs—the annexation of territories;[20] the recognition of new governments;[21] the termination of treaties;[22] and the recognition of states of insurgency, belligerency, or war—were deemed nonjusticiable "political questions."[23]

TABLE 4.1   SENATE REJECTION OF PROPOSED TREATIES

DATE OF VOTE	COUNTRY	SUBJECT
March 9, 1825	Columbia	Suppression of African slave trade
June 11, 1836	Switzerland	Property rights
June 8, 1844	Texas	Annexation
June 15, 1844	Germany	Commercial reciprocity
May 31, 1860	Mexico	Transit and commercial rights
June 27, 1860	Spain	Cuban claims commission
April 13, 1869	Britain	Arbitration of claims
June 1, 1870	Hawaii	Commercial reciprocity
June 30, 1870	Dominican Republic	Annexation
January 29, 1885	Nicaragua	Interoceanic canal
April 20, 1886	Mexico	Mining claims
August 21, 1888	Britain	Fishing rights
February 1, 1889	Britain	Extradition
May 5, 1897	Britain	Arbitration
March 19, 1920	Multilateral	Treaty of Versailles
January 18, 1927	Turkey	Commercial rights
March 18, 1934	Canada	St. Lawrence Seaway
January 29, 1935	Multilateral	World Court
May 26, 1960	Multilateral	Law of the Sea Convention
March 8, 1983	Multilateral	Montreal Aviation Protocol
October 14, 1999	Multilateral	Comprehensive Test Ban

Source: U.S Senate Library.

This classical understanding of the constitutional basis for the practice of foreign relations was generally embraced by legal scholars, such as Edward S. Corwin, Quincy Wright, and others.[24] Indeed, as legal historian G. Edward White emphasizes, as late as the early 1920s when Quincy Wright published his influential *The Control of American Foreign Relations* (1922), treaties remained regarded as the principal means of conducting foreign affairs.[25]

Notably, Quincy Wright undertook his book in response to the ongoing debate over the Senate's rejection of the Treaty of Versailles. In summarizing the constitutional law and politics of foreign relations at the time, he glimpsed at what was beyond the horizon when acknowledging the growing role of the president. "In foreign affairs," Wright wrote, "the controlling force is the reverse of that in domestic legislation. The initiation and development of details is with the president, checked only by the veto of the Senate or Congress upon completed proposals."[26] Nonetheless, executive agreements were still not recognized as having the same status as treaties and they remained exceptional, rather than typical, exercises of foreign affairs powers. But, the Court and the country were in the midst of a not yet fully understood constitutional transformation, as it were, on the brink of a new world order.

Dislodging the Classical Understanding and Legitimating Presidential Dominance

As Quincy Wright foresaw, though perhaps not fully appreciated, in motion were developments that would destabilize and dislodge the classical understanding of the central place of the treaty-making power and transform the roles of the president and Congress in foreign affairs. Moreover, in retrospect, in a series of rulings the Supreme Court did as much or more than Congress or the president to legitimate the transformation of the conduct of foreign affairs into one of presidential dominance.

Admittedly, the position advanced here runs contrary to some historical reconstructions that trace the transformation to the presidency of Franklin D. Roosevelt from 1933 to 1945,[27] or to post–World War II geopolitical forces arising out of the Cold War preoccupation with combating the former Soviet Union.[28] Building on Ackerman's provocative theory of popular sovereignty in *We the People* (1991) that "constitutional moments," like the battle over the New Deal, usher in profoundly fundamental changes that reconfigure constitutional law and politics, Bruce Ackerman and David Golove argue that the conduct of foreign relations was transformed in the 1930s and 1940s in ways that legitimate the rise of executive agreements and presidential predominance in foreign affairs thereafter.[29]

It bears noting that Ackerman and Golove advanced their theory in response to the heated controversy over the process for authorizing accession to the North American Free Trade Agreement (NAFTA) and the World Trade Organization (WTO), neither of which were submitted for ratification by two-thirds vote of the Senate. Instead, the president negotiated and signed both agreements as so-called "executive-congressional agreements," after which simple majorities of both houses of Congress approved them pursuant to what was termed "fast-track authority."[30]

To be sure, the process by which the wide-ranging NAFTA and WTO agreements were approved underscores how dramatically the classical understanding of the treaty-making power has given way to presidential dominance in foreign affairs. That transformation remains well summed up in the words of Justice George Sutherland, writing for the Court in *United States v. Curtiss-Wright* (1936): The president, in his words, is the "sole organ of foreign affairs."[31] Yet, the transformation, arguably, began well before *Curtiss-Wright*, FDR's presidency, and the geopolitical forces that later came into play with the Cold War.

Looking back, *Curtiss-Wright* in certain respects merely built on precedents and practices legitimating congressional delegation of, and acquiescence in, greater presidential power in foreign affairs. Like *Field v. Clark*,

Curtiss-Wright upheld a congressional delegation of power, authorizing the president to suspend arms sales to Paraguay and Bolivia if necessary to promote peace in the region. As Justice Sutherland noted in his opinion for the Court, and several contemporaneous decisions striking down early New Deal legislation delegating power to the executive branch underscored, the Court would have invalidated such a delegation of power in domestic affairs.[32]

The classical understanding of the respective powers of the president and Congress in foreign affairs had been incrementally breaking down during the three decades preceding *Curtiss-Wright* due to increasing congressional delegation of power to the president, in both domestic and foreign affairs; growing presidential frustration with dealing with the Senate in obtaining its consent to treaties;[33] and the Court's rulings in cases like *Field v. Clark*. Significantly, after the turn of the century, not only did Congress delegate more authority to the executive branch, but also presidents increasingly negotiated executive agreements, which gradually became a more common practice. President Wilson (1913–1921), for example, negotiated about the same number (54) as Teddy Roosevelt, while Republican President Calvin Coolidge (1923–1929) doubled that number with 120, exceeding all previous presidents.[34]

Furthermore, over two decades before writing *Curtiss-Wright*, Justice Sutherland had championed a revisionist theory of the Constitution, including extraconstitutional powers for the president in foreign affairs. Admittedly, except for *Curtiss-Wright*, Justice Sutherland remains chiefly remembered as a conservative jurist, who voted with a bare majority of the Court to strike down early New Deal delegations of power to the executive branch.[35] That precipitated the 1937 constitutional crisis over FDR's "Court-packing plan" and the Court's "switch-in-time-that-saved-nine."[36] Thereafter, Sutherland remained identified as one of the "Four Horsemen" who, along with Justices Willis Van Devanter, James McReynolds, and Pierce Butler, dissented from the Court's post-1937 rulings upholding New Deal delegations of power, and who rode with those justices in a horse-drawn coach to the Court on oral argument days—hence "the Four Horsemen."[37]

Yet, as Utah's Republican Senator in 1909, Sutherland published a Senate document, reissued as an essay entitled "The Internal and External Powers of the National Government" in the influential *North American Review*.[38] There, he presaged *Curtiss-Wright* in challenging the classical understanding of the constitutional constraints on the conduct of foreign affairs. A decade later in a series of lectures at Columbia University, published as *Constitutional Power and World Affairs*, he refined what he termed a "radically more liberal" theory of sovereignty. Sovereignty, according to him, was divided between internal, domestic affairs, on the one hand, and external, foreign affairs on the other.[39] With respect to the former, the national government's powers were restricted to specifically enumerated provisions of the Constitution and limited by principles of federalism and sovereign state police powers. Whereas, in foreign affairs the national government possessed sovereign and exclusive, even extraconstitutional, powers.

"A striking example" of the bifurcation of sovereignty and the division of constitutional power in domestic and foreign affairs, according to Sutherland's revisionist theory, was the then recently concluded Migratory Bird Treaty of 1918, protecting birds migrating between Canada and the United States. "In the absence of the treaty," Sutherland acknowledged, "the subject [the killing of migratory birds] is one beyond the powers of Congress, since wild game is not the property of the Nation but of the states in their public capacity for the common benefit of the people."[40] However, pursuant to a treaty Congress might legislate on the matter and the executive branch enforce regulations banning the killing of migratory birds over the objection that that amounted to asserting extraconstitutional authority infringing on sovereign state police powers.

Sutherland's constitutional revisionism not only anticipated his eventual opinion in *Curtiss-Wright*, but also the Court's expansive reinterpretation, and virtual abandonment of the federalism concerns of the classical understanding, in *Missouri v. Holland* (1920).[41] Missouri indeed challenged the regulations enacted pursuant to the Migratory Bird Treaty as a violation of the powers "reserved to the States" under the Tenth Amendment. There was no denying that prior decisions affirmed that birds were the property of states.[42] At the time Congress's power over interstate commerce had also not been interpreted so broadly as to justify treating birds as articles in interstate commerce. In sum, in the absence of the treaty, Congress had no power to enact, and the executive branch no power to enforce, the contested regulations.

Writing for the Court in *Missouri v. Holland*, Justice Oliver Wendell Holmes did not dispute that in the absence of the treaty Congress lacked power to regulate migratory birds. Nonetheless, he deemed the regulation to reflect "a national interest of very nearly the first magnitude"; suggested there was something like an inherent federal police power stemming from its sovereignty over external foreign affairs; and found no explicit constitutional limitation on the treaty-making power in the Supremacy Clause. Justice Holmes dismissed the federalism challenge by observing that the case "must be considered in the light of our whole experience and not merely in that of what was said a hundred years ago." And in that light with his typical rhetorical flourish, he swept aside the Tenth Amendment claim, explaining: "To put the claim of the State upon title [to the birds] is to lean upon a slender reed. . . . The whole foundation of the State's rights is the presence within their jurisdiction of birds that yesterday had not arrived, tomorrow may be in another State and in a week a thousand miles away."[43]

Missouri v. Holland, thus, effectively brushed aside traditional federalism concerns about state sovereignty as a limitation on the conduct of foreign affairs and lodged the latter squarely within the exclusive sovereign domain of the national government. Indeed, Justice Holmes swept so broadly that the treaty-making power appeared unlimited.

Although Justice Sutherland neglected to mention *Missouri v. Holland*, he built on it and swept no less broadly in *Curtiss-Wright* when writing into constitutional law his revisionist theory of the president as the "sole organ" in foreign affairs. Drawing on and extending *Field v. Clark* when upholding the statute authorizing the president to proclaim a ban on foreign arm sales, he went out of his way to demolish what remained of the classical understanding of the conduct of foreign affairs. Moreover, in replacing the orthodox constitutional view with his revisionist theory of the national government's external sovereignty and complete, plenary power in foreign affairs, he rested on a flawed rendering of legal history.

According to Justice Sutherland, after the Revolutionary War the national government's external sovereignty derived directly from the British Crown. Whereas, he claimed, the national government's powers in domestic affairs were rooted in and limited by the Constitution. That reinterpretation is, of course, ahistorical—an example of "law office history"—since the states exercised power over both domestic and foreign affairs under the Articles of Confederation.

Nevertheless, having established that in foreign affairs the national government enjoys a monopoly—unchecked and unregulated by the Constitution—Justice Sutherland next asserted boldly that the president "is the sole organ of the federal government in the field of international relations—a power which does not require as a basis for its exercise an act of Congress. . . ."[44] In other words, here, the president could have proclaimed the arms embargo even without Congress's authorization.

. Besides turning somersaults with the history of the founding to justify that result, he strategically lifted out of context a quote from John Marshall. As a member of the House of Representatives in 1800, Marshall defended President John Adams's request for the extradition of a British subject pursuant to the Jay Treaty. Marshall argued that the president was "the sole organ of the nation in its external relations," since "the demand of a foreign nation can only be made on him. He possesses the whole Executive power." Yet, Marshall clearly aimed to establish only that the president was bound to carry out treaties. For, he continued with reasoning along the lines of that justifying the exercise of judicial review in his famous opinion in *Marbury v. Madison* (1803): "[The President] is charged to execute the law. A treaty is . . . a law. He must, then, execute a treaty, where, he, and he alone, possesses the means of executing it."[45] However, Marshall's "sole organ" reference in Justice Sutherland's hands was used to support the much more sweeping, even contrary proposition: Presidential powers in foreign affairs are plenary, and neither derive from nor are limited by Congress.

Still, Justice Sutherland was not quite done. Five months after *Curtiss-Wright* was handed down, another case arrived at the Court, which afforded him another opportunity to write for the Court and to further advance his revisionist theory of presidential power. *United States v. Belmont* (1937) involved a challenge to the Litvinov Agreement of 1933—an exchange of letters between FDR and Soviet Commissar of Foreign Affairs Maxim Litvinov.[46] It granted the Soviets diplomatic recognition in exchange for settlement of some of the Russian government's outstanding debts. At the time, Congress remained opposed, as it had been since the Bolshevik Revolution in 1917, to diplomatic recognition of the Soviet government. And FDR negotiated the Litvinov Agreement as a "sole executive agreement," basically, a protocol not submitted for ratification by the Senate. One of the most important parts of the agreement was the Soviets' assigning to the government all money due under U.S. court decisions to the Russian government from U.S. citizens.

In *United States v. Belmont*, the federal government had sued to recover funds deposited in 1918 by the Petrograd Metal Works Company with a private banker, August Belmont and Company in New York. The Petrograd Metal Works Company had been appropriated and nationalized by the Soviet government in 1918. And under the Litvinov Agreement, the company's assets in New York would be assigned to the national government. Belmont's executors, though, refused to release the funds on several grounds: The account was located in New York, not on Soviet territory; New York courts did not enforce expropriation decrees affecting property within the state; and, finally, to transfer the funds under the Litvinov Agreement would violate the Fifth Amendment's prohibition against the government's taking private property without just compensation. A district court agreed to dismiss the suit and, after the Court of Appeals for the Second Circuit affirmed, the government appealed to the Supreme Court.

Belmont raised issues both of federalism (whether the Litvinov Agreement trumped state laws and policies) and of separation of powers (whether the agreement was valid and enforceable). Justice Sutherland quickly disposed of each. The matter of federalism was dismissed out of hand at the outset of his opinion with the rather astonishing observation: "We do not pause to inquire whether in fact there was any policy of the State of New York to be infringed, since we are of the opinion no state policy can prevail against the international compact here involved."[47] In short, traditional federalism concerns of the classical understanding of the conduct of foreign affairs had completely disappeared, buried by Justice Sutherland's revisionist theory in *Curtiss-Wright* of internal and external sovereignty. Citing *Missouri v. Holland* in support, Justice Sutherland thought: "It is inconceivable that [state constitutions, state laws, and state policies] can be interpreted as an obstacle to the effective operation of a federal constitutional power" in foreign affairs.[48]

Turning to the separation of powers issue, Justice Sutherland relied on the holding in *Curtiss-Wright* that governmental power over external, foreign affairs "is vested exclusively in the national government." Largely overlooking the apparent conflict between the Litvinov Agreement and the Fifth Amendment's just compensation clause, he simply declared that the Supremacy Clause made all international agreements—protocols, compacts, congressional-executive agreements, and sole executive agreements—the supreme law of the land.

Justice Sutherland's rather cursory analysis in support of such a sweeping ruling invited some immediate criticism from legal scholars.[49] But, it nonetheless elevated executive agreements to the status of internationally binding compacts, buttressed his revisionist constitutional theory of presidential predominance, and extended an invitation for presidents to make more endruns around the Senate and the treaty-making power.

If doubts remained about the constitutional transformation taking place and the triumph of presidential predominance after *Curtiss-Wright* and *Belmont*, they were soon laid to rest in another case involving the government's claim to assets under the Litvinov Agreement. In 1934 the government sought to recover the assets of the New York branch of the First Russian Insurance Company and sued Louis H. Pink, the state superintendent of insurance. Pink's attorneys contended that the Litvinov Agreement was not binding in the face of conflicting state laws because it lacked either congressional approval as legislation or Senate approval as a treaty. The separation of powers issue at stake in *United States v. Pink* (1942) had been foreshadowed but still not squarely addressed in *Belmont*.[50]

United States v. Pink was argued just days after the bombing of Pearl Harbor, which undoubtedly weighed on the minds of the justices just as World War II would the next year when the Court upheld a curfew for Japanese Americans in *Hirabayashi v. United States* (1943) and, the following year, upheld their internment in *Korematsu v. United States* (1944).[51] Relying principally on *Curtiss-Wright* and *Belmont* in his opinion for the Court in *Pink*, Justice William O. Douglas reaffirmed that the president is "the sole organ" in foreign affairs, and ruled that "international compacts and agreements [such] as the Litvinov Assignment have a similar [constitutional] dignity [to that of treaties]."[52] Given *Curtiss-Wright* and *Belmont*, in *Pink* the Court almost inexorably legitimated sole executive agreements as possessing the same constitutional status as treaties, in spite of their not complying with the constitutionally prescribed procedures for ratification by the Senate. Justice Douglas also suggested that challenges to such agreements, along with presidential predominance in foreign affairs more generally, should be treated as nonjusticiable "political questions." For, he read *Belmont* to establish that "the conduct of foreign affairs is committed by the Constitution to the political branches of the federal government; that the propriety of the exercise of that power is not open to judicial inquiry. . . ."[53] Notably, only Chief Justice Stone dissented in *Pink*.

Given the Court's rulings from *Field v. Clark*, to *Missouri v. Holland*, and then *Curtiss-Wright*, *Belmont*, and *Pink*, the constitutional transformation of the conduct of foreign affairs into one of presidential predominance should not be surprising. In the first three decades of the twentieth century, as already noted, Congress increasingly delegated power to the president in foreign and domestic affairs. At the same time, presidents became increasingly frustrated in dealing with the Senate over treaty ratification. And the Court's rulings on the treaty-making power and executive agreements served to legitimate, and constitutionalize, what had been emerging as an increasingly common political practice.

CONGRESS AND PRESIDENTIAL PREDOMINANCE IN FOREIGN AFFAIRS

In light of the Court's rulings, little wonder that during his thirteen years in office FDR almost doubled the number of executive agreements of previous presidents in signing 609. His successor, Harry Truman (1945–1953), though, outdid him in just seven years by entering into over twice as many (1,466).[54] Since 1945, as illustrated in Figure 4.1, the number of executive agreements has steadily climbed, dwarfing that of treaties and reinforcing presidential inclinations to make endruns around the Constitution's prescription for treaty making and ratification by two-thirds vote of the Senate.

After World War II the number of executive agreements not only increased dramatically, but they also covered a broader range of subjects, binding the country prospectively in international relations, and came to be used interchangeably with Article 2 treaties. In historical perspective, in spite of the controversy in the early 1990s over the process for obtaining congressional

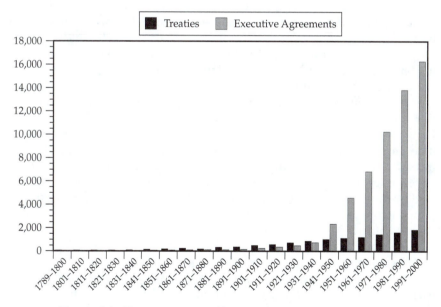

FIGURE 4.1   TREATIES AND THE RISE OF EXECUTIVE AGREEMENTS

Source: Lawrence Margolis, *Executive Agreements and Presidential Power in Foreign Affairs* (New York: Praeger, 1986), Table 1, pp. 101–106, and as updated from data from the U.S. Department of State, Treaty Office (August 2000).

approval for ascension into NAFTA and the WTO, as earlier noted, the practice of presidents overcoming the obstacle of trying to win Senate ratification of treaties had already become well established. Recall that in 1945 President Truman avoided the treaty-making process when obtaining the approval of simple majorities of both houses of Congress for the Bretton Woods Agreements of 1944, which established the World Bank and the International Monetary Fund (IMF). And in 1948 Truman signed a sole executive agreement that brought the United States into compliance with the General Agreement on Tariffs and Trade (GATT), which remained in effect until it was replaced by the 1994 GATT. Truman undertook these and other executive agreements because of persistent congressional opposition to commitments to international organizations and due to Congress's tendency toward protectionism for domestic economic interests.[55] Nonetheless, Truman's practice, buttressed by the Court's rulings, became the established pattern for latter presidents, Republican and Democratic alike.

In response to the rise in the number of executive agreements, in the early 1950s Congress debated various versions of the proposed Bricker Amendment to the Constitution. Sponsored by Republican Senator John Bricker, the amendment would have amended Article 6 so as to overrule the Court's earlier decisions and deny the supremacy of executive agreements and treaties over state or federal laws.[56]

More successful, Congress enacted the Case Act of 1972, requiring the Secretary of State to transmit to Congress within sixty days "any international agreement, other than a treaty." That act also provides that if national security would be jeopardized by making an agreement public, the president may transmit it under an injunction of secrecy to the Senate and House of Representatives committees on foreign affairs. Subsequently, though, the Senate discovered that the administrations of Richard M. Nixon and Gerald R. Ford failed to always comply with the act, and thus in 1977 and 1978 the Congress broadened the act and tightened the reporting requirements. Finally, in response to continued problems with compliance with the Case Act, in 1987, Congress provided that if an international agreement is not reported to Congress within sixty days, "then no funds authorized to be appropriated by this or any other Act shall be available after the end of that sixty-day period to implement that agreement until the text of that agreement has been so transmitted."[57]

The Court, for its part, in a couple of decisions did step back somewhat from its expansive reading of presidential power. In *Reid v. Covert* (1957), the Court finally held that executive agreements and treaties may not deprive individuals of their Fifth and Sixth Amendment guarantees in the Bill of Rights, thereby reversing the contrariwise position taken by a majority of the justices just the year before in *Reid v. Covert* (1956). Writing for the Court, Justice Hugo L. Black ruled that executive agreements and treaties may not confer power "on the Congress or any other branch of Government, which is free from restraints of the Constitution."[58]

In an unrelated though important ruling involving congressional and presidential powers in both domestic and foreign affairs, the Court also dealt Truman a blow and reaffirmed the power and role of Congress in the famous *Steel Seizure* case, *Youngstown Sheet & Tube Company v. Sawyer* (1952).[59] During the undeclared war in Korea, a labor dispute threatened to shut down steel mills. Claiming that a strike would affect our military and national security interests, Truman issued an executive order directing his Secretary of Commerce, Charles Sawyer, to seize and operate the mills. He did so instead of invoking the Taft-Hartley Act, which provided for a cooling-off period in labor–management disputes and was passed over a presidential veto just hours before Truman issued his order. In addition, when enacting the Taft-Hartley Act, Congress had specifically considered and ultimately rejected the idea of authorizing the president to stop strikes.

Writing for the Court, as he did in *Reid v. Covert*, Justice Black firmly rejected the president's claims to "inherent power" and to plenary powers as commander in chief. In his words, "the president's power, if any, to issue the order must stem either from an act of Congress or from the Constitution itself."[60] Yet, even that seemingly straightforward understanding of the Constitution proved as controversial within as without the Court. Chief Justice Fred Vinson and Justices Stanley Reed and Sherman Minton dissented. And each of the other five justices in the majority (Justices William D. Douglas, Felix Frankfurter, Harold Burton, Tom Clark, and Robert Jackson) filed separate concurring opinions, taking more or less pragmatic positions recognizing the need for political expediency in foreign affairs. Of these concurrences, Justice Jackson's remains the most celebrated and instructive.

In *Youngstown*, Justice Jackson expressly rejected Justice Sutherland's theory in *Curtiss-Wright* as *"dictum"* and read that decision to simply affirm the power of Congress to delegate broad authority to the president over foreign commerce. He recalled the earlier classical understanding, when rejecting the president's claim to broad, inherent emergency powers. As Justice Jackson explained, the president's "powers are not fixed but fluctuate" among three categories:

1. When the President acts pursuant to an express or implied authorization of Congress, his authority is at its maximum, for it includes all that he possesses in his own right plus all that Congress can delegate. . . .

2. When the President acts in absence of either a congressional grant or denial of authority, he can only rely upon his own independent powers, but there is a zone of twilight in which he and Congress may have concurrent authority, or in which its distribution is uncertain. . . .

3. When the President takes measures incompatible with the express or implied will of Congress, his power is at its lowest ebb, for then he can rely

only upon his own constitutional powers minus any constitutional powers of Congress over the matter.[61]

Justice Jackson left no doubt that Truman's order fell into the third category and, because it ran afoul of the will of Congress when enacting the Taft-Hartley Act, it failed to survive judicial scrutiny.

Likewise, in the "Pentagon Papers" case, *New York Times Company v. United States* (1971), the Court rejected President Nixon's claim to an "inherent power" to safeguard national security interests when seeking a court-ordered injunction against the publication of excerpts from a forty-seven-volume secret history of the United States' involvement in the war in Vietnam.[62] In separate opinions, five members of the Court—Justices Black, Douglas, Thurgood Marshall, Byron White, and Potter Stewart—arguably took the position that the president has no inherent powers in domestic affairs and may only seek an injunction against publications based on a congressional authorization, as in the Atomic Energy Act of 1954.[63]

However, subsequently in *Dames & Moore v. Regan* (1981) the Court upheld President Jimmy Carter's executive orders, issued without congressional authorization, suspending claims against Iran that were then pending in U.S. courts.[64] In 1979, following the Iranian taking of U.S. diplomats as hostages, Carter declared a national emergency, as permitted under the International Emergency Economic Powers Act (IEEPA), and froze all assets of Iran within U.S. jurisdiction. Subsequently, he signed the Declaration of Algiers, which was never submitted for congressional approval. Under the terms of that agreement, Iran agreed to release the hostages in exchange for the termination of all litigation against it; the transfer of all its assets in the U.S. to the Bank of England; and to having all claims against it settled by the International Claim Tribunal in the Hague, not by U.S. courts. Dames & Moore had a pending suit in federal district court against Iran for breach of contract and sought the payment of $3.4 million for services rendered. As in *Belmont* and *Pink*, attorneys for Dames & Moore contended that the executive orders freezing Iranian assets and suspending pending claims in U.S. courts exceeded the president's statutory and constitutional authority.

Writing for the Court in *Dames & Moore*, Justice William H. Rehnquist, who had clerked for Justice Jackson in 1952 and 1953, drew heavily on Jackson's concurring opinion in *Youngstown Sheet & Tube*. He found that the president had statutory authority under the IEEPA to freeze Iranian assets, and thus those orders fell within Jackson's first category of claims to presidential power. However, he found no such authority for Carter's ordering the suspension of pending claims against Iran, which fell into the second category of claims to presidential power.

While underscoring both "the necessity to rest the decision on the narrowest possible ground" and the unique nature of the emergency in responding to the hostage crisis, Justice Rehnquist nevertheless did not revive the classical understanding of strict interpretation of the president's powers. Instead, unlike Justice Jackson in *Youngstown*, he emphasized the need for political expediency in presidential actions in foreign affairs:

> We are obviously deciding only one more episode in the never-ending tension between the President exercising the executive authority in a world that presents each day some new challenge with which he must deal and the Constitution under which we all live and which no one disputes embodies some sort of system of checks and balances.[65]

And on that basis he upheld the president's actions, observing that "where, as here, we can conclude that Congress acquiesced in the president's action, we are not prepared to say that the president lacks the power to settle such claims."[66]

The Court in *Dames & Moore*, as Louis Fisher put it, "strained to uphold an agreement it could not possibly overturn, given the foreign policy implications."[67] Yet, it also reflected the demise of the classical understanding of the conduct of foreign affairs and the post–World War II judiciary's virtually complete deference to presidential predominance in foreign affairs. That change in understanding spearheaded in *Curtiss-Wright*, *Belmont*, and *Pink* became even more widely accepted and less critically challenged by the courts in the latter half of the twentieth century.

Another indication of the displacement of the classical understanding of the powers and roles of the president and Congress in foreign affairs is reflected in the second and third *Restatement of the Foreign Relations Law of the United States*.[68] In the second *Restatement*, published in 1965, executive agreements were deemed to have to either rest on congressional approval or be related to a president's independent constitutional authority, as commander in chief, for example; as such, they were considered to supercede state, but not federal, laws.[69] By contrast, in 1986 the third *Restatement* acknowledged that the president may make any agreement on any subject matter, either as a treaty or an executive agreement, and both supercede state and federal laws.[70]

Furthermore, in the latter half of the twentieth century, the Supreme Court in at least four other interrelated ways buttressed presidential predominance by exhibiting even greater judicial deference to the executive branch, and leaving it largely to Congress to check the president.

First, in the potentially very significant case of *Goldwater v. Carter* (1979), the Court, with Justices Harry Blackmun, Brennan, and White dissenting, summarily vacated the lower court's ruling and rejected a challenge by Arizona's Republican Senator Barry Goldwater and other senators to President Carter's unilateral suspension of a mutual defense treaty with Taiwan.[71] Senator Goldwater maintained that the Senate should approve treaty terminations, since it ratifies them. The issue of who has constitutional authority to terminate treaties is, obviously, an important one and one that the Constitution does not specifically address, arising instead from the constitutional silence on the subject.

Like *Youngstown* and the Pentagon Papers case, *Goldwater v. Carter* fragmented the Court. In a concurrence, Justice Lewis F. Powell contended that the matter was not ripe for judicial resolution. In his view, the Senate or Congress as a whole had failed to assert its opposition and, thus, there was not yet a true institutional conflict between the president and Congress for the Court to adjudicate. By contrast, in another concurring opinion joined by Chief Justice Warren E. Burger and Justices Stewart and Stevens, Justice Rehnquist countered that the matter was a "political question" for the president and Congress, not the courts, to decide. Indeed, distinguishing *Youngstown* and quoting approvingly from *Curtiss-Wright*, Justice Rehnquist suggested that the political questions doctrine applies broadly to the area of foreign affairs. Dissenting Justices Blackmun and White objected to summarily disposing of the case and would have granted review and heard oral arguments on the merits. Only dissenting Justice Brennan addressed the merits of the case and, however, would have upheld the power of the president to unilaterally terminate treaties.

Second, besides broadly applying the political questions doctrine to foreign affairs, the Court under Chief Justice Rehnquist (1986–present) has indicated that it no longer considers members of Congress to have standing to challenge the constitutionality of legislation,[72] or presidential initiatives and actions like that in dispute in *Goldwater v. Carter*. In recent years the Court has repeatedly refused to grant review of lower court decisions rejecting congressional standing to challenge, under the War Powers Resolution of 1973,[73] the president's commitment of troops abroad, in the Persian Gulf War, for instance, and ordering the bombing of Bosnia and Kosovo.[74]

Third, the Court has held that the judiciary should generally defer to the president when the executive branch reinterprets ambiguous legislation and treaties,[75] even when that reinterpretation runs contrary to the will of Congress,[76] or completely disregards provisions of a treaty.[77] The political problems and institutional conflict between the president and Congress arising from the executive branch's reinterpretation of treaties were dramatized in 1988 during the controversy over Senate ratification of the Inter-Range Nuclear Force (INF) Treaty.[78] Yet, in all probability the Court will not address the matter of treaty reinterpretation, because it would either invoke the political question doctrine or deny congressional standing in suits filed over such disputes.

Finally, although the Rehnquist Court in the 1990s has significantly curbed congressional power in deference to the states,[79] it shows no inclination to revive the federalism concerns of the classical understanding of the conduct of foreign affairs. The Court continues to uphold the need for "the nation to speak with one voice" in foreign affairs, when striking down state laws that conflict with treaties, international agreements, and other federal legislation.[80]

In conclusion, during the first few decades of the twentieth century the Supreme Court legitimated the constitutional transformation of the conduct of foreign affairs, and at the outset of the twenty-first century the Court appears reluctant to revisit and enforce constitutional limitations on the president in foreign affairs. As a result, as political scientist Aaron Wildavsky, among others, observed: "The United States has one President, but it has two presidencies; one presidency is for domestic affairs, and the other is concerned with defense and foreign policy."[81] Thus, it remains left largely for Congress to curb the president through its other, not inconsiderable, powers over spending and oversight of the executive branch.

NOTES

1. Merrill Jensen, *The Articles of Confederation* (Madison: University of Wisconsin Press, 1940).
2. Max Farrand, *The Framing of the Constitution of the United States* (New Haven, CT: Yale University Press, 1913), p. 131; and Jack Rakove, *Original Meanings: Politics and Ideas in the Making of the Constitution* (New York: Knopf, 1996), pp. 262–267.
3. James Madison, *Notes on Debates in the Federal Convention of 1787* (Columbus, OH: Ohio University Press, 1966), p. 532; and Max Farrand, ed., *The Records of the Federal Convention of 1787*, 4 vols. (New Haven, CT: Yale University Press, 1911), p. 58.
4. See *The Federalist Nos. 68 and 75*; Lee Ackerman, "Executive Agreements, the Treaty-Making Clause, and Strict Constructionism," 8 *Loyala of Los Angeles Law Review* (1975), pp. 587–617; and Louis Fisher, *Constitutional Conflicts between Congress and the President*, 3rd ed. (Lawrence, KS: University of Kansas Press, 1991), pp. 216–217.
5. Rakove, *Original Meanings: Politics and Ideas in the Making of the Constitution*; William J. Brennan, Jr., "The Constitution of the United States: Contemporary Ratification," in *Judges on Judging*, ed. David M. O'Brien (Chatham: Chatham House Publishers, 1997); Laurence Tribe, "Taking Text and Structure Seriously: Reflections on Free-Form Method in Constitutional Interpretation," 108 *Harvard Law Review* (1995), p. 1221; and David M. O'Brien, "The Framers' Muse on Republicanism, the Supreme Court, and Pragmatic Constitutional Interpretation," 93 *The Review of Politics* (1991), p. 251.
6. Robert H. Bork, "Foreword," in *The Fettered Presidency: Legal Constraints on the Executive Branch*, ed. L. Gordon Crovitz and Jeremy A. Rabkin (Washington, D.C.: American Enterprise Institute, 1989); and L. Gordon Crovitz and Jeremy A. Rabkin, eds., *The Fettered Presidency: Legal Constraints on the Executive Branch* (Washington, D.C.: American Enterprise Institute, 1989).
7. *United States v. Curtiss-Wright*, 299 U.S. 304 (1936), pp. 316–317.
8. Dumas Malone, *Jefferson the President, First Term 1801–1805* (Boston: Little Brown, 1970), pp. 253–259 and 351–361.
9. Wallace McClure, *International Executive Agreements* (New York: Columbia University Press, 1941), p. 31.
10. Lawrence Margolis, *Executive Agreements and Presidential Power in Foreign Affairs* (New York: Praeger, 1986), pp. 101–106.
11. Charles C. Hyde, "Agreements of the United States Other Than Treaties," 17 *Green Bag* (1905), p. 229.
12. *Little v. Barreme*, 6 U.S. 170 (1804); *Brown v. United States*, 12 U.S. 110 (1814); *The Prize Cases*, 67 U.S. 635 (1862); and *Ex Parte Milligan*, 71 U.S. 2 (1866).
13. *Marbury v. Madison*, 5 U.S. 137 (1803); *Luther v. Borden*, 48 U.S. 1 (1849); and *The Prize Cases* (1862).
14. *Geofrey v. Riggs*, 133 U.S. 258 (1890), p. 267.
15. *Field v. Clark*, 143 U.S. 649 (1892).
16. Ibid.
17. *Geogrey v. Riggs*, (1890) and *Ware v. Hylton*, 3 U.S. 199 (1796).
18. *Holmes v. Jennison*, 39 U.S. 540 (1840); *The License Cases*, 46 U.S. 504 (1847); and *The Passenger Cases*, 48 U.S. 283 (1849).
19. *Prevost v. Greneaux*, 60 U.S. 1 (1856).
20. *Jones v. United States*, 137 U.S. 202 (1890).
21. *Doe v. Braden*, 57 U.S. 635 (1853).

22. *The Three Friends*, 166 U.S. 1 (1897).
23. *The Prize Cases* (1862) and *The Protector*, 79 U.S. 700 (1871).
24. Charles Henry Butler, *The Treaty-Making Power of the United States* (New York: Banks Law Publishing, 1902); William E. Mikell, "The Extent of the Treaty-Making Power of the President and Senate of the United States," 57 *University of Pennsylvania Law Review* (1909), p. 435; Edward S. Corwin, *National Supremacy: Treaty Power v. State Power* (New York: Holt and Company, 1913); and Quincy Wright, *The Control of American Foreign Relations* (New York: Macmillan, 1922).
25. Edward G. White, "The Transformation of the Constitutional Regime of Foreign Affairs," 85 *Virginia Law Review* (1999), p. 1.
26. Wright, *The Control of American Foreign Relations*, pp. 149–150; and Clinton Rossiter, *The Supreme Court and the Commander in Chief* (Ithica: Cornell University Press, 1976).
27. Bruce Ackerman and David Golove, "Is NAFTA Constitutional?" 108 *Harvard Law Review* (1995), p. 799; and David Golove, "Treaty-Making and the Nation: The Historical Foundations of the Nationalist Conception of the Treaty Power," 98 *Michigan Law Review* (2000), p. 1075.
28. Joel R. Paul, "The Geopolitical Constitution: Executive Expediency and Executive Agreements," 86 *California Law Review* (1998), p. 671.
29. Ackerman and Golove, "Is NAFTA Constitutional?"
30. *Restatement (Third) of the Foreign Relations Law of the United States* (Philadelphia: American Law Institute, 1987); and Harold Hongju Koh, "The Fast Track and United States Foreign Policy," 18 *Brooklyn Journal of International Law* (1992), p. 143.
31. *United States v. Curtiss-Wright Export Corporation*, 299 U.S. 304 (1936).
32. *Panama Refining Company v. Ryan*, 293 U.S. 388 (1935); *Schecter Poultry Corporation v. United States*, 295 U.S. 495 (1935); and *Carter v. Carter Coal Company*, 298 U.S. 238 (1936).
33. Theodore Roosevelt, *American Ideals* (New York: Putnam, 1920), p. 551.
34. Margolis, *Executive Agreements and Presidential Power in Foreign Affairs*, p. 104.
35. Hadley Arkes, *The Return of George Sutherland* (Princeton: Princeton University Press, 1994).
36. William Leuchtenburg, *The Supreme Court Reborn: The Constitutional Revolution in the Age of Roosevelt* (New York: Oxford University Press, 1995).
37. David M. O'Brien, *Storm Center: The Supreme Court in American Politics*, 5th ed. (New York: Norton, 2000), pp. 56–61.
38. George Sutherland, *Constitutional Power and World Affairs* (New York: Columbia University Press, 1919).
39. Ibid., p. 21.
40. Ibid., p. 154.
41. *Missouri v. Holland*, 252 U.S. 416 (1920).
42. *Greer v. Connecticut*, 161 U.S. 519 (1896).
43. *Missouri v. Holland* (1920).
44. *United States v. Curtiss-Wright Export Corporation* (1936), p. 320.
45. John Marshall, *Annals of the First Congress*, vol. 6 (Washington, D.C.: Gales & Seaton, 1800), pp. 596–619.
46. *United States v. Belmont*, 301 U.S. 324 (1937).
47. Ibid, pp. 327 and 332.
48. Ibid.
49. Edwin Borchard, "Confiscations: Extraterritorial and Domestic," 31 *American Journal of International Law* (1937), p. 675; Philip Jessup, "The Litvinov Agreement and the Belmont Case," 31 *American Journal of International Law* (1937), p. 481; and Stefan Reisenfeld, "The Powers of Congress and the President in International Relations," 25 *California Law Review* (1937), p. 643.
50. *United States v. Pink*, 315 U.S. 203 (1942).
51. *Hirabayashi v. United States*, 320 U.S. 91 (1943); *Korematsu v. United States*, 323 U.S. 214 (1944); and William H. Rehnquist, *All the Laws but One: Civil Liberties in Wartime* (New York: Knopf, 1998).
52. *United States v. Pink* (1942), pp. 229–230.
53. Ibid., pp. 22–23.
54. Margolis, *Executive Agreements and Presidential Power in Foreign Affairs*, pp. 104–105.
55. John Jackson, "The General Agreement on Tariffs and Trade in United States Domestic Law," 66 *Michigan Law Review* (1967), p. 249; and Ronald Brand, "The Status of General Agreement on Tariffs and Trade in U.S. Domestic Law," 26 *Stanford Journal of International Law* (1990), p. 479.

56. John Witton and J. Edward Fowler, "Bricker Amendment—Fallacies and Danger," 48 *American Journal of International Law* (1954), p. 23.
57. Fisher, *Constitutional Conflicts between Congress and the President*, 3rd ed., pp. 242–243.
58. *Reid v. Covert*, 354 U.S. 1 (1957), p. 16.
59. *Youngstown Sheet & Tube Company v. Sawyer*, 343 U.S. 579 (1952); and Maeva Marcus, *Truman and the Steel Seizure Case* (New York: Columbia University Press, 1977).
60. *Youngstown Sheet & Tube Company v. Sawyer* (1952), p. 585.
61. Ibid., p. 637.
62. *New York Times Company v. United States*, 403 U.S. 670 (1971).
63. Peter Junger, "Down Memory Lane: The Case of the Pentagon Papers," 23 *Case Western Law Review* (1971), p. 3; and David M. O'Brien, *The Public's Right to Know: The Supreme Court and the First Amendment* (New York: Praeger, 1981), pp. 150–170.
64. *Dames & Moore v. Regan*, 453 U.S. 654 (1981).
65. Ibid, pp. 662 and 668.
66. Ibid.
67. Fisher, *Constitutional Conflicts between Congress and the President*, 3rd ed., p. 241.
68. *Restatement (Second) of the Foreign Relations Law of the United States* (Philadelphia: American Law Institute, 1965); and *Restatement (Third) of the Foreign Relations Law of the United States* (1987).
69. *Restatement (Second) of the Foreign Relations Law of the United States* (1965), pp. 117–120.
70. *Restatement (Third) of the Foreign Relations Law of the United States* (1987), p. 303.
71. *Goldwater v. Carter*, 444 U.S. 996 (1979).
72. *Raines v. Byrd*, 521 U.S. 811 (1997).
73. John Hart Ely, *War and Responsibility: Constitutional Lessons of Vietnam and Its Aftermath* (Princeton: Princeton University Press, 1993); and Thomas Frank and Edward Weisband, *Foreign Policy by Congress* (New York: Oxford University Press, 1979).
74. *Lowry v. Reagan*, 676 F. Supp. 333 (D.C. Cir. 1987); *Dellums v. Bush*, 752 F. Supp. 1141 (D.D.C. 1990); and *Campbell v. Clinton*, 203 F. 3d 19 (9th Cir. 2000).
75. *Chevron v. Natural Resources Defense Council*, 467 U.S. 837 (1984).
76. *Rust v. Sullivan*, 500 U.S. 173 (1991).
77. *United States v. Alvarez-Machain*, 504 U.S. 655 (1992).
78. David M. O'Brien, *Constitutional Law and Politics: Struggles for Power and Governmental Accountability*, 4th ed. (New York, Norton, 2000), pp. 248–250; and Fisher, *Constitutional Conflicts between Congress and the President*, 3rd ed., pp. 234–237.
79. David M. O'Brien, "How the Republican War over 'Judicial Activism' Has Cost Congress," in *Congress Confronts the Court: The Struggle for Legitimacy and Authority in Lawmaking*, ed. Colton Campbell and John F. Stack, Jr. (Lanham: Rowman & Littlefield Publishers, Inc., 2001).
80. *United States v. Locke*, 529 U.S. 89 (2000) and *Crosby v. National Foreign Trade Council*, 530 U.S. 3 (2000).
81. Aaron Wildavsky, "The Two Presidencies," 4 *Trans-Action* (December 1969), p. 230; and Rossiter, *The Supreme Court and the Commander in Chief* (1976), p. 126.

5

A TALE OF TWO TREATIES

THE PRACTICAL POLITICS
OF TREATY RATIFICATION IN THE U.S. SENATE

C. LAWRENCE EVANS AND WALTER J. OLESZEK

On October 13, 1999, the U.S. Senate rejected the Comprehensive Nuclear Test Ban Treaty on a mostly party-line vote of 48 to 51. The overwhelming defeat of the proposed agreement stunned the Clinton administration, as well as many close observers of American foreign policy. To be sure, serious questions had been raised about the substantive merits of the proposed accord, particularly its enforceability and implications for the U.S. nuclear arsenal. But many lawmakers initially believed that a bipartisan consensus on the measure was achievable, if only the administration and Republican leaders could work together to strike an agreement about the details for implementing the treaty.

In the months leading up to the vote, however, partisan confrontation and gamesmanship dominated attempts at cooperation. Indeed, a last-ditch effort by the administration and congressional Democrats to simply postpone the vote—and thus avoid the embarrassment of outright Senate rejection of a major international treaty—was sidetracked by the procedural maneuvers of Majority Leader Trent C. Lott (R-Miss.), and a coalition of Republican conservatives. According to many observers, the treaty's demise was in part the result of the intense partisanship that has characterized Capitol Hill in recent years, residual GOP bitterness toward the president in the wake of impeachment, and burgeoning unilateralist sentiments among congressional Republicans.

Still, among other points, we argue in this chapter that the strategic goals of the Republican leadership were only part of the test-ban story. Along with Republican distrust of the Clinton administration, the outcome of the fight also resulted from strategic miscalculations made by Democratic leaders at both ends of Pennsylvania Avenue. For one, Senate Democrats chose to transform the treaty into a party-message issue, substantially complicating efforts at bipartisan accommodation. In addition, the Clinton White House failed to aggressively lobby and negotiate with key Republican leaders about how the treaty would be implemented until immediately prior to the vote. Moreover, the political dynamics on the nuclear test ban treaty can only be understood within the context of the ratification fight on the Chemical Weapons Convention, an equally consequential treaty that had been successfully ratified by the Senate just two years previously.

The central premise of this chapter is that the different, but related, fates of the chemical weapons and nuclear test ban treaties can provide us with useful insights about the politics of treaty consideration in the contemporary Senate, as well as about interbranch bargaining on foreign policy matters more generally. For instance, what factors shape party strategies during treaty ratification fights? Which administration tactics are associated with successful ratification efforts, and which ones tend to fail? How important are grassroots mobilization campaigns in the treaty ratification process? To address these and related questions, we train a microscope on the two accords, relying for evidence on congressional documents, media accounts, and a number of interviews with White House and Senate staff.[1] Our main conclusion is that Senate decision making on international treaties and other foreign policy matters can no longer be usefully distinguished from the broader legislative game, which often is characterized by intense partisanship and an emphasis on public relations and procedural maneuvering within the chamber over each party's message agenda. In the pages that follow, we consider each treaty in turn, beginning with Senate action on the Chemical Weapons Convention in 1993–1997, and then chamber consideration of the nuclear test ban treaty during 1997–1999. We close by summarizing the implications of our analysis for treaty ratification politics and foreign policy making in the contemporary Senate.

CHEMICAL REACTIONS IN THE SENATE

The fundamental purpose of the Chemical Weapons Convention (CWC) is the global elimination of chemical weapons within twenty years. Specifically, the CWC aims to institute a worldwide ban on the development, production, and stockpiling of poison gases and weapons. In addition, the treaty requires the destruction of both chemical weapon stockpiles and production facilities and, to prevent cheating, allows spot checks and on-site monitoring by international inspectors.

Negotiations to achieve these objectives began in 1968 among forty nations at the Conference on Disarmament held in Geneva, Switzerland. The United States and the then U.S.S.R—the world's two largest producers and stockpilers of chemical weapons—also pursued bilateral negotiations from 1976 to 1980, when the United States ended the discussions for lack of progress. The question of verification—how to insure compliance and prevent the covert production of these weapons—proved to be among the most difficult issues for the two superpowers to resolve. Despite concerns about verification, the perceptions that Saddam Hussein might use chemical weapons against allied troops and Israel during the 1991 Gulf War generated substantial momentum for completing the negotiations. In September 1992, the forty nations that were a party to the Geneva Conference on Disarmament agreed on a draft of the CWC and transmitted it to the United Nations, where it was approved by the General Assembly and opened to all nations for signature.

A week before the end of George Bush's presidency, on January 13, 1993, at a Paris meeting, the United States and more than 120 other nations signed the CWC.[2] On November 23, 1993, President Bill Clinton submitted the CWC to the Senate for its advice and consent.[3] Under Senate Rule XXV, the CWC was referred to the Committee on Foreign Relations. This Senate rule grants the panel exclusive jurisdiction over "treaties and executive agreements, except reciprocal trade agreements." Other committees may conduct hearings on the subject matter of treaties, as occurred in the case of the CWC, but only Foreign Relations may report treaties for Senate consideration. Worth mentioning is that under Senate Rule XXXVII, all decisions of the Senate with regard to a treaty "shall be reduced to the form of a resolution of ratification, with or without amendments." It is this resolution which must attract the constitutional two-thirds vote of the Senate for a treaty to be approved.

The relationship between the president and the Senate over treaty making is often characterized by a complex combination of cooperation and conflict, with the outcome hinging on a variety of factors and strategic calculations. The CWC encountered its share of hurdles, but it eventually won the Senate's approval despite strong opposition from an intense minority of lawmakers, including Foreign Relations Chairman Jesse Helms (R-N.C.). He viewed the CWC as fatally flawed, loophole-ridden, and unverifiable.

STARTS AND STOPS: 1994–1996

Senate action on the CWC began on March 22, 1994, more than a year after the treaty was submitted to it, when the Foreign Relations Committee began hearings. The delay occurred because the Senate was occupied with other issues, including consideration of a treaty (START II) between the United States and Russia aimed at reducing the deployment of strategic nuclear weapons. During the panel's hearings on the CWC, the administration requested the Senate to approve the treaty before July 17, 1994, "to allow international implementation of the pact to begin by early 1995."[4] However, given electoral and other imperatives, the Senate did not take up the CWC in 1994. In fact, for the next two years the treaty failed to win approval. A few key factors contributed to this outcome.

Helms Takes Charge   Republicans scored a big victory in the November 1994 elections, which meant that Senator Helms took over from Claiborne Pell (D-R.I.), as Foreign Relations chairman. Helms and the Clinton administration soon clashed over a number of foreign policy issues, including the chairman's initiative to reorganize the State Department. Helms proposed, for instance, the elimination of the Agency for International Development, the Arms Control and Disarmament Agency, and the United States Information Agency. Administration opposition to Helms's bill triggered a deliberate "slow down" in the work of the Foreign Relations Committee. For four months in 1995 Senator Helms played "hostage politics." He prevented action on all the administration's ambassadorial nominations and all treaties until Democrats agreed to act on his plan for revamping the State Department. To force action on the CWC, Senate Democrats in late 1995 began to filibuster a State Department authorization bill.

Finally, on December 7, 1995, the Senate agreed to a unanimous consent agreement (UCA) negotiated by Helms and Senator John F. Kerry (D-Mass.), which ended the panel's "work stoppage." (UCAs are the procedural accords that Senators use to structure floor consideration of legislation.) In exchange for Foreign Relations action on eighteen ambassadors and the START II treaty, the Senate would vote on a revised version of Chairman Helms's State Department reauthorization plan by mid-December 1995. In addition, as Chairman Helms requested, "if the Chemical Weapons Convention has not been reported by the close of business on April 30, 1996, that convention [will] be discharged from the Foreign Relations Committee and placed on the Executive Calendar."[5] Subsequently, Minority Leader Tom A. Daschle (D-S.D.) asked Majority Leader Robert J. Dole (R-Kan.) his schedule for taking up the CWC. "It would be my intention," stated Dole, "that the Senate would consider the convention in a reasonable time period once the convention is on the Executive Calendar."[6] Although Chairman Helms agreed to act on the CWC, he remained opposed to it and indicated his intent to try and kill it. "I cannot imagine," he said, "that the Senate will be prepared to take [favorable] action on such a treaty."[7]

Good Prospects, Little Focus   Except for Senators and administration officials who focus on defense or international issues, the CWC was not the subject of extensive legislative or public consideration. "Very little thought has been given to it," remarked Senator Richard G. Lugar (R-Ind.), a leading member and former chairman of the Foreign Relations Committee. "[Senate action on the CWC is] not polarized at this point, and probably still open for discussion."[8] In fact, given the array of favorable forces behind it, the expectation among many senators and the White House was that the treaty would win easy Senate adoption once it was brought to the floor in 1996.

For instance, the CWC enjoyed a bipartisan imprimatur having been negotiated by the Reagan and Bush administrations and now backed by President Clinton. In addition, top military leaders endorsed the CWC as did executives of major chemical corporations, whose facilities would be subject to the treaty's verification requirements. Further, while many Senators recognized that the treaty had defects—the impossibility of insuring 100 percent compliance by signatory nations, for instance—they agreed with the oft-cited adage that the perfect should not exclude the good. "The question we must ask is not whether [the CWC] has flaws . . . but whether its strengths out-weigh its flaws," stated Senator Nancy Landon Kassebaum [now Baker]. "I be-lieve they do."[9]

Lott Becomes Majority Leader   On April 25, 1996, the Foreign Relations Committee reported the CWC by a 13 to 5 vote. Scheduling Senate action on the treaty became problematic, however. Majority Leader Dole, the pre-sumptive GOP presidential nominee, left the Senate to campaign full-time for the presidency. On June 12, 1996, Trent Lott was elected majority leader to re-place Dole, and his position on the CWC was unclear. Needless to say, con-servative Republicans encouraged Lott to ignore Dole's scheduling commitment on the CWC.

To force Lott's hand, Senate Democrats decided to take a "hostage"—the defense authorization bill, which the Senate took up on June 18, 1996. Their strategy was simple: offer dozens of amendments to delay final action on a measure that Lott wanted to process rather quickly. The stalling tactic pre-cipitated informal negotiations between the two sides. Eight days after the Senate began debate on the defense bill, Lott successfully propounded a UCA which stipulated "that the majority leader, after consultation with the Democratic leader, will, prior to September 14, 1996, proceed to executive session to consider . . . the Chemical Weapons Convention."[10] The agree-ment also permitted Lott to offer two amendments to the resolution of rat-ification; however, the contents of Lott's two amendments were left deliberately vague other than to state that they would address the subject matter of the treaty.

Lott, in effect, provided himself with leeway and leverage to change the terms of the CWC if subsequent political circumstances warranted that effort. This feature of the UCA also provided a way for Lott to attract the consent of conservative Senators for the agreement. Amendments, it is worth noting, only require a majority vote for approval unlike the constitutional two-thirds required for final passage of the resolution of ratification.

Senate debate on the CWC was slated to begin September 12, 1996, and to conclude the next day. Opponents and proponents of the treaty worked diligently to muster support for their position. "I think it's going to be a full-scale battle," said CWC supporter Sam A. Nunn (D-Ga.) who recognized the fervency of the senatorial opponents.[11] Unbeknownst to advocates of the treaty, Senator Jon L. Kyl (R-Ariz.) had been working behind-the-scenes since spring 1999—meeting individually with most Senate Republicans and coordinating with outside groups—to defeat the treaty. For example, the antitreaty forces successfully solicited support for their position from former Reagan and Bush officials, including Bush's Secretary of Defense, Dick Cheney. Meanwhile, Sen-ator Helms's committee staff spearheaded a grassroots campaign against rat-ification that featured the faxing of almost 1,000 press releases to local media outlets across the country.[12]

CWC's Initial Demise   On September 12, 1996, GOP presidential nominee Dole wrote to Lott and voiced his strong objections to the CWC, especially relating to enforcement and verification.[13] Dole's letter eroded Senate Republican support for the treaty and assured that there would be insufficient votes for its approval. Both uncommitted Senate Republicans and GOP treaty supporters backed away from the CWC, in part to avoid handing Clinton a political victory during his presidential reelection campaign.[14] Lott and Kyl also let it be known that they were working on an amendment to the resolution of ratification that would accommodate Dole's views on the treaty. Their amendment stated that the United States would comply with the CWC only if all nations signed it and the Central Intelligence Agency certified they could catch any cheaters.

Realistically, neither of these conditions could be met. If the amendment was approved, it would block U.S. participation in the CWC. Facing defeat, the Clinton administration decided to temporarily shelve the treaty. Majority Leader Lott agreed to Secretary of State Warren Christopher's request to postpone action on the treaty. As Senator Lugar declared: "The whole process was politicized in a way that would be harmful to our foreign policy. This is not a good time for the debate."[15] The treaty's almost certain rejection meant that the CWC was returned to the calendar of the Foreign Relations Committee.

To sum up, then, the treaty's problems in 1996 resulted from several key factors. First, the CWC became embroiled in presidential politics and support for it evaporated among GOP senators, who were themselves split over the pact between their moderate and hard-line wings. Second, outside activists helped to mobilize influential opponents, such as several former Republican secretaries of defense, whose concerns with the CWC provided political cover to wavering Republicans to oppose the treaty. Third, the Clinton administration's efforts on behalf of the treaty were too little and too late, probably because they were overconfident of success. Who, after all, could vote against eliminating poison gas? Senator Lugar called the administration's strategy an ill-planned effort. On the CWC, as often occurs on various political and policy matters, an intense minority prevailed over a diffuse majority. Fourth, the administration made little progress on resolving issues that aroused the concern of many GOP senators. Significantly, it appeared to these lawmakers that their misgivings were not taken seriously by the administration. Finally, the administration failed to win the backing of the majority leader. As Majority Leader Lott noted: "I worked closely with Senators Helms, Kyl, and others in opposition to the treaty. Had we not canceled the vote [on the CWC], I would have voted against it, and I believe that it would have failed."[16]

ANOTHER CHEMICAL TEST SUCCEEDS

The year 1997 provided a much different result with respect to the CWC. On April 24, the Senate voted 74 to 26 to approve the treaty. Twenty-nine Republicans (out of fifty-five) joined all forty-five Democrats for ratification.

How the administration turned a stinging 1996 defeat into a major success the next year was the product of several strategic calculations, not to mention sheer hard work and close consultation with critical Senators, especially Majority Leader Lott.

In January 1997, top White House national security officials agreed that the president needed to undertake a full-court press if the CWC was to be approved by the Senate. Clinton agreed with their unanimous recommendation, saying: "We cannot afford to fail."[17] Senator Lugar urged the president to "put a politically savvy person in charge and pursue [CWC's ratification] as if it were a political campaign."[18] From Senator Joseph R. Biden (D-Del.), the ranking minority member on the Foreign Relations Committee, came the suggestion to work closely with both Lott and Senator Helms. Clinton followed all of these recommendations.

As for making the CWC a major foreign policy priority as his second term began, President Clinton used the "bully pulpit" of the State of the Union address. On February 4, 1997, the president appeared before a joint session of Congress during prime time to present his agenda to the Congress and the American public. Clinton urged the Senate to ratify the CWC. The president said the following:

> This treaty has been bipartisan from the beginning, supported by Republican and Democratic administrations and Republican and Democratic Members of Congress and already approved by 68 nations. But if we do not act by April 29th, when this convention goes into force with or without us, we will lose the chance to have Americans leading and enforcing this effort. Together we must make the Chemical Weapons Convention law, so that at least we can begin to outlaw poison gas from the Earth.[19]

With April 29 a clear deadline for action and the role of the United States as a world leader at stake—not to mention economic sanctions against domestic chemical industries if the treaty was not ratified—the president made clear that ratification of the CWC was a top priority. Failure to approve the treaty, he implied, would put the United States in the company of nations like Iraq and Libya. Inaction would also hamper the nation's ability to encourage others to destroy their chemical weapons stockpiles.

From the outset of the 105th Congress (1997–1999), the administration put its top officials in charge of shepherding the treaty to passage. Secretary of State Madeleine Albright courted Senator Helms personally, visiting North Carolina with him, testifying many times before his committee, and informally consulting with the chairman countless times. She wanted to assure Helms that the administration was listening to his concerns about the CWC and that the president was sensitive to the chairman's parallel interests, such as reorganizing the State Department. Everyone understood that Helms had the ability to keep the treaty locked up in his committee. While his resistance to the CWC might not change, the administration's close consultations with Helms could encourage him to allow a vote on the treaty. Albright, too, was making numerous speeches and appearances around the country to mobilize public support for the CWC. Senator Biden was also conducting intensive negotiations with Chairman Helms, trying to accommodate and answer his concerns. Together, they "hammered out more than 20 amendments to the resolution designed to address some of the criticisms raised by GOP conservatives."[20]

National security adviser Samuel "Sandy" Berger and other administration arms control experts negotiated on a regular basis in person or by telephone with Senator Lott and other GOP lawmakers. "Berger was willing to task other people in the administration, matching a particular Republican's concerns with people from downtown who could address those concerns," said a congressional official.[21] From January 1997 to the day of the final vote, the administration kept the pressure on senators and worked to generate grassroots support. Public attacks on the treaty were answered quickly; Berger, Albright, and Secretary of Defense William Cohen appeared regularly on radio and television to promote the CWC; and White House ceremonies, with Clinton presiding, were staged with former Republican presidents (Bush and Ford) and Cabinet officers (James A. Baker, for instance) as well as high-ranking military officers, such as Colin Powell, the former chairman of the Joint Chiefs of Staff (and current Secretary of State).[22]

A major public relations and political coup for the administration was Bob Dole's endorsement of the CWC. A GOP senator informed the White House that Dole had seen an administration briefing on C-SPAN (the Cable Satellite Public Affairs Network) and came away favorably impressed with what he had heard about the treaty. The next sequence of events occurred: On Saturday, Clinton telephoned Dole and asked for his support; on Monday, Clinton sent a foreign policy expert to personally brief Dole; on Tuesday, the president sent Dole a letter asking for his backing; and on Wednesday morning, with only about an hour's notice and on the day the Senate began debate on the CWC, Dole appeared with Clinton at the White House and endorsed the treaty. "Is it perfect?" he asked. "No. But I believe there are now adequate safeguards to protect American interests."[23]

Senate Democrats Press for Action   Many Senate Democrats, mindful of the April 29 deadline, kept urging the majority leader to schedule action on the CWC. In mid-March, for example, Minority Leader Daschle stated: "We're determined to get a date for the Chemical Weapons Convention, and unless we get some sort of a date, we're not going to be inclined to move any additional legislation . . . this week."[24] During Senate debate on March 19, Senator Jeff Bingaman (D-N.M.) said: "I think we are to the point where it is not responsible for the Senate to go on with its other business if we cannot get agreement among Senators to bring up this very important matter on a timely basis."[25] Majority Leader Lott kept assuring all Senators that negotiations were continuing and that the CWC could be brought up before the so-called "drop dead" date.

About three weeks before the CWC took effect, Minority Leader Daschle "threatened that Democrats would delay up to 32 separate and unrelated issues, including support for a ballistic missile defense system [a top GOP priority], until the Republicans agreed to allow the CWC to go for a vote before the full Senate."[26] Daschle ended his threat when it appeared that Lott would schedule a vote within a week or so. "There is no agreement to schedule a vote on the Chemical Weapons Convention," stated Lott. However, "I am meeting with senators and representatives of the administration tomorrow and hope we can conclude an agreement" to take up the treaty.[27]

About ten days later, on April 17, Majority Leader Lott presented a detailed UCA to the Senate, which no lawmaker objected to. "I must say this is the longest and the most complicated unanimous-consent agreement that I have worked on since I have been majority leader," exclaimed Lott.[28] Under its terms, the CWC was automatically discharged from the Foreign Relations Committee, placed on the Executive Calendar, and slated to be taken up by the Senate at 10 AM on April 23. Senator Helms went along with the accord "because the procedure for voting is 'the best shot we've got' to defeat or nullify the treaty."[29]

Clinton and Lott   There seems little question that if the CWC was to be ratified President Clinton needed the support of Majority Leader Lott. Clinton recognized that with forty-five solid Democratic votes, he still needed twenty-two Republicans if the Senate was to approve the CWC. Press accounts indicated that Lott, who remained undeclared until the very end, might swing as many as seventeen Republican votes for the treaty if he decided to vote for it.[30] Clinton knew, too, that it would be virtually impossible to get Helms to report the CWC unless he had Lott in his corner.

Lott, in the end, supported the treaty, and several factors influenced his decision. First, just as Clinton was starting his second term, Lott was beginning his first full term as majority leader. He wanted to establish a record of accomplishment as a "statesman" who was being mentioned as a possible 2000 GOP presidential candidate. And with Speaker Newt L. Gingrich's (R-Ga.) political star in apparent eclipse because of his controversial role in triggering two government shutdowns in late 1995 and early 1996, Lott was positioned to be the most influential GOP leader on Capitol Hill. Second, Lott wanted to demonstrate that he, and not Jesse Helms, was leading the Senate. He worried, too, about negative voter reaction if Republicans were blamed for rejecting a treaty banning chemical weapons and poison gases.

Third, Lott viewed his support of the CWC as a "bargaining chip" that he could use when he had to negotiate with the president about budget issues, tax cuts, and other Republican priorities. After his vote Lott said he demonstrated courage and bipartisanship in backing the treaty, "Now we're going to see if the president shows similar courage against his [electoral] base and leadership" when it comes time to resolve other contentious issues.[31] Finally, on the day the Senate approved the treaty, Lott asserted that, "the United States is marginally better off with it than without it."[32] Lott, of course, realized that he would alienate his conservative allies in and outside the Congress, but he was willing to take that risk. For instance, conservative Paul Weyrich, president of the Free Congress Foundation, described Lott as "the doormat for Bill Clinton" and a "dead letter for any future in national politics."[33]

At the outset of the 105th Congress (1997–1999), Lott made it clear to the administration that progress on the CWC required progress on GOP priorities, especially those supported by Helms, such as State Department reorganization and United Nations reform. In short, Clinton had to make concessions to Senate Republicans if he was to win approval of CWC, and he was willing to accommodate many of their concerns. For example, after consultation with Gore, Clinton announced on April 17 a major reorganization of the foreign policy bureaucracy—a priority of Senator Helms. The "reinvention" involved the integration of the arms control agency and the information agency into the State Department; the Agency for International Development remained a separate entity, but its director now would report to the Secretary of State rather than to the president. The administration's change paralleled the plan Helms proposed two years earlier. Although Helms said he still opposed the CWC, an administration official said the reorganization would create "an environment in which more people will be favorably inclined" to vote for the treaty.[34]

Throughout the first months of 1997 until treaty ratification, Lott and Clinton were in constant communication. Not only was the president dialing Lott almost daily, Clinton was telephoning numerous senators to urge their support for the treaty.[35] Lott also established an informal working group of nine Senate Republicans, including Helms, to work with top Clinton officials on changes to the CWC that could address many of their problems. Out of these discussions came thirty-three proposed changes designed to allay GOP concerns; twenty-eight of these provisos were accepted by Clinton and five so-called "killer" amendments were turned down by the Senate. On the morning of the final vote, Lott even convinced Clinton to issue a letter promising that the United States would withdraw from the CWC if it compromised U.S. national security. The letter helped provide political cover for Republicans who backed the treaty.[36]

THE SENATE GOES NUCLEAR

From the role played by Senators Lott and Helms to mixed signals from the Clinton administration, most of the political dynamics that characterized the CWC resurfaced in the 106th Congress (1999–2001) during Senate consideration of the Comprehensive Nuclear Test Ban Treaty (CTBT). A ban on nuclear testing had been a national arms control priority at least since the Eisenhower administration. This effort took on heightened significance during the 1962 Cuban missile crisis when the United States and the then U.S.S.R. came close to a nuclear showdown. The next year the Kennedy administration signed the Limited Test Ban Treaty, which prohibited nuclear explosions in space, in the atmosphere, and under water. Subsequent presidents also took steps to extend the ban on nuclear testing. Finally, with the end of the Cold War and the breakup of the Soviet Union, international pressure mounted to enact a comprehensive nuclear test ban treaty.

The Conference on Disarmament—the multilateral forum for negotiating arms control treaties, as in the CWC case—also took the lead in approving a comprehensive test ban proposal. In August 1996, the Conference had a draft treaty in hand, and on September 10, 1996, the UN General Assembly voted 158 to 3 (Libya, India, and Bhutan voted against) "to seek ratification of a treaty permanently banning the testing of all nuclear weapons."[37] Two weeks later President Clinton signed the treaty, which prohibited all nuclear explosions and provided an international monitoring network to verify compliance.[38]

THE SENATE RECEIVES THE CTBT

On September 22, 1997, Clinton officially submitted the CTBT to the Senate for ratification. In his message to the Senate, the president characterized the treaty as "a signal event in the history of arms control" and pointed out that it had been "under consideration by the international community for 40 years. . . . Therefore, I urge the Senate to give early and favorable consideration to the Treaty and its advice and consent to ratification as soon as possible."[39] In response to Clinton, Chairman Helms said: "I recommend that you do not hold your breath."[40]

President Clinton knew that he would face stiff opposition from many of the same conservative Republicans who opposed him on the CWC. Chairman Helms, for instance, raised familiar arguments against the nuclear treaty: It was unverifiable, it undermined the reliability of the nation's nuclear arsenal, and it was unenforceable. Many Republicans, too, did not want any action on the treaty until the United States developed an antimissile nuclear space shield to protect the nation against a missile attack.

To rebut some of these criticisms, Clinton instructed the Department of Energy to develop technological ways (computer simulations, for example) to test the reliability of the country's nuclear stockpile without the need for explosions. Clinton also saw another potential benefit of the technology initiative: Much of the laboratory work would be done in New Mexico's two nuclear weapons labs represented by a potential ally of the administration on this issue—GOP Senator Pete V. Domenici of New Mexico—who might be influenced by the generous funding earmarked for the two facilities.[41]

Still, in October 1999, the Senate rejected the CTBT on a largely party-line vote, with Republican internationalists such as Domenici and Lugar voting no. Not only did the treaty fail to attract a simple majority, it fell nineteen votes short of the two-thirds necessary for ratification. Only four moderate Republicans—John H. Chafee of Rhode Island, James M. Jeffords of Vermont (now an Independent), Gordon H. Smith of Oregon, and Arlen Specter of Pennsylvania—voted with forty-four Democrats for the treaty.[42]

FACTORS BEHIND THE DEFEAT

Rejection of the CTBT was a major defeat for Clinton. To provide some historical perspective, since the Republic began, only 20 of 1,523 treaties have been turned down by the Senate.[43] As Senator Jon Kyl, a leading treaty opponent, phrased it: "For the first time since it rejected the Versailles Treaty seventy-nine years before, the Senate turned down a major international treaty," because "a majority of senators believed the treaty was fundamentally flawed."[44] Several key factors contributed to the treaty's rejection, including miscalculations by Democrats and adroit maneuvers by Majority Leader Lott and Senate Republicans. Why did the CWC and the CTBT each fare differently in the Senate?

Different Political Context Unlike the CWC, which was endorsed by Republican and Democratic presidents, the CTBT was clearly identified with the Clinton administration. Republican Presidents Reagan and Bush opposed a nuclear test ban; thus, Senate Republicans had no party stake in the treaty's adoption. Furthermore, where there was a willingness in 1997 for moderate Republicans, Majority Leader Lott, and Clinton to cooperate on the CWC, that was not the case two years later.

The year 1999 was an intensely partisan year. Not only were the important November 2000 elections on the horizon, but the year began in the Senate with one of the most divisive events in recent American politics: the Senate trial of President Clinton following his impeachment by the House. Unsurprisingly, the hostility that existed between most Senate Republicans and President Clinton contributed to the downfall of the CTBT. The CTBT, sometimes called the Holy Grail of treaties by arms control advocates, was not to be a legacy of the Clinton administration. Senator Pat Roberts (R-Kan.) even referred to Clinton's call for action on the treaty as a "legacy trip" to ensure a major foreign policy victory before he leaves office.[45] These political tensions made it especially difficult for the two sides to reach agreement on when or how to deal with the treaty. As Minority Leader Daschle explained: "It's an understandable frustration that [Senate Republicans have] not fared very well in their legislative battles with this president over the past eight years. So maybe it's payback time."[46] Unfortunately, he said, the treaty "has become a partisan matter. There are some [Republicans] who don't want to give President Clinton a victory."[47] Or as Senator Joseph I. Lieberman (D-Conn.) put it: "Something unusual and unsettling has happened to our politics when party lines divide us so clearly and totally on a matter such as this. That's not the way it used to be in the United States Senate and it's not the way it should be."[48]

Chairman Helms's Role During consideration of the CWC, Helms remained a staunch opponent to the very end, but at least he negotiated with the administration and with Lott and others to permit the CWC to be discharged from his committee. He also held hearings on the CWC and won certain concessions from the administration. Helms's role with respect to the CTBT was somewhat different.

First, Helms made it clear that the CTBT was not a priority for his panel. He wrote Clinton on January 21, 1998, and asked why "your Administration has been unwisely and unnecessarily engaged in delay in submitting these treaties [amendments to the 1972 Anti-Ballistic Missile (ABM) treaty and the Kyoto Protocol on global warming] to the Senate for its advice and consent." Neither treaty was likely to be approved by the Senate. Helms added the following:

> Mr. President, let me be clear. I will be prepared to schedule Committee consideration of the CTBT only after the Senate has had the opportunity to consider and vote on the Kyoto Protocol and the amendments to the ABM treaty. When the Administration has submitted these treaties, and when the Senate has completed its consideration of them, then, and only then, will the Foreign Relations Committee consider the CTBT.[49]

True to his word, Helms scheduled no hearings specifically on the treaty in 1998 and one, reluctantly, in 1999 only a few days before the Senate defeated it. Democrats repeatedly complained that Helms was not holding hearings on the CTBT. Helms responded by arguing that there were fourteen hearings where different witnesses discussed the measure. Senator Biden, the ranking Democrat on Foreign Relations, rejected the Chairman's contention: "But the idea that we have had hearings on this treaty is not true. . . . [W]e have had hearings on other subjects that implicate the Comprehensive Test Ban Treaty. . . . But we have never had a hearing on the Comprehensive Test Ban Treaty."[50] Disappointed that Foreign Relations had not conducted comprehensive hearings on the treaty, Minority Leader Daschle stated, "It is my intention, as Democratic leader, to conduct hearings of my own as part of the Democratic Policy Committee to ensure that we do have experts in Washington to express themselves."[51]

Helms, in brief, never wavered in his adamant resistance to the CTBT, and, unlike on the CWC, he was not under any pressure from Lott or moderate Republicans to facilitate Senate action on the nuclear treaty. An outside event also bolstered Helms's opposition to the treaty. During the week of May 11, 1998, India set off a series of underground nuclear explosions. "India's actions demonstrate that the Comprehensive Test Ban Treaty, from a non-proliferation standpoint, is scarcely more than a sham."[52] India's nuclear tests provided Helms with another excuse to continue postponing action on the CTBT.

Inadequate Lobbying by the Administration   In 1997, the Clinton administration went all-out to win Senate ratification of the CWC. This was not the case with the CTBT. The president became fully engaged only when it was too late to make a difference. In 1998, in his January 27 State of the Union address, President Clinton urged the Senate to approve the treaty "this year."[53] However, the treaty became sidetracked by the impeachment imbroglio, the

India nuclear explosions, the 1998 elections, and other matters. The administration expended little sustained effort to move the treaty.

Two senators, Biden and Specter, circulated a "Dear Colleague" letter in 1998, and urged their colleagues to sign it. The purpose of the letter was to encourage Chairman Helms to hold hearings on the treaty. In addition, on September 1, 1998, Senator Specter forced a test vote on the treaty. He offered an amendment to the foreign operations appropriations bill that would provide funding for a CTBT preparatory commission. The amendment was adopted 49 to 44, but the margin was far short of the two-thirds needed for treaty ratification. Significantly, Majority Leader Lott expressed dismay with the amendment and with the treaty itself. "The last thing the United States needs is another arms control treaty," he exclaimed.[54]

The next year, Clinton again recommended in his January 19 State of the Union address that the Senate ratify the CTBT. "I ask the Senate to take this vital step: Approve the treaty now, to make it harder for other nations to develop nuclear arms, and to make sure we can end nuclear testing forever."[55] However, the Clinton administration remained preoccupied with other issues. Senator Lugar "harshly criticized the Clinton administration for failing to educate Senators on the complex terms of the test ban."[56] A Senate Democratic aide noted: "We all recognize the need [for the Administration] to do more. [The White House] felt that the treaty wasn't going anywhere. So it was a question of priorities."[57] Arms control advocates pointed out that Clinton "has not yet made ratification a public issue or fought hard for it in Congress."[58] One pro-treaty advocate bluntly stated: "They just completely dropped the ball. You can't say it's a top priority for foreign policy and then do nothing with it for two years."[59]

The president finally took personal charge of the ratification campaign, but this occurred only about a week before the conclusive Senate vote. Top administration officials, including Vice President Gore, urged treaty adoption in various public forums. The president met with reporters, mobilized his national security team, and spoke extensively with members. His Chief of Staff and National Security adviser made numerous telephone calls to senators. The Secretary of State, the Defense Secretary, and the chairman of the Joint Chief of Staffs went to Capitol Hill to lobby lawmakers. As in the first phase of the CWC, it was another instance of too little and too late by the administration. Clinton was unable to generate public pressure or momentum for the CTBT despite some opinion polls indicating that 75 percent of registered voters favored the nuclear test ban treaty.

Lott Outmaneuvers the Democrats Lott had played a crucial role in the success of the CWC, but in the process incurred the wrath of conservative Senate Republicans. They believed the majority leader had been too much the deal maker and accommodator—recall, for example, that Lott in 1996 delayed action on the CWC at the administration's request—and whose support for the

CWC led to its approval. "I've been paying the price for that vote every since," said Lott.[60] In contrast, Lott staunchly opposed the nuclear treaty, and actions by Senate Democrats afforded him the chance to refurbish his conservative credentials on international security issues.

By fall 1999, "message politics" had become central to the procedural infighting on the CTBT. In both chambers, congressional Republicans and Democrats devise formal message agendas, which are comprised of the issues, proposals, and policy symbols that legislators believe will resonate for their party among voters.[61] In September 1999, the Senate Democratic Message Team—an informal group of Democratic members charged with developing and publicizing the party message—decided that the Republicans' failure to schedule floor action on the CTBT would make a useful message item for the Democratic party.[62] Senator Byron L. Dorgan of North Dakota, cochairman of the Senate Democratic Policy Committee, Joseph Biden, and other Democrats took to the floor to denounce the alleged delaying tactics by Helms and Lott. On September 8, for example, Dorgan threatened to tie up the Senate unless Lott scheduled action on the treaty. Knowing full well that unanimous consent is the *modus operandi* of the Senate, Dorgan declared: "I intend to plant myself on the floor like a potted plant and object . . . to the routine business of the Senate until . . . this treaty [is brought] to the floor for a debate and a vote."[63] Administration officials, however, viewed the taunting by Senate Democrats as "freelancing," and not part of a coordinated strategy with the White House.[64]

Senate Democrats believed their "gridlock strategy" would either force the treaty to the floor where, in a reprise of the CWC vote, moderate Republicans would join with them to produce the required two-thirds for ratification, or enable them to use the treaty as a message issue and score campaign points against Republicans in the November 2000 elections. As Senator Biden remarked about his home-state colleague, GOP Senator William V. Roth, who was facing a difficult reelection contest: "Bill Roth says he will vote against the treaty. Bingo! That's $200,000 worth of ads" against his campaign.[65] Senator Biden also had a resolution he was planning to offer requesting that Foreign Relations hold hearings in 1999 with a Senate vote slated by March 31, 2000, injecting the issue into the presidential campaign.

What Senate Democrats did not realize, though, was that Lott already had the votes to reject the treaty. Since spring 1999, a small group of conservative Republicans, led by Senators Kyl and Paul Coverdell of Georgia had conducted their own informal "whip counts" and lined up GOP opposition to the treaty. In May, Kyl told Lott that he had thirty-four Republican votes against the treaty. Lott informed Helms that he could safely report the CTBT to the floor where it would be rejected. Chairman Helms responded: "Get me more."[66] So Kyl, Coverdell, and others continued to round up votes against the treaty. Thus, when Senate Democrats decided to try to compel Lott to take up the treaty, he was ready for them. In fact, he surprised the Democrats, including the White House, by calling for expedited action on the treaty.

On September 30, 1999, Majority Leader Lott asked unanimous consent that the CTBT be discharged from the Foreign Relations Committee, that the Senate begin consideration at 10 AM on October 6, that each party leader be allowed to offer one relevant amendment, that there be ten hours of debate on the treaty, and that no other amendments, reservations, and the like be in order to the treaty. "I think this treaty is bad, bad for the country and dangerous," stated Lott, "but if there is demand that we go forward with it, as I have been hearing for 2 years, we are ready to go."[67] A surprised Daschle objected, saying ten hours of debate was insufficient and that the October 6 timetable did not allow adequate time for lawmakers to prepare for the debate. Chairman Helms observed: "I am absolutely astonished our friends across the aisle refuse to agree to the majority leader's unanimous consent agreement" to bring the treaty to the floor for a vote.[68]

The next day, Lott asked that the treaty be taken up on October 8 and that there be fourteen hours of debate on the treaty with an additional four hours, equally divided, to debate each leader's amendment. Daschle did not object to the unanimous consent request.[69] "We feel we have no choice," he said. "This may be the best that we can get. . . . We'll take it."[70] The die was now cast for the Senate to vote within a two week period on the CTBT, and Senate Democrats were beginning to recognize that they did not have the votes for ratification. Despite their grumbling about the short time frame, Democrats accepted Lott's terms because, as Senator Carl Levin (D-Mich.) explained: "They put us in the position of looking like we didn't want the treaty to come up if we opposed that kind of extremely rapid consideration."[71] Or as a Senate Democratic aide put it: "It became difficult for the Democrats to say we can't do this, we would have looked stupid demanding hearings, demanding a vote and then complaining about the process."[72] In short, Lott's surprise unanimous consent request had maneuvered Democrats into a procedural cul de sac from which they could neither retreat nor advance.

It soon became apparent to everyone that the treaty was doomed to defeat if the Senate voted on it. Thus, lawmakers on both sides of the aisle tried to find a graceful way to avoid that result, fearing it would be a diplomatic embarrassment to the United States and encourage nuclear proliferation. "There are international ramifications for killing it," remarked Senator Domenici.[73] However, neither party wanted to be seen as backing away from their commitment to vote on the treaty, which set in motion a series of efforts to try and avoid the vote.

In exchange for postponing the vote, Majority Leader Lott demanded a pledge from Clinton that the Democrats would not attempt to bring the treaty up on the Senate floor until after the 2000 elections.[74] Daschle and the White House rejected Lott's proposal. Chairman Helms upped the ante and stated that Clinton must request, in writing, that the treaty be withdrawn and not be taken up again during his presidency. Desperate to avoid the treaty's defeat, Clinton sent the letter to Lott and asked that the vote on the treaty be postponed. Lott's spokesperson then said this was only a first step and that

Clinton must agree not to bring the treaty up again in the 106th Congress (1999–2001). "As the majority leader has stated all along, agreement must be reached that it not come up again at any time in this Congress."[75] The White House refused to go along with this condition.

Meanwhile, other initiatives were underway with respect to Senate action on the CTBT. Senators John W. Warner (R-Va.) and Daniel P. Moynihan (D-N.Y.) circulated a letter requesting that Lott put off the vote. The letter attracted sixty-two senatorial signatures, including twenty-four Republicans. In response, three conservative GOP senators—Tim Hutchinson of Arkansas, Robert C. Smith of New Hampshire, and James M. Inhofe of Oklahoma—sent a letter to Lott stating they would object to any request to delay the vote.[76] (It is important to underscore that the UCA governing consideration of the treaty could only be dropped or modified by unanimous consent.) Senator Daschle also wrote to Lott and pledged that Democrats would not bring the treaty up again in the 106th Congress unless there were "unforeseen circumstances." Lott reviewed the letter with Senators Helms, Kyl, Coverdell, and Inhofe, and the consensus of the group was that Daschle's proposal was unacceptable.[77] The bipartisan letter also had no effect on postponing the vote.

Senate Democrats even tried a parliamentary maneuver to stop debate on the treaty. Under Senate rules, treaties and nominations are placed on an Executive Calendar and considered in a Senate forum called "executive session." Regularly, the Senate moves back-and-forth between its regular "legislative session," where bills and other matters are debated, to executive session for the consideration of treaties or nominations. If a senator objects to the usual unanimous consent request to move from one public forum to the other, then Majority Leader Lott, or his designee, can accomplish that goal by offering a nondebatable motion. The motion requires majority approval. The Democratic plan was that if this motion was rejected, the Senate would not be able to take up the treaty and its outright defeat could be avoided. Majority Leader Lott, concerned about this possibility, "warned Republican lawmakers during their weekly policy luncheons that a vote with Democrats [on this procedural motion] would be tantamount to party disloyalty."[78] When Lott made the motion to shift the Senate from legislative session to executive session, it was a strict party-line vote of 55 to 45.[79] Republicans decided to stick with their leader, which meant that the treaty could not be set aside by a procedural vote.

The bottom line: all 100 Senators needed to agree to postpone the vote. However, delay was not the goal of many conservative Republicans. They wanted to kill the treaty outright, and they insisted that the vote take place. This flawed treaty "will not improve with age," said Senator Kyl.[80] Ironically, once Senate Democrats accepted Lott's UCA, Chairman Helms and his allies, including the Majority Leader, gained absolute control over the final outcome, absent some dramatic change in the voting predilections of Senators—and this did not occur.

After defeat of the treaty, President Clinton railed against hard-line Republicans in the Senate and called the episode "partisan politics of the worst kind," which Lott vehemently denied.[81] Senate–White House hostility intensified when it became known that Secretary of State Albright had informed foreign governments that the United States would still honor the treaty despite its rejection. In response, Majority Leader Lott exclaimed: "If the administration persists in maintaining that the United States is bound as a matter of international law to a treaty that has been rejected by the Senate, then there will be profound implications for the relationship between the president and the Senate on foreign policy matters."[82] After the treaty's defeat, President Clinton requested General John Shalikashvili, former chairman of the Joint Chiefs of Staff, to outline how the next administration might be able to ratify the accord.

CONCLUSION

Both the Chemical Weapons Convention and the Comprehensive Nuclear Test Ban Treaty were major international agreements, significant foreign policy initiatives of the Clinton administration, and broadly supported by the public. Many of the same strategic and political forces also characterized Senate consideration of the two accords. But the different fates that befell the treaties before the Senate generate some important lessons about the practical exigencies of treaty ratification in the contemporary Congress. We close this chapter by highlighting five broad points.

First, public support for the two treaties tended to be broad, but not deep. Ordinary citizens lack the information and the expertise necessary to form firm preferences about the logistics and details of most international agreements. Thus, even major treaties are ripe for opposition and possible defeat by minority coalitions with intense preferences. Spin control and issue framing are an important part of this process. In the current political and communications environments, proponents and opponents are likely to engage in outside strategies on major treaties. That is, they conduct grassroots mobilization efforts aimed at shaping public opinion, and thus the incentives confronted by legislators on Capitol Hill.

Second, for treaties that relate directly to international security matters, the pivotal actors within Congress tend to be senior Republican internationalists, such as Richard Lugar and Pete Domenici. It is critical for administration officials to consult and work with these members early in the ratification effort, or even before, during the process of international negotiation. Such tactics characterized the CWC but not the CTBT. With the inauguration of George W. Bush, the internationalist wing of the GOP will be less likely to desert the President on foreign policy matters, but these members remain the key coalition on these issues within the Senate. (Interestingly, this configuration contrasts sharply with international trade agreements, where the pivotal coalition tends to be free-trade Democrats.)

Third, if a treaty or other foreign policy matter becomes intertwined in message politics and campaign strategizing, the ratification process will be transformed from a positive-sum (e.g., "partisanship ends at the water's edge") to a zero-sum game, and the likelihood of a Senate endorsement falls accordingly. Thus, it often is a mistake for presidents to push for Senate approval during a presidential election year, or when relations between the two congressional parties are dominated by an upcoming campaign. Senate acceptance of the CWC only became politically feasible after the 1996 presidential elections. Likewise, the rancorously partisan environment of the 106th Congress helped doom the CTBT.

Fourth, the president's party in the Senate often has to play procedural hardball to avoid obstructionist tactics on major treaties. The process of treaty consideration has now become inseparable from the partisan maneuvering that characterizes the Senate agenda more generally. In the contemporary Senate, individual members use a range of procedural tactics to keep initiatives they oppose off of the committee and floor agendas. In recent years, Foreign Relations Committee Chairman Helms has taken the lead in blocking Senate consideration of treaties he opposes. Minority Leader Daschle typically has responded with retaliatory threats to hold up policy initiatives supported by Helms and other conservative Republicans. Even with a Republican in the White House, such procedural infighting is likely to continue in some form within the narrowly divided Senate of the 107th Congress (2001–2003).

Fifth, and by far most important, the president must play a central and critical role in the ratification of international treaties. The executive branch has special prerogatives and responsibilities in the area of foreign policy. Thus, Senate endorsement of a major treaty typically depends on early, systematic, and aggressive lobbying by the White House—even if a treaty is the result of longer-term negotiations stretching back across many administrations. Often, the administration will need to work with interested senators on possible reservations, conditions, and perhaps amendments to a treaty, subject to the constraint that such changes or conditions not undermine international support for the accord. Throughout the ratification process, the prospects of the CWC and the CTBT were directly tied to the intensity of administration lobbying and bargaining with senators. On the CTBT, the opposition effort spearheaded by Senator Kyl raised significant obstacles to successful ratification. But the primary factor behind the treaty's demise was the failure of the Clinton administration to effectively reach out to Republican internationalists and build a bipartisan supporting coalition on the Senate floor.

For the president and the Congress on foreign policy matters, the U.S. Constitution indeed may be "an invitation to struggle." But for these and other issues, our constitutional framework also serves as an invitation to negotiation and accommodation between the branches—a feature that presidents will forget at their own political peril.

NOTES

1. More concretely, both authors together spoke at length with a former director of legislative liaison in the Clinton White House, as well as with top aides to the Senate Majority and Minority Leaders. In addition, one of us (Evans) posed questions about one or both treaties during interviews with a broadly representative sample of Senate chiefs of staff.
2. Several nations, including Iraq and Libya, refused to sign the treaty.
3. The ten-month delay in transmitting the CWC to the Senate probably was associated with the transition activities of a new administration.
4. Elizabeth Palmer, "Senate Panel Opens Hearings on Chemical Weapons Pact," *Congressional Quarterly Weekly Report*, 26 March 1994, p. 756.
5. *Congressional Record*, 104th Cong., 1st sess., December 7, 1995, 35893.
6. Ibid., 35894.
7. Carroll Doherty, "Senate Slashes Agency Budgets, Confirms 18 Ambassadors," *Congressional Quarterly Weekly Report*, 16 December 1995, p. 3821.
8. Pat Towell, "Administration Begins New Drive for Chemical Weapons Treaty," *Congressional Quarterly Weekly Report*, 30 March 1996, p. 893.
9. Ibid.
10. *Congressional Record*, 104th Cong., 2nd sess., June 28, 1996, S7293.
11. Donna Cassata, "Chemical Weapons Treaty Nears Climactic Vote," *Congressional Quarterly Weekly Report*, 7 September 1996, p. 2534.
12. Carla Anne Robbins, "Chemical-Weapons Treaty Shapes Up as Messy Battle," *Wall Street Journal*, 14 February 1997, p. A-16.
13. Adam Clymer, "Dole Pressures the Senate to Kill Poison Gas Treaty," *New York Times*, 13 September 1996, p. A-1.
14. Towell, "Chemical Weapons Ban Delayed as Dole Joins Objectors," p. 2607.
15. Clymer, "Dole Pressures the Senate to Kill Poison Gas Treaty," p. A-23.
16. *Congressional Record*, 105th Cong., 1st sess., April 24, 1997, S3602.
17. Alison Mitchell, "How the Votes Were Won: Clinton's New G.O.P. Tactics," *New York Times*, 25 April 1997, p. A-10.
18. Peter Baker and Helen Dewar, "Clinton-Lott Connection Emerges in Treaty Fight," *Washington Post*, 26 April 1997, p. A-12.
19. *Public Papers of the Presidents of the United States, William J. Clinton, 1997, Book I* (Washington, D.C.: U.S. Government Printing Office, 1998), 116.
20. *CQ Monitor*, "Democrats Change Tactics on Chemical Weapons Treaty," 9 April 1997, p. 5.
21. Peter Baker and Helen Dewar, "Clinton-Lott Connection Emerges in Treaty Fight," p. A-12.
22. Needless to say, Chairman Helms had his own parade of political celebrities—Donald Rumsfeld, James Schlesinger, and Caspar Weinberger are examples of politicians who criticized the treaty.
23. Mitchell, "How the Votes Were Won: Clinton's New G.O.P. Tactics," p. A-10.
24. Nancy Roman, "Daschle Warns against Treaty Delay," *Washington Times*, 20 March 1997, p. A-4.
25. *Congressional Record*, 105th Cong., 1st sess., March 19, 1997, S2503.
26. Martin Sieff, "Lott Sees Possible Vote on Treaty," *Washington Times*, 9 April 1997, p. A-13.
27. Ibid.
28. *Congressional Record*, 105th Cong., 1st sess., April 17, 1997, S3326.
29. Helen Dewar, "Senate Sets Chemical Arms Pact Vote," *Washington Post*, 18 April 1997, p. A-10. Senator Robert C. Byrd, (D-W.Va.) the chamber's senior Democrat, former majority and minority leader, and acknowledged parliamentary expert, seemed ready to object to the UCA because he had not seen the lengthy agreement. Quickly, Minority Leader Daschle defused the potential for objection by pointing out that Democrats had been notified of the agreement's terms on four different occasions. First, he said, the UCA had been sent to all Senate Democratic offices forty-eight hours ago; second, the Democratic Caucus discussed it; third, all relevant committee staff aides and interested senators had reviewed the UCA within the last twenty-four hours; and, fourth, "we have explained it again in a policy committee [meeting] just about two and one-half hours ago." Senator Daschle also made sure that Vice President Al Gore was presiding at strategic times to cast any tie-breaking votes and to remind any potential Democratic defectors of the importance the administration placed on treaty approval.

30. Ibid., p. A-10.
31. Brian Bloomquist, "Senate Approves Chemical-Arms Treaty," *Washington Times*, 25 April 1997, p. A-4.
32. *Congressional Record*, 105th Cong., 1st sess., April 24, 1997, S3603.
33. Donna Cassata, "For Lott, a Chance to Rise above the Fray," *Congressional Quarterly Weekly Report*, 26 April 1997, p. 975.
34. John Harris and Thomas Lippman, "Clinton Agrees to Shift Foreign Policy Agencies," *Washington Post*, 18 April 1997, p. A-10.
35. John Harris and Helen Dewar, "Clinton Works Phones to Push Chemical Treaty," *Washington Post*, 17 April 1997, p. A-4.
36. Pat Towell, "Chemical Weapons Ban Approved in Burst of Compromise," *Congressional Quarterly Weekly Report*, 26 April 1997, p. 973. Lott also scheduled a bill sponsored by Senator Kyl, which the Senate passed on April 17 by a largely party-line vote of 54 to 44, to do by statute what the treaty planned to accomplish.
37. Jonathan Weisman, "Nuclear Test Ban Treaty Up Next," *Congressional Quarterly Weekly Report*, 14 September 1996, p. 2608.
38. Pat Towell, "Clinton Signs Test Ban," *Congressional Quarterly Weekly Report*, 28 September 1996, p. 2770.
39. *Public Papers of the Presidents of the United States, William J. Clinton, 1997, Book II* (Washington, D.C.: U.S. Government Printing Office, 1999), pp. 1209–1213.
40. Jonathan Weisman, "President Submits Nuclear Test Ban, Seeks Critical Mass of Senate Votes," *Congressional Quarterly Weekly Report*, 27 September 1997, p. 2325.
41. Ibid., p. 2,326.
42. Democratic Senator Byrd voted "present," something he had never done before, because he wanted more time to consider the treaty. Robert C. Byrd, "Advise and Consent? Not This Time," *New York Times*, 15 October 1999, p. A-31.
43. R. W. Apple, Jr., "The G.O.P. Torpedo," *New York Times*, 14 October 1999, p. A-1.
44. Senator Jon Kyl, "Maintaining 'Peace through Strength': A Rejection of the Comprehensive Test Ban Treaty," *Harvard Journal on Legislation* (summer 2000), p. 325.
45. Helen Dewar, "Senate on 3 Fronts in Treaty Vote," *Washington Post*, 8 October 1999, p. A-24.
46. Ibid.
47. Sumana Chatterjee, "Politics Splashing Noisily beyond 'the Water's Edge,'" *CQ Daily Monitor*, 12 October 1999, p. 5.
48. Helen Dewar, "Democrats Push Delay on Treaty," *Washington Post*, 13 October 1999, p. A-4.
49. *Congressional Record*, 106th Cong., 1st sess., September 30, 1999, S11667.
50. Ibid.
51. *Congressional Record*, 106th Cong., 1st sess., October 1, 1999, S11820.
52. Chuck McCutcheon, "India's Nuclear Detonations Rattle Clinton's Arms Control Strategy," *Congressional Quarterly Weekly Report*, 16 May 1998, p. 1320.
53. *Public Papers of the Presidents of the United States, William J. Clinton, 1998, Book II* (Washington, D.C.: U.S. Government Printing Office, 1999), p. 118.
54. *Congressional Record*, 105th Cong., 2nd sess., September 1, 1998, S9770.
55. *Weekly Compilation of Presidential Documents*, January 25, 1999, p. 84.
56. Richard Cohen, "The Senate Goes Ballistic," *National Journal*, 9 October 1999, p. 2890.
57. Ibid.
58. Eric Schmitt, "Democrats Ready for Fight to Save Test Ban Treaty," *New York Times*, 30 August 1999, p. A-1.
59. Charles Babington and Michael Grunwald, "President Requests Treaty Vote Deferral," *Washington Post*, 12 October 1999, p. A-4.
60. Eric Schmitt, "Why Clinton Plea on Pact Left Lott Unmoved," *New York Times*, 15 October 1999, p. A-11.
61. C. Lawrence Evans, "Committees, Leaders, and Message Politics," in *Congress Reconsidered*, 7th ed., ed. Lawrence C. Dodd and Bruce I. Oppenheimer (Washington, D.C.: CQ Press, 2001).
62. Not-for-attribution interviews conducted by C. Lawrence Evans with selected Senate chiefs of staff, October 1999.
63. *Congressional Record*, 106th Cong., 1st sess., September 8, 1999, S10541.
64. John Broder, "Quietly and Dexterously, Senate Republicans Set a Trap," *New York Times*, 14 October 1999, p. A-11.
65. Cohen, "The Senate Goes Ballistic," p. 2890.

66. Broder, "Quietly and Dexterously, Senate Republicans Set a Trap," p. A-11.

67. *Congressional Record*, 106th Cong., 1st sess., September 30, 1999, S11667.

68. Ibid., S11670. It is interesting to note that critics of the treaty released a letter from former Senator Dole, who called the treaty "an ill-conceived and misguided arms control agreement." See Eric Schmitt, "Both Parties Seek a Graceful Way to Put Off a Nuclear Treaty Vote," *New York Times*, 6 October 1999, p. A-8.

69. *Congressional Record*, 106th Cong., 1st sess., October 1, 1999, S11820.

70. "Senate to Take Up Nuclear Test Ban Treaty on Oct. 12," *Washington Times*, 2 October 1999, p. A-4.

71. Broder, "Quietly and Dexterously, Senate Republicans Set a Trap," p. A-11.

72. Ibid.

73. Schmitt, "Both Parties Seek a Graceful Way to Put Off a Nuclear Treaty Vote," p. A-1.

74. Ibid., pp. A-1, A-8.

75. Art Pine, "Clinton Asks Again to Put off Test-Ban Treaty Vote," *Los Angeles Times*, 10 October 1999, p. A-1.

76. Neil King and Jeffrey Taylor, "Both Parties Want Other Side to Put Off Tuesday's Vote on Nuclear Test Ban," *Wall Street Journal*, 7 October 1999, p. A-32.

77. *Congressional Record*, 106th Cong., 1st sess., November 10, 1999, S14579.

78. Sumana Chatterjee, "No Deal Yet on Delaying Test Ban Treaty Vote," *CQ Daily Monitor*, 13 October 1999, p. 2

79. *Congressional Record*, 106th Cong., 1st sess., October 13, 1999, S12504–S12505.

80. Helen Dewar, "Democrats Push Delay on Treaty," *Washington Post*, 13 October 1999, p. A-4.

81. Charles Babington, "Clinton Uses Treaty Defeat to Fault GOP Partisanship," *Washington Post*, 15 October 1999, p. A-16.

82. Bill Gertz, "Lott Hits Clinton Stance on Nuke Pact," *Washington Times*, 3 November 1999, p. A-1.

6

ALARMS AND PATROLS

LEGISLATIVE OVERSIGHT IN FOREIGN AND DEFENSE POLICY

CHRISTOPHER J. DEERING[1]

In 1791, General Arthur St. Clair led an "army" of regulars and militia into what was then the Northwest Territory (Ohio, Indiana, Illinois, and Michigan).[2] More than half of the 1,400 men in his command were killed or wounded on November 4 when an inferior force of Little Turtle's Miamis (along with allies) ambushed the army's encampment.[3] News of the disastrous expedition quickly reached President Washington and spread in the national press. A dismayed President Washington refused St. Clair's request for a military inquiry—which the general believed would exonerate him. Congress responded by opening investigative hearings to fix blame in the affair, St. Clair being their clear target. Instead, the congressional investigation demonstrated that St. Clair was largely blameless in the episode. It was the quartermaster general, the quality of the supplies he provided, and the poor quality of the soldiers that were to blame.[4] St. Clair resigned. Quartermaster General Samuel Hodgdon, was replaced.[5] Washington appointed Anthony Wayne commander in chief for the territory. And, over objections from staunch opponents of a standing army, northern, mostly Federalist legislators succeeded in granting Washington's request for a doubling of the regular army.

In December 1979, the Baltimore *Sun* reported that sexual harassment was common at the U.S. Army's Fort Meade. In February the House Armed Services Committee's Personnel Subcommittee held hearings at which five Army enlisted women and base officers testified. In spite of the women's complaints, the officers assured legislators that the incidents were isolated. Congress took no action. In 1992, press attention to the so-called Tailhook scandal received nationwide attention. Once again, Congress held hearings. The Pentagon pursued a lengthy investigation of its own. And the Senate postponed Navy promotions (which it handles as confirmations). Through-out 1996 and 1997, a series of sensational stories appeared in the national press about sexual harassment in the U.S. military. In 1998, the House National Security Committee and the Senate Armed Services Committee held hearings and strengthened legislation regarding sexual harassment in the military.[6]

By one estimate, roughly half of the investigations undertaken by Congress in the nineteenth century were focused on activities related to the armed forces of the United States.[7] Like the disastrous St. Clair expedition and sexual harassment at Fort Meade, nearly all of these were triggered by an alarm of some sort or other. Contrast these examples, however, with an 1877 statute whereby Congress required that *any* military construction project in excess of $20,000 be approved by Congress prior to commencement.[8] This placed the executive branch and the military in the position of coming before the legislature each and every year to request approval for even the smallest projects. Needless to say, this sort of annual review placed the executive branch on a very short leash, for it knew that legislators could pick and choose among the various actions they proposed.

Does Congress have a preference for investigative oversight? Or is the latter requirement for close, annual scrutiny closer to its *modus operandi*? Unlike civilian departments and agencies, it may be difficult for Congress to delegate its oversight responsibilities to third parties. Hence, we might ask, is there a basic difference in motivations and behavior where foreign and military policy are concerned? Indeed it might well be that even between foreign policy on the one hand and military policy on the other there are differences in incentives. Primary responsibility for oversight of foreign and military policy—by statute and by tradition—falls to the two foreign policy committees (House International Relations and Senate Foreign Relations), the two military committees (House Armed Services and Senate Armed Services), and to subcommittees of the two appropriations committees (defense, military construction, and foreign operations).[9]

To investigate the nature of oversight in foreign and defense policy, this chapter commences by examining more closely the nature of the oversight function. It then offers three ways to view that oversight effort. First, whether police patrols or fire alarms are being used, hearings remain fundamental to Congress's efforts to understand and control administration. Thus a review of the absolute and relative levels of effort is in order. Second, Congress's use of its authorization power will be examined—or more specifically, the reassertion of that authority in the postwar era. And third, although there is, to my knowledge, no systematic effort to treat patrols and alarms empirically,[10] some circumstantial evidence on these techniques will help improve our understanding of Congress's choices between the two alternatives.

OVERSEEING OR OVERLOOKING:
BASIC NOTIONS OF LEGISLATIVE OVERSIGHT

By wide agreement and historical precedent, it is the legislature's role to watch and control the government. But should it do so only retrospectively by investigating administrative malfeasance and shirking? Should it do so prospectively through legislative design and statutory guidance? Or is there another way? For more than a century, reactive investigations seemed the method of choice. But then the state was relatively small, it touched only a modest portion of the populace, and then only in fairly localized ways.[11] If a scandal occurred, form a committee and get to the bottom of it. But the state of the twentieth century was larger, more powerful, and more intrusive in people's lives. Efficiency in such a large organization (or organizations) requires delegation, flexibility, and yet accountability at the same time. What is Congress to do?

Delegation is the "cheap" solution. Wait for problems to occur; then come riding to the rescue.[12] Meddling provides another alternative. Write legislation in a way that ties bureaucrats' hands but at the cost of "snafus" needing remedies anyway. For one scholar, it was the latter remedy that seemed to attract Congress:

> The *Statutes at Large* and the annual appropriation acts are cluttered with a mass of detailed prohibitions and limitations upon administrative action. They represent in part a process of legislation by exasperation. Unfortunately, these often petty restrictions tend to continue and to accumulate. They hamper good administration and miss the mark as a means of control.[13]

Written today, this passage would surprise few observers of legislative–executive relations. Many might even add that this is an apt description of the now popular notion of legislative "micromanagement." But these words were written near the close of World War II.[14] Not that the writer was the first to worry about such things or about how Congress ought to properly exercise its undeniable right of investigation. Nearly twenty years earlier another congressional observer worried about the lack of interest in investigations, given their importance as a supplement to appropriations and lawmaking, and an alternative to impeachment.[15] And only a couple of years after that did someone else list supervision of the administration as one of three basic congressional functions. In pursuing this task, however, the legislature could not depend solely upon the "casual information" provided by constituents, interests, and newspapers.[16] Rather, formal mechanisms needed to be employed to ascertain directly from administrators how programs were being carried out.

The tradition of investigations, traced to Parliament's use of investigating committees long before the American Revolution, implies an *ex post* character to the activity.[17] That is, English investigating committees, Royal commissions, and American select or special committees always appeared in response to a perceived or actual problem rather than in anticipation of one. Several have chronicled the litany of department, agency, and administration investigations produced by Congress, some taking Congress's investigatory power largely as given, at least insofar as precedent was concerned, with others departing from that tradition in asking for more. The public administration tradition of the 1920s and 1930s advocated a scientific approach to federal administration. It is not surprising, therefore, that White would at once decry "legislation by exasperation" and demand more systematic control of administration. Nonetheless, his sympathies (as he readily admits) were with greater capacity for administration.

For their part, contemporary observers are accustomed to distinguishing between *prospective* and *retrospective* oversight.[18] Indeed, the whole idea of oversight proffered by twentieth-century public administrators is slightly at odds with that of investigations. Not that investigations should disappear, but proper legislative construction and review should provide a system that ensures competence and responsibility. Congress gave statutory voice to oversight in the Legislative Reorganization Act of 1946. The act requires *standing* committees, dramatically pruned by the act itself, to assure "continuous watchfulness" over the execution of laws by departments and agencies within their jurisdictions.[19] Although oversight would be undertaken subsequent to legislative enactments it was to be proactive rather than reactive. Standing committees were not to wait for things to go wrong; rather, they were to observe actively the execution of the laws. Moreover, they were required to provide a report of their activities pursuant to the Section 190(d) requirement.

In 1984, two scholars introduced a metaphor to capture these alternatives. Legislators, they argued, could either engage in "police patrols" (the requirement of the 1946 Act and the desire of many public administrators) or they could provide mechanisms to sound "fire alarms" (which in turn might trigger active investigations).[20] They go on to suggest that legislators will prefer the efficiency of alarms to the drudgery of patrols.[21] More concretely, they will prefer to wait for a St. Clair disaster, a Tailhook episode or, worse, a September 2001–style terrorist attack, rather than searching for or preventing one. Either way hearings and subsequent legislation are the mechanisms for response. In response to these scholars, another has asserted that it is hasty to assume that fire alarm oversight will predominate, suggesting the evidence appears to favor a predominance of police patrol oversight.[22]

In reality, patrols are made possible by, and the scut work falls to, the legislative staff who prepare the hearings, write the reports, and draft much of the legislation. Informally, it is the staff (albeit as ghostwriters) who make most of the contacts with departments and agencies. And it is staff increases, first in the late 1940s and more dramatically in the 1970s, that have made this possible. Even a quick review of recent activities reports (mandated by the 1946 Reorganization Act and subsequent legislation) shows a certain sensitivity to the requirements for "continuous watchfulness." For example, the biennial report of the House International Relations Committee commences with a lengthy recitation of the statutory and institutional authority for its oversight effort.[23] Equally telling, the House Armed Services Committee offers this language to introduce its oversight plan:

> While most of the committee's oversight agenda was designed to serve primarily in support of the annual authorization bill, much of the committee's most demanding oversight activity was *event-driven* and not subject to prior planning.[24]

What does "event driven" mean? In a subsequent section titled "Additional Oversight Activities," the opening phrases illustrate the order of events:

> In the wake of the devastating bombing of the Khobar Towers complex in Dhahran, Saudia Arabia . . .

> . . . the circumstances surrounding the shootdown of an American F-16 fighter over Bosnia.

> In response to widespread concerns regarding the analytical rigor which was employed in compiling the Administration's 1995 National Intelligence Estimates . . .

> In the wake of the tragic killings of a black civilian couple by three white soldiers from the Army's 82nd Airborne Division . . .

> . . . an in-depth review of the April 14, 1994, downing of two Army UH-60 Black Hawk helicopters by Air Force F-15 fighters over Northern Iraq.[25]

Now there is no reason to expect the committee staff to adopt the metaphors and language applied by political scientists, but they actually come very close in distinguishing routine oversight attendant to the annual defense authorization bill (with each subcommittee holding its own set of hearings in preparation for that legislation) and event-driven oversight in response to crises and other occurrences.

So how does Congress oversee the executive when it comes to foreign and defense policy? What tools should it, and does it, employ? Observers of the process offer several solutions. Congress can employ investigations as it has done from the St. Clair episode in 1792 up to and beyond the inevitable string of hearings regarding the terrorist attacks on the World Trade Center and Pentagon. Congress has launched a formal investigation into every war in which the United States has participated with the exception of the Spanish–American war. No doubt investigations will continue. But Congress also has fashioned other devices in an attempt to assure continuous watchfulness. And it mixes alarms and patrols in creative ways to pursue that end.

OVERSIGHT IN THE POST–WORLD WAR II ERA

Oversight of all sorts is achieved through congressional hearings, so the most direct way to examine Congress's absolute and relative levels of oversight effort is to look at those hearings. A remarkable data set gathered for the purpose of exploring legislative agendas codes all of the entries in the Congressional Information Service's *CIS/Annual* from 1946 to 1994. This data offers a comprehensive picture of legislative hearings by committee and by topic and allows an estimate of the overall level of effort and the proportion of the effort by different committees.

OVERSIGHT OVERTIME: HEARING PATTERNS SINCE WORLD WAR II

True to popular wisdom, and in spite of the 1946 admonition to exercise "continuous watchfulness," total House hearings declined during the postwar years and bottomed out in the 86th to 90th Congresses (1959–1969). Thus, hearings of all kinds reflect the general impression that the House receded from its oversight responsibilities only to "reawaken" during the era of Vietnam and Watergate.[26] From the 80th to the 85th Congress (1947–1959) total hearings exceeded 1,000 for each two-year period while total hearing days exceeded 3,000 in five of the six congresses. See Table 6.1 for details.

TABLE 6.1 TOTAL HOUSE AND SENATE HEARINGS
AND HEARING DAYS (80TH TO 103RD CONGRESS)

CONGRESS	HOUSE HEARINGS (HEARING DAYS)	HOUSE FOREIGN AND DEFENSE HEARINGS (HEARING DAYS)	SENATE HEARINGS (HEARING DAYS)	SENATE FOREIGN AND DEFENSE HEARINGS (HEARING DAYS)
80th	1,857 (4,206)	498 (1,016)	796 (1,996)	196 (458)
81st	1,337 (2,461)	359 (978)	856 (2,416)	203 (518)
82nd	1,078 (3,019)	250 (886)	704 (2,050)	191 (609)
83rd	1,326 (3,228)	315 (985)	1,172 (2,406)	260 (561)
84th	1,450 (3,674)	300 (982)	1,026 (2,346)	318 (608)
85th	1,547 (3,762)	345 (974)	927 (2,292)	200 (461)
86th	778 (2,803)	211 (886)	907 (1,988)	142 (351)
87th	776 (2,795)	189 (803)	1016 (2,236)	158 (477)
88th	758 (2,901)	179 (695)	905 (2,147)	159 (522)
89th	864 (3,050)	204 (661)	1,004 (2,456)	137 (374)
90th	800 (2,691)	183 (583)	1,062 (2,473)	150 (342)
91st	1,108 (4,393)	218 (838)	1,362 (3,269)	165 (454)
92nd	1,073 (3,702)	221 (787)	1,201 (2,858)	155 (501)
93rd	1,363 (4,308)	287 (1,030)	1,448 (3,325)	205 (529)
94th	1,753 (5,192)	326 (1,057)	1,449 (3,064)	209 (555)
95th	1,984 (5,283)	391 (1,135)	1,583 (3,303)	225 (515)
96th	2,201 (5,337)	436 (1,241)	1,628 (3,075)	218 (527)
97th	2,164 (4,671)	408 (1,027)	1,524 (2,615)	228 (504)
98th	2,174 (4,205)	412 (1,002)	1,379 (2,246)	229 (417)
99th	2,108 (3,791)	443 (942)	1,084 (1,819)	197 (371)
100th	2,303 (3,765)	505 (1,001)	1,238 (2,081)	178 (428)
101st	2,456 (3,865)	498 (943)	1,411 (2,204)	207 (428)
102nd	2,316 (3,694)	487 (895)	1,280 (1,934)	235 (463)
103rd	1,492 (2,330)	303 (525)	1,103 (1,607)	184 (333)
Total	37,066 (90,086)	7,959 (21,872)	28,065 (58,206)	4,749 (11,306)

Source: Unless otherwise noted the data reported here and in subsequent tables and/or figures are the author's compilations using data collected by Baumgartner and Jones (2000) for the *Policy Agendas Project*.

But the Senate picture is not so clear. For the first three postwar congresses, Senate hearings remained at relatively low levels only to rebound in the 83rd and 84th Congresses (1953–1955 and 1955–1957). But from that point on, there is a relatively constant level of oversight effort by the Senate—though its greatest level of effort occurs in the 93rd to the 97th Congresses (1973–1983). Although House hearings exceed Senate hearings in a clear majority of the postwar congresses, the Senate's hearing output was superior to the House's for eight straight congresses—from 1959 to 1974. But in only one congress, the 84th, did Senate hearings on foreign and defense exceed those of the House (and that by a narrow margin and with fewer days).

The proportion of all hearings on defense, foreign affairs and foreign aid, and foreign trade is displayed in Figures 6.1 and 6.2. Several trends are apparent. First, although congressional attention to foreign aid rose dramatically relative to the prewar era, attention to defense policy was easily the predominant focus of foreign and defense hearings. But, second, that proportion dropped quite steadily before bottoming out in the 88th to 90th Congresses (1963–1969). Third, at that point all three categories of hearings commence (or continue) a steady climb that lasts more than two decades before falling sharply in the 103rd Congress (1993–1995).[27]

Why did hearing levels decline initially in the House? Largely because the amount of "housekeeping" needed in the immediate postwar period declined. A closer look at the subject matter of defense hearings shows that the number of hearings on personnel and dependents, on installations and land transfers, and

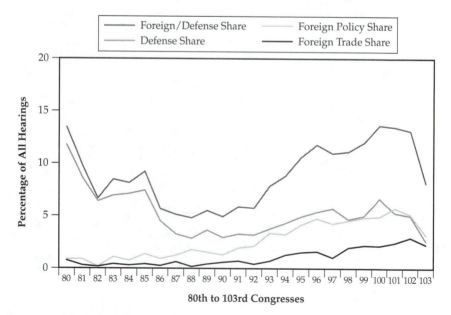

FIGURE 6.1   HOUSE FOREIGN AND DEFENSE POLICY HEARINGS

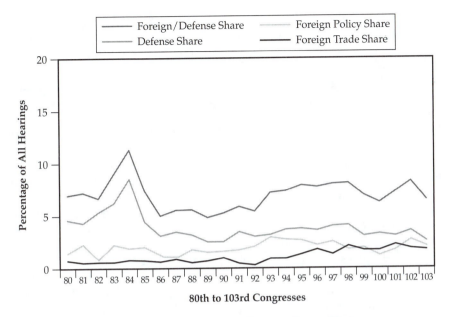

FIGURE 6.2 SENATE FOREIGN AND DEFENSE POLICY HEARINGS

on military claims, declined dramatically. Indeed, from the 83rd to the 85th Congresses (1953–1959) over 400 hearings occurred on those topics. In the next three congresses only 138 occurred. A roughly similar pattern obtains in the Senate. Regardless, the low levels of hearings in both chambers between the 86th and the 92nd Congresses (1959–1973) is due to a decline in defense hearings rather than foreign policy hearings, which started and remained at relatively low levels.

Overall, these trends conform to our general impressions of the postwar era. The high proportion of hearings in the immediate aftermath of World War II reflected the onset of the Cold War and postwar defense issues. But that concern dissipated as the Cold War wore on and was crowded out, ultimately, by Great Society concerns. By the end of the Johnson administration, however, Congress once again turned, in largely equal measure, to foreign *and* defense matters. Throughout the entire period, trade hearings, clearly the most narrowly defined of these three categories, remained proportionately smaller—albeit with an unmistakable, if modest, upward trend after the 92nd Congress (1971–1973).[28] It is also the case that defense issues made up the largest portion of hearings among these three without exception in the Senate and with only a handful of exceptions in the House.

OVERSIGHT ACROSS COMMITTEES

Given the forgoing, namely that foreign and defense hearings comprise about 10 percent of all hearings during the postwar era, it is no surprise to learn that the appropriations, foreign policy, and armed services committees in the two chambers are leaders in this kind of activity. Across the entire period, the House Appropriation Committee is easily the most prolific in terms of total hearing days (hardly surprising given that it is, essentially, thirteen committees) and ranks second, behind Resources, in total hearings (see Table 6.2 for details). House Foreign Affairs and Armed Services are fairly close behind but edged out by Judiciary and Commerce and, in the case of Foreign Affairs, Government Operations (the House's principal oversight committee) for total hearings. Armed Services ranks second in total hearing days, however, with Foreign Affairs fifth.

Once again, the picture on the Senate side is a bit fuzzier. Six committees held more hearings than Appropriations, Armed Services, and Foreign Relations. As in the House, Appropriations had the largest number of hearing days, followed by Judiciary, Commerce, and Labor, leaving Armed Services and Foreign Relations in the middle of the pack in terms of hearing effort. In both cases Senate Foreign Relations and Armed Services rank behind all the major committees except Finance, Environment, and Agriculture.

Differences between the House and Senate, reflected among committees and over time, are hardly surprising. The average senator sits on three or four committees and another eight or so subcommittees. Couple this with a chamber that is less than a quarter the size of the House and, even with slightly fewer standing committees, there simply are not enough members to mount the kind of effort that exists in the House. In addition, however, both the Armed Services Committee and the Foreign Affairs Committee in the House became reactivated after reforms in that chamber decentralized power in the early 1970s. So much for the overall load; who tackles the lion's share when we examine just foreign and defense policy hearings?

Figures 6.3 (on page 122) and 6.5 (on page 124) track the proportion of all foreign and defense hearings held by the appropriations, armed services, and foreign policy committees and by all other committees combined. Figures 6.4 (on page 122) and 6.6 (on page 124) track just defense policy hearings. In the House the most obvious trend is the expanded level of activity by Foreign Affairs and the diminished proportion of all activity accounted for by Armed Services. It is important to emphasize that these are shares of the total—a total that has increased as noted earlier. Nonetheless, Foreign Affairs' share of all foreign and defense hearings expands significantly with the 91st Congress (1969–1971), a point that is coincident with House committee reforms and the end of the Bretton Woods system. The absolute level of hearings accounted for by Armed Services has changed rather little during that time period. Meanwhile the number of hearings in Foreign Affairs jumps ahead of Armed Services in the 92nd Congress (1971–1973) and remains that way through the present.

Not surprisingly, the Foreign Affairs Committee holds few hearings on strictly defense-related issues, but it has staked a claim to arms control issues and military force in foreign policy. It is somewhat surprising that in neither foreign nor defense policy do these three panels have a monopoly. In fact, as

Table 6.2 House and Senate Standing Committees Ranked by Number of Hearings, 1946–1994

House Committees	Hearings	Days of Hearings	Senate Committees	Hearings	Days of Hearings
Natural Resources	3,317	4,882	Judiciary	2,954	6,863
Appropriations	3,192	16,523	Energy & Natural Resources	2,945	4,131
Energy & Commerce	2,962	6,605	Commerce, Science, Trans.	2,538	5,158
Judiciary	2,618	5,113	Labor & Human Resources	2,258	4,398
Armed Services	2,549	7,183	Banking, Housing, & Urban Aff.	2,019	3,679
Government Affairs	2,327	4,785	Governmental Affairs	1,907	3,565
Foreign Affairs	2,316	5,682	Appropriations	1,720	8,765
Education & Labor	2,047	5,794	Armed Services	1,614	3,782
Science, Space & Tech.	1,843	4,135	Foreign Relations	1,614	3,243
Agriculture	1,764	3,800	Finance	1,506	2,449
Banking, Finance & Urban Aff.	1,633	3,536	Environment & Public Works	1,258	2,487
Ways and Means	1,504	3,263	Agriculture, Nutrition, Forestry	1,042	1,932
Merchant Marine & Fisheries*	1,406	3,499	District of Columbia*	983	1,224
Post Office & Civil Service*	1,403	2,940	Small Business**	713	1,318
Public Works & Transportation	1,139	2,970	Post Office*	554	953
Small Business	887	1,856	Rules and Administration	300	515
Veterans' Affairs	858	1,512	Veterans' Affairs	239	334
District of Columbia*	729	1,377	Budget**	147	387
Un-American Activities*	503	1,173	Aeronautical & Space Sciences*	138	264
Budget**	370	661	Select Intelligence**	49	123
Rules	218	355			
House Administration	174	295			
Select Intelligence**	41	120			
Standards of Off. Conduct**	12	41			

Note: Committees marked with an asterisk no longer exist. Committees marked by a double asterisk have not existed during the entire period. Miscellaneous select and special committees have been excluded so total hearings and hearing days do add to the same totals as in Table 6.1. Committee names used herein are those as of the 103rd Congress (1993–1995).

121

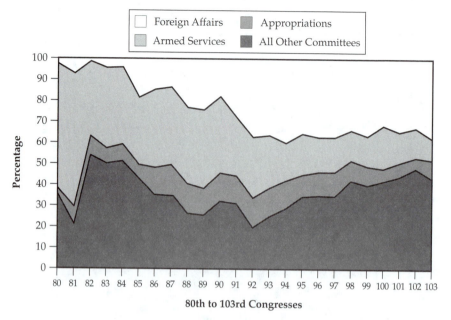

FIGURE 6.3   HOUSE FOREIGN AND DEFENSE POLICY HEARINGS
BY COMMITTEE (80TH TO 103RD CONGRESS)

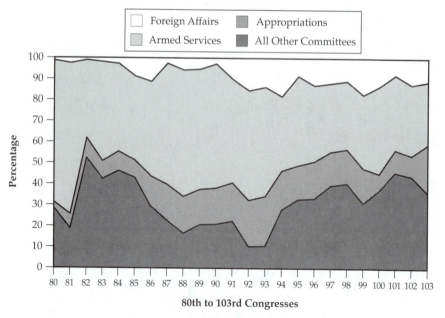

FIGURE 6.4   HOUSE DEFENSE POLICY HEARINGS
BY COMMITTEE (80TH TO 103RD CONGRESS)

Figures 6.3 and 6.4 make clear, the committees' dominance in these areas has eroded with 40 percent of all foreign and defense hearings and nearly 40 percent of defense hearings being held by "other" committees. The jurisdictional sanctity of Armed Services and Foreign Affairs is hardly complete. This is not the case for Appropriations, of course, since money bills must be reported by that panel. Thus, Appropriations' share of the load here is lower (though hearing days are higher) and constant throughout the postwar period.

Though not without fluctuation, hearing patterns in the Senate are much more stable throughout the period (see Figures 6.5 and 6.6 on page 124). None of the three committees, nor all of the others combined, dramatically increases or decreases its share of foreign and defense hearings or defense hearings alone. Appropriations' share is larger than that of the House committee, but that is to be expected given the smaller base against which it is measured. Armed Services' proportion remains nearly constant throughout these five decades. And in the Senate, as in the House, Appropriations, Armed Services, and Foreign Relations have nothing like a lock on the foreign and defense business in that chamber.

AUTHORIZATIONS AND APPROPRIATIONS: THE ULTIMATE OVERSIGHT?

Insofar as foreign and military policy are concerned, the founders provided the strictest possible limit with regard to the standing army—and hence the ultimate in oversight. Because of their fear of a standing army, the Constitution requires that "no appropriation of money to [the Army] shall be for a longer term than two years (Article I, Section 8, Clause 12)." In practice, of course, Congress has gone even further, for all of the government, by annually appropriating virtually every dime that is spent. But the founders and the early Congress were particularly concerned about the army. Indeed, there is no similar constitutional proscription applying to the Navy, which follows in the next clause (Clause 13) but without the limit on appropriations. As to authorizations, that is a relatively recent development.

The establishment of the Departments of War and of State numbered among Congress's first acts in July and August 1789. (A Navy Department would follow, but not until 1798.) Both departments had broadly written responsibilities, but neither really amounted to much in the early years. Those of the former included land and naval forces (including ships and supplies) and Indian affairs.[29] Subsequent congressional enactments permitted the Department of War to recruit up to certain ceilings, but these were rarely achieved. The situation at the Department of State was, if anything, even worse. Washington and Adams took personal control of virtually all diplomatic endeavors rendering the Secretary of State just that, a secretary. In addition, the department was distracted by a variety of chores—the census, a mint, patents, and aid to seaman.[30] So neither in size nor power did either department constitute any sort of threat to the legislature's power. And that is precisely how most members of Congress wanted it to be.

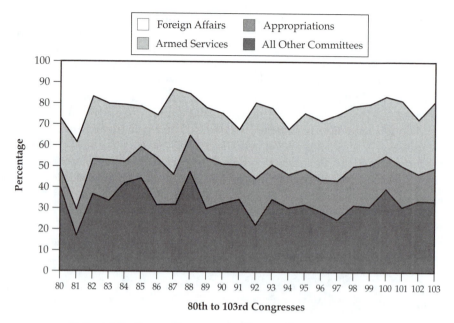

FIGURE 6.5 SENATE FOREIGN AND DEFENSE POLICY HEARINGS
BY COMMITTEE (80TH TO 103RD CONGRESS)

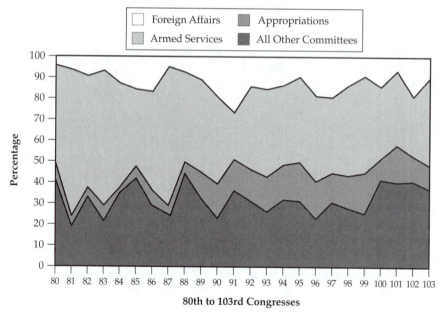

FIGURE 6.6 SENATE DEFENSE POLICY HEARINGS
BY COMMITTEE (80TH TO 103RD CONGRESS)

As with most committees the institutional role (and import) of the Foreign Relations and Armed Services Committees is closely tied to money. During the 73rd Congress (1933–1935) the foreign policy committees authorized the expenditure of $103,000. In the decade immediately following World War II, these same two committees constructed and passed annual foreign aid bills that authorized the expenditure of more than $50 billion. In one congress alone, the 83rd (1953–1955), the committees authorized $8 billion dollars.[31] The dramatic shift in the amount of money authorized by Foreign Affairs and Foreign Relations was, of course, more than matched by the Armed Services committees for defense. And for both sets of committees, these authorizing activities were critical elements of their institutional power. That said, the trends for the two panels would run in opposite directions.

DEFENSE AUTHORIZATIONS (BACK TO THE "BIG SHOW"?)

Throughout most of the nineteenth and the first half of the twentieth century, defense legislation provided liberal grants of authority to the military departments to provide for the national defense. And, in the immediate post–World War II era, little had changed. For example, before 1962 the committees authorized the military services an aggregate active-duty personnel ceiling of 5 million even though actual peacetime, active-duty personnel levels rarely reached half these authorized levels.[32] Likewise, the Secretary of the Air Force was authorized to "procure 24,000 serviceable aircraft or 225,000 airframe tons . . . as he may determine."[33] That is it. No elaboration. A simple grant of authority to buy airplanes, lots of airplanes. With these broad grants of authority, the defense committees simply ceded any annual influence over military policy to their agents in Defense or to the defense appropriations subcommittees. As one Pentagon wag put it: "It's the Armed Services Committee that gives you the hunting license and the Appropriations Committee that gives you the rabbits."[34] At the time, the license was perpetual, but the rabbits were rationed annually.

Prior to World War II, the practice of open-ended authorization was of little consequence because neither the standing army nor the navy ever amounted to much. As a result, any substantial change in the size or character of the military establishment—most importantly, mobilization for war—required participation by these committees. By the end of World War II, these circumstances had changed dramatically. From 1947 until the outbreak of the Korean War, peacetime, active-duty, military personnel averaged 1.8 million. From the end of the Korean War until 1965, they averaged 2.8 million. By contrast, active-duty personnel averaged only 285,000 from 1920 to 1940.[35]

After World War II, the impact of open-ended grants of authority, and the presence of a large standing army, was to eliminate the Armed Services Committees from any serious role in national security policymaking. By contrast, Foreign Relations' annual foreign aid authorization bill gave that panel a consistent opportunity to influence policy. Only in military construction, 100 percent of which was authorized annually, did Armed Services have a comparable role. By the early 1960s, therefore, the committees faced a dual threat to their power. The Pentagon was authorized to operate within very permissive programmatic authority, a circumstance that reduced Armed Services to the status of defense cheerleader. Meanwhile the Appropriations subcommittees undermined the authority of Armed Services by establishing a pattern of *annual* appropriations—a process that frequently also included programmatic guidance.

Thus, the committee seized upon the procedural device of annual authorization of appropriations to ensure their capacity to effectively participate in defense policymaking. The trend toward annual reauthorization began in 1959 with the so-called Russell Amendment—named after the venerable chair of the Senate Armed Services Committee, Richard Russell of Georgia. The Russell Amendment required the annual authorization of appropriations for the procurement of aircraft, missiles, and naval vessels:[36]

> No funds may be appropriated after December 31, 1960, to or for the use of any armed force of the United States for the procurement of aircraft, missiles, or naval vessels unless the appropriation of such funds has been authorized by legislation enacted after that date. (Sec. 412, subsection (b), PL 86-149)

From 1962 through 1982 the annual authorization requirement was expanded eleven more times (see Box 6.1 for the current requirements). By one estimate, only 2 percent of defense appropriations required annual authorization in 1961—virtually all accounted for by military construction. Today the figure stands, effectively, at 100 percent. Each year, therefore, the Armed Services Committees produce a "must pass" piece of legislation, the annual defense authorization bill. This bill authorizes the appropriation of roughly 15 percent of the annual federal budget—$289 billion in fiscal year 2000. Unlike the foreign aid bill, this bill has been passed successfully in all but one year for the past three decades or more. Indeed, existing law virtually requires passage.

Samuel P. Huntington's characterization of defense policymaking, published in 1961, gives a clear sense of the two-track system established by the defense committees. On strategic and crisis policy, open-ended grants permitted the president and Defense Department a relatively free hand in policymaking attended by fire alarm oversight. On structural policy, however, close monitoring accompanied by something very close to police patrol oversight became the norm.[37] Indeed, although military construction was a small portion of annual defense spending, 100 percent of it was authorized annually.[38] At bottom, this meant that, except in military construction, the committees made no consistently effective use of their legislative powers and had no procedures in place to ensure Pentagon responsiveness. Moreover, the unity of opinion was such that the committee could only reinforce the Pentagon's views on national security policy. The result, of course, was that opinion elites shaped public opinion in a consistent fashion.

BOX 6.1   TITLE 10—ARMED FORCES

SEC. 114. ANNUAL AUTHORIZATION OF APPROPRIATIONS

(a) No funds may be appropriated for any fiscal year to or for the use of any armed force or obligated or expended for

    (1) procurement of aircraft, missiles, or naval vessels;

    (2) any research, development, test, or evaluation, or procurement or production related thereto;

    (3) procurement of tracked combat vehicles;

    (4) procurement of other weapons;

    (5) procurement of naval torpedoes and related support equipment;

    (6) military construction;

    (7) the operation and maintenance of any armed force or of the activities and agencies of the Department of Defense (other than the military departments);

    (8) procurement of ammunition; or

    (9) other procurement by any armed force or by the activities and agencies of the Department of Defense (other than the military departments); unless funds therefor have been specifically authorized by law.

(b) In subsection (a)(6), the term "military construction" includes any construction, development, conversion, or extension of any kind which is carried out with respect to any military facility or installation.

SEC. 115. PERSONNEL STRENGTHS: REQUIREMENT FOR ANNUAL AUTHORIZATION

(b) No funds may be appropriated for any fiscal year to or for

    (1) the use of active-duty personnel or full-time National Guard duty personnel of any of the armed forces (other than the Coast Guard) unless the end strength for such personnel of that armed force for that fiscal year has been authorized by law; or

    (2) the use of the Selected Reserve of any reserve component of the armed forces unless the end strength for the Selected Reserve of that component for that fiscal year has been authorized by law.

Source: 10 United States Code Section 114.

Note: The defense budget is broken into five categories: procurement, military construction, personnel, research and development, and operations and maintenance.

The move to annual authorization marks an important shift in the potential and actual influence of the Armed Services committees. It ends open-ended grants, ensures yearly participation, increases the anticipated responsiveness of the Pentagon, shifts the committees to more of a police-patrol style of oversight while preserving the fire alarm option, and moves the committees into strategic as well as structural policymaking. Annual authorization is not entirely cost free, however, since it ensures that both committee members and nonmembers may dabble in procurement politics. Sufficient examples exist to make this an area of concern, but the most recent evidence suggests that the stylized image of benefits accruing to committee members is overdrawn.[39]

FOREIGN RELATIONS AUTHORIZATIONS (LITTLE SIR ECHO?)

As Armed Services' role expanded through the late 1960s and into the 1970s, the foreign policy committees suffered a comparable decline. Ideological and partisan differences regarding foreign aid ultimately ended in stalemate as the committees were unable to report a foreign aid bill that could garner majority support in the chamber. Foreign aid programs did not disappear, but the committees' influence was ceded to the Foreign Operations subcommittees of the Appropriations committees. Weakly led and without an annual authorization bill, Foreign Relations had become a shadow of its former self. As Senator Christopher J. Dodd (D-Conn.) put it: "By frittering away its authorizing function, the Foreign Relations Committee became a largely irrelevant debating society."[40]

To arrest this decline the foreign policy committees simply emulated Armed Services by expanding their use of the State Department authorization bill.[41] In 1971, the Senate Foreign Relations Committee added an amendment to the FY 1972 foreign aid bill (which contained both economic and military assistance) requiring periodic reauthorization of the State Department, the United States Information Agency, the Arms Control and Disarmament Agency, and assorted other foreign relations operations and institutions. Up to this point, State (and the much younger USIA), had operated under permanent authorizations. The legislation passed early in 1972 and later that year Congress also passed the necessary reauthorizing legislation for the various foreign relations activities. Two years later, Congress refined this process by requiring the president to submit annually three major pieces of legislation—a foreign aid proposal, a military aid proposal, and a foreign relations proposal (for State, USIA, ACDA, etc.). That legislation has passed nearly every year since then.

But gains on this front were offset by two other developments. First, since the early 1980s Congress generally has failed to pass a foreign aid bill. And, since that is where the money is, the foreign policy committees have largely ceded their leverage (and hence their capacity for oversight) to the Appropriations committees.[42]

Second, the foreign relations authorization bill has become a target for legislating foreign policy by amendment. Indeed, in some years one whole title of the bill has simply been called "Miscellaneous Foreign Policy Provisions." In 1999, for example, the Senate version of the foreign relations authorization bill included nine titles on everything from the basic authorization (Title I) to Russian business management education (Title IX). The bill totaled 231 pages and its short title, the "Admiral James W. Nance Foreign Relations

Authorization Act, Fiscal Years 2000 and 2001," served as a memorial to the deceased former staff director of the Senate Foreign Relations Committee.[43] In this case, "miscellaneous provisions" can be found in Title VII, all twenty-eight of them (see Box 6.2 on page 130 for examples). It is here therefore that the Senate expresses its sense of U.S. policy on everything from organ harvesting in China (we're against it), to self-determination in East Timor (we're for that), to the use of children as combatants in armed conflicts (we're against that as well). This is not to say that the measure is entirely trivial. Far from it, Congress weighs in on foreign policy issues in important ways in the context of this bill. But, much more than is the case with the defense authorization bill (it, too, is a target for policy amendments), this foreign relations legislation has been a mixed blessing as a vehicle for policy oversight.

THE NEW OVERSIGHT

During the 1970s, a popular expression arose on Capitol Hill among advocates of a greater role for Congress in foreign and defense policy. It went: "If we have to be in on the crash landings then we should be in on the takeoffs that precede them." This oft-repeated mantra soon became statutory as Congress fashioned what some called the "new oversight." This new oversight is active rather than passive and emphasizes not just third parties but a requirement for actual participation in policymaking.[44] Annual authorizations are a big part of that pattern but it also includes report requirements, notifications, and other anticipatory techniques.

But rather than a wholly new invention (few things are truly new on Capitol Hill after all), the new oversight was a much more aggressive use of techniques that can be traced to the 1877 requirement for consultation on all military construction projects. Congress included very similar language in the Military Construction Act of 1951, requiring military departments to "come into agreement" with the Armed Services committees prior to completing any real estate transaction in excess of $25,000.[45] Now certainly there was no institutional memory of the 1877 requirement but the "come into agreement" language could not have been forgotten—even though softened subsequently to a prior report requirement—by the 1960s. By the 1970s, therefore, Congress was prepared to enhance its participation in takeoffs through the use of a variety of reporting requirements (frequently bolstered by legislative veto provisions). The following are illustrative but far from exhaustive of the trend.

- The Case-Zablocki Act of 1972 required that all executive agreements be reported to Congress (classified if necessary) within sixty days.
- The War Powers Resolution of 1973 required that the president report any use of U.S. military forces, limit that use to sixty days, absent explicit congressional consent to continue, and terminate military operations at any time pursuant to a congressional resolution.

- The Nelson-Bingham Amendment of 1974 required that all major arms sales be reported to Congress prior to submitting a "letter of offer" to the recipient nation. Congress could then, by passage of a concurrent resolution of disapproval within thirty days, block the sale.
- The Hughes-Ryan Amendment of 1974 required the president and the CIA to report any covert activity in a "timely manner." The requirement, thus, gave Congress an opportunity to block or terminate such activities.

Box 6.2   S. 886

Section 1. Short Title; Table of Contents

(a) Short Title.—This act may be cited as the "Admiral James W. Nance Foreign Relations Authorization Act, Fiscal Year 2000 and 2001."

Title VII—MISCELLANEOUS PROVISIONS

[The following are selected examples of the sections included in Title VII.]

Sec. 701. Prisoner Information Registry for the People's Republic of China.

Sec. 705. Sense of Congress regarding organ harvesting and transplanting in the People's Republic of China.

Sec. 721. Denial of entry into the United States of foreign nationals engaged in establishment of forced abortion or sterilization policy.

Sec. 724. Waiver of certain prohibitions regarding the Palestine Liberation Organization.

Sec. 726. United States policy with respect to Nigeria.

Sec. 727. Partial liquidation of blocked Libyan assets.

Sec. 730. Sense of Congress on the use of children as soldiers or other combatants in foreign armed forces.

Sec. 734. Prohibition on the return of veterans' memorial objects to foreign nations without specific authorization in law.

Sec. 735. Support for the peace process in Sudan.

Sec. 736. Expressing the sense of the Congress regarding the treatment of religious minorities in the Islamic Republic of Iran, and particularly the recent arrests of members of that country's Jewish community.

Sec. 739. Sense of Senate regarding child labor.

Sec. 740. Reporting requirement on worldwide circulation of small arms and light weapons.

Source: S. 886, 106th Congress, 1st sess., June 30, 1999.

Note: S. 886 was incorporated into a similar House bill (H.R. 2415) and pocket vetoed by President Clinton. Another version of the bill was introduced in the House and later incorporated into H.R. 3194 (an appropriations bill) that became Public Law 106-113.

Relatively few have claimed that these and other reporting requirements, with or without legislative vetoes, have been successes. Indeed, some have argued that the War Powers resolution in particular actually ceded constitutionally granted legislative powers to the executive (see Louis Fisher's chapter in this volume, for example). Moreover, the Supreme Court, in *Immigration and Naturalization Service v. Chadha* (1983) seemed to sweep away the legislative veto as a viable tool for congressional use.[46]

Undeterred, however, Congress continues to utilize artfully worded legislative vetoes to force executive agents to report to Congress prior to taking particular actions defined in statutes. Perhaps the most arcane of these is the legislative requirement for reporting to appropriate congressional committees prior to "reprogramming" appropriated funds. Reprogramming occurs when an executive agent moves money from one purpose or program to another without specific statutory authorization. Reprogramming increased after 1949 because Congress consolidated numerous appropriations accounts into larger catch-all categories. But it soon became alarmed at the liberal use of these funds by departments and agencies—not least of which the Pentagon. In the 1950s, Congress informally required consultation, then semiannual reports, and, finally, formal notification for any reprogramming. Today, the "Budget Guidance Manual" used at the Pentagon outlines explicit procedures that are to be followed so as to adhere to congressional wishes regarding reprogramming.[47]

Taken in concert with annual authorizations, these requirements for reports and financial management force the executive departments to anticipate legislative reactions to even relatively minor policy changes. In aggregate, they form the backbone of Congress's police patrol approach to oversight. And, interestingly enough, they depend in large part upon the State and Defense Departments monitoring themselves, lest they later be forced to report on some transgression or other that may have been committed.

ALARMS OR PATROLS? SOME CIRCUMSTANTIAL EVIDENCE

On August 24, 2001, President George W. Bush announced from near his ranch in Crawford, Texas that he was nominating Air Force General Richard B. Myers to be the new Chairman of the Joint Chiefs of Staff. The nomination attracted scant press attention and virtually no questions at the ensuing press conference. Within a week the Senate Armed Services Committee arranged a nomination hearing for Myers as part of its advice and consent responsibilities. Two days prior to the hearing, on September 11, 2001, terrorists hijacked four American airliners. The first two planes were subsequently crashed into New York's World Trade Center, the third into the Pentagon, and the fourth into an open field near Pittsburgh, Pennsylvania. The four plane crashes killed the planes' crews, the passengers, and thousands of people on the ground. Two days later

Myers's hearing went on as scheduled but was commandeered by shocked senators as a forum on the military's immediate response, or lack thereof, to the hijackings. Of particular interest to the senators was whether the military could have done anything to intercept the doomed aircraft.[48] What started off as a completely mundane appointment hearing, spiced up only by the possibility of a bit of partisan posturing, suddenly became the first available committee forum for consideration of one of the most devastating events in American history. Needless to say, the legislative response to those dramatic events didn't stop there or solely with the Senate Armed Services Committee.

It should be clear at this point that legislators employ a mixture of techniques to monitor administrative activities and compliance with legislative intent. Left unanswered, however, is the question of Congress's preference for police patrols or for fire alarms. On the surface, the adoption of annual authorizations suggests that it is the former. And yet, at least as a general rule, several argue that fire-alarm oversight is "likely to be more effective" and that "fire-alarm techniques" will predominate.[49] This assumption carefully notes that fire-alarm techniques do not preclude police-patrol techniques and, further, that fire-alarm techniques do not guarantee superior service to the public interest. In an extension of this work, others have offered a more formal analysis that suggests legislators are more likely to prefer patrols when they are uncertain about the level of "hidden" knowledge possessed by administrators.[50] For the most part, legislators have a relatively difficult time structuring alarms that will allow third parties an opportunity to monitor the executive since, by definition, a great deal of what goes on in foreign and defense policy is classified (though truer of the latter than the former). Thus, we might well expect that Congress will be more inclined to mix patrols with legislative constraints and depend somewhat less on alarms.

Fire-alarm oversight involves the delegation of oversight to third parties. Strictly speaking, therefore, nothing Congress does itself, save the delegation, falls into that category. Still, if alarms are pulled, Congress must respond in some way by investigating, holding hearings, legislating, or whatever. Evidence of fire-alarm techniques might be found in two ways. First, if Congress establishes formal or informal mechanisms to induce monitoring by third parties, that would be evidence of a dependence on some level of fire-alarm oversight. Second, if Congress responds to alarms—again, the St. Clair investigation, Tailhook, and the September 11 attacks are examples—that would be evidence that it pays attention to alarms once they are pulled.

One of the most obvious cases of Congress establishing a fire-alarm oversight mechanism, though not in foreign and defense policy, was the National Environmental Policy Act of 1969 that empowered citizens to bring lawsuits against development projects that failed to file proper environmental impact statements. That is, rather than monitor development projects itself, Congress delegated that role to third parties and also gave them the tools to act. Now clearly, Congress will have a much more difficult time delegating oversight authority to third parties when it comes to foreign and defense policy, at the very least because of the classified nature of the subject matter. If that is the case, or if Congress does not fear the amount of hidden information possessed by its national security agents, then fire-alarm oversight should be less prominent than it might be in other areas of domestic policymaking.

A couple of examples of such delegations stand out.

- In 1969, Congress passed the Freedom of Information Act which directs government agencies to make public certain kinds of information (which they might otherwise retain in a confidential manner) and provides a mechanism for citizens to request the release of information possessed by government agencies. The act's mechanism has been used to force the release of large amounts of previously classified national security information.

- In 1988, Congress passed the Base Closure and Realignment Act that provided a mechanism for reducing the number of military installations, mostly within the United States. A principal feature of that act (and subsequent reenactments) was to delegate the selection of sites to be closed, reduced, or realigned to an appointed commission. While the commission's decisions could be made behind closed doors, they were to hear testimony from witnesses, and its decisions would be made public prior to going into effect.

- In 1989, Congress passed the Whistle-blower Protection Act designed to shield government employees from retaliation for exposing (to the press or to Congress) instances of waste, fraud, and abuse in the federal government. In 1999, Congress passed the Intelligence Authorization Act which included language protecting employees of intelligence agencies under whistle-blower procedures. Previously, rather than protection, employees divulging classified information (even if their intent was to correct some wrongdoing) were themselves subject to prosecution.

In each of these cases, Congress empowered third parties to help review decisions being made by its executive branch agents. That is, they gave them the capacity to pull fire alarms and alert legislators to the possibility that congressional preferences or legal mandates were not being carried out. Were a complete catalogue of such mechanisms available, some measure of legislative dependence on fire-alarm oversight would be achieved.

A more indirect measure of dependence on fire alarms can be achieved by returning to hearings themselves. If Congress is more likely to depend upon patrols, in national security or any other area, then evidence of that might be found in the number of hearings that are triggered by alarms and the number that appear to be a part of routine patrols. Earlier, several examples of patrol language and alarm language from the House National Security Committee's activities report were given. If that report is illustrative then, by a very rough estimate about one-third of the hearings (but a smaller proportion of total days) identified by the committee fall into the category of fire alarms.[51]

TABLE 6.3   POLICE-PATROL AND FIRE-ALARM OVERSIGHT HEARINGS:
FOREIGN POLICY AND DEFENSE COMMITTEES, 104TH CONGRESS (1995–1996)

COMMITTEE	POLICE PATROL PERCENTAGE (N)	FIRE ALARM PERCENTAGE (N)
House:		
National Security	.81 (16)	.19 (3)
International Relations	.60 (134)	.40 (53)
Senate:		
Armed Services	.83 (42)	.17 (7)
Foreign Relations	.78 (37)	.22 (8)

Source: Author's data coded from *CIS Abstracts* (1995, 1996, 1997).
Note: Treaties, nominations, markups, and business meetings excluded.

An alternative measure, but again one that has not been thoroughly exploited or validated is to examine hearing abstracts and code hearings as either "routine" or "event driven." Data for the House and Senate defense and foreign policy committees for one congress, the 104th (1995–1997), is contained in Table 6.3. For that congress, at least, the predominance of patrol-type oversight is fairly clear. Even in the case of the House International Relations, which has a noticeably higher level of alarm-type oversight, the balance is substantially in favor of patrols. Again, this data is, at this point, just circumstantial, but it suggests that legislators (at least committee members) may put more effort into patrols than some have suggested.

CONCLUSION

It has long been remarked, with encomiums to Jefferson, that a free press always will be a bulwark against the transgressions of government. But in 1929, some students of Congress counseled against too great a dependence on "casual information" in the monitoring of administrative action. In the 1950s, it was popular to note that neither the defense nor the foreign policy committees were popular because constituents just did not care much about defense and foreign policy—though they might care a lot about that military base in their district. And yet, Gordon reports that even then–Representative Daniel J. Flood (D-Pa.) could boast of a network of constituent-informants that the congressman referred to as "Flood's spies."[52] Thus, third-party oversight is likely to remain an important element in triggering legislative review.

The history of the postwar era is one of ebb and flow in legislative attention to foreign and military policy. Cold war consensus clearly put a damper on Congress's willingness to interfere with executive prerogatives in national security—a circumstance the executive was only too willing to exploit.[53] But Congress fought back doggedly, if not completely successfully, to fashion the "new oversight." In this, as in many areas of legislative behavior, therefore, we must say that Congress isn't nearly as bad as "they" say it is; but it is not as good as it might be either.

NOTES

1. Thanks go to Steve Balla, Lou Fisher, and Jim Lindsay for sharing their ideas during the preparation of this chapter. Most of the hearings data used here were originally collected by Frank R. Baumgartner and Bryan D. Jones, with the support of National Science Foundation grant number SBR 9320922, and were distributed through the Center for American Politics and Public Policy at the University of Washington and/or the Department of Political Science at Penn State University. Neither NSF nor the original collectors of the data bear any responsibility for the analysis reported here.
2. St. Clair previously had been appointed governor of the territory.
3. Though anticipated by St. Clair's officers (who did not, however, report their concerns) the attack commenced after the troops had been dismissed from their morning parade. The encampment was on a Wabash River tributary fifty miles south of present-day Fort Wayne, Indiana. Fort Wayne was constructed at the site of the Miami village of Kekionga, St. Clair's destination. Estimates of the number of Miamis (and their allies) vary, but 1,100 to 1,400 seems about right. St. Clair's casualties in the battle numbered 914 including 630 dead. In addition, half of the 200 "camp followers," made up of wives, children, and prostitutes" also were killed. For additional details on St. Clair's expedition and the subsequent congressional investigation see Wilbur Edel, *Kekionga! The Worst Defeat in the History of the U.S. Army* (Westport, CT: Praeger, 1997).
4. Contracts by the quartermaster general went to cronies. Saddles and packing rigs purchased for the horses fit large eastern horses quite well, but were much too large for smaller, frontier horses. The recruits, by all accounts, were very much from the bottom of the barrel. See Edel, *Kekionga!*
5. Replaced but apparently not totally disgraced. Hodgdon's replacement, James O'Hara, returned him to his old position as commissary of military stores. This position was later elevated by President Washington to a superintendency and Hodgdon remained until Jefferson became president (<http://www.qmfound.com/Samuel_Hodgdon.htm>). So, while Hodgdon bore the brunt of Congress's wrath, he remained in the good graces of the administration. A biographer of St. Clair's is less kind: ". . . Quartermaster Hodgdon failed in every respect. He deserved to be court-martialed, tried, condemned, and executed. Yet, after full exposition of his criminal neglect, he was continued at the head of the department for years." William Henry Smith, ed., *The St. Clair Papers*, vol. 2 (Cincinnati: Robert Clarke & Co., 1882), p. 301.
6. For background see Juliana Gruenwald, "Women in the Military: Mission in Progress," *Congressional Quarterly Weekly Report*, 16 August 1997, pp. 1662–1666.
7. See Marshall E. Dimock, *Congressional Investigating Committees* (Baltimore: Johns Hopkins Press, 1929).
8. Elias Huzar, *The Purse and the Sword: Control of the Army by Congress through Appropriations, 1933–1950* (Baltimore: Johns Hopkins University Press, 1950), p. 224.
9. House committee names have changed somewhat frequently during the postwar era. Sometimes this reflected reorganization or clarification of jurisdictions. At other times it has been more politically motivated. I will generally use the more longstanding names here: hence, House Foreign Affairs instead of House International Relations and House Armed Services instead of House National Security. But the reader should be aware that alternative references are, nonetheless, to the same panels. Senate Foreign Relations and Senate Armed Services have remained constant in the period examined here.
10. Joel D. Aberbach, *Keeping a Watchful Eye: Politics of Congressional Oversight* (Washington, D.C.: Brookings Institution, 1990). This is something of an exception.
11. Steven Skowronek, *Building the New American State: The Expansion of National Administrative Capacities, 1877–1920* (Cambridge, MA: Cambridge University Press, 1982).

12. Morris P. Fiorina, *Congress—Keystone of the Washington Establishment* (New Haven, CT: Yale University Press, 1987).
13. Leonard D. White, "Congressional Control of the Public Service," *American Political Science Review* 39 (1945), p. 3.
14. White's observations were part of his APSA presidential address. The address itself went undelivered because the annual convention was canceled "on account of travel and hotel congestion." White, "Congressional Control of the Public Service," p. 1.
15. George B. Galloway, "The Investigative Function of Congress," *American Political Science Review* 21 (February 1927), p. 50.
16. Dimock, *Congressional Investigating Committees*, p. 17.
17. In 1571, to be precise, when Parliament authorized a series of committees to investigate disputed elections. Dimock, *Congressional Investigating Committees*, p. 48.
18. See, for example, Aberbach, *Keeping a Watchful Eye: Politics of Congressional Oversight*; Mathew D. McCubbins and Thomas Schwartz, "Congressional Oversight Overlooked: Police Patrols versus Fire Alarms," *American Journal of Political Science* 28 (1984), pp. 165–179; and Morris S. Ogul, "Overseeing Oversight: New Departures and Old Problems," *Legislative Studies Quarterly* 15 (1990), pp. 5–24.
19. Today, that language (now reading "shall review and study, on a continuing basis") is at 2 U.S.C. 190d. It was originally contained in Sec. 136 of the Legislative Reorganization Act of 1946.
20. McCubbins and Schwartz, "Congressional Oversight Overlooked: Police Patrols versus Fire Alarms," pp. 165–167.
21. The ultimate in police-patrol oversight might well have been achieved prior to the current Constitution when Continental Congress committees actually traveled and encamped with General Washington during the Revolutionary War. Louis Smith reports, for example, that the Continental Congress created at least seventeen committees to oversee the Revolutionary War effort—on cannon, muskets, hospitals, clothing, beef, and saltpeter—before later consolidating them into a Board of War and a Maritime Committee. Louis Smith, *American Democracy and Military Power: A Study of Civil Control of the Military Power in the United States* (Chicago: University of Chicago Press, 1951), p. 178.
22. Aberbach, *Keeping a Watchful Eye: Politics of Congressional Oversight*, pp. 97–104.
23. House Committee on International Relations, *Legislative Review of Activities of the Committee on International Relations: One Hundred Fifth Congress*, 105th Cong., 2nd sess., 1999; H. Rept. 105-838, pp. 1–6.
24. House Committee on National Security, *Report of the Activities of the Committee on National Security for the One Hundred Fourth Congress*, 104th Cong., 2nd sess., 1997, H. Rept. 104-884, p. 35, emphasis added.
25. Committee on National Security, *Report of the Activities of the Committee on National Security for the One Hundred Fourth Congress*, pp. 39–44.
26. Much like Bayliss, Manning did with the conflation of international and domestic policies of roughly the same era, coining the term "intermestic" affairs; these two oft-quoted stimuli might be elided to form "WaterNam." While such macrolevel causal analysis is frequently overdrawn, there is something to be said for the *nom de cause*. Manning, "The Congress, the Executive, and Intermestic Affairs: Three Proposals," *Foreign Policy* 55 (January 1977), pp. 306–324. Indeed, there is a general argument, not pursued here, that domestic sources of foreign policy drove increased oversight across the board. Seyom Brown (1974) is frequently associated with this notion. Brown, *New Forces in World Politics* (Washington: Brookings Institution, 1974).
27. House hearings on foreign affairs and foreign aid exceed those for defense in only three congresses, the 101st to 103rd. If foreign trade is combined with this category, however, then the overall number and proportion of foreign policy hearings exceeds defense in every Congress since the 87th (1961–1963).
28. Commencement of this upward trend is coincident with the end of the so-called Bretton Woods system that effectively tied the West's economic regime to the U.S. dollar. Trade issues, in the wake of this change, became much more important. See Manning, "The Congress, the Executive, and Intermestic Affairs: Three Proposals," 1977.
29. On War's duties see Leonard D. White, *The Federalists: A Study in Administrative History* (New York: The Macmillan Company, 1948), p. 125. It should be noted that responsibility

for naval affairs was an "empty gift" since all major U.S. warships had been sold. The only vessels owned by the government were the so-called revenue cutters—precursors of today's Coast Guard—and these belonged to the Treasury. White, *The Federalists: A Study in Administrative History*, p. 157.

30. Ibid., pp. 128–144.
31. This tidbit is from Holbert N. Carroll, *The House of Representatives and Foreign Affairs* (Boston: Little Brown and Company, 1966), p. 20.
32. Barry M. Blechman, *The Politics of National Security: Congress and U.S. Defense Policy* (New York: Oxford University Press, 1990), pp. 29–30.
33. Bernard K. Gordon, "The Military Budget: Congressional Phase," *Journal of Politics* 23 (1961), pp. 691–692. The circumstance was repeated in similarly broad fashion for missiles, naval vessels, and other munitions.
34. Ibid., p. 692.
35. For additional details on the size of the national army historically, see Christopher J. Deering, "Congress, the President, and Military Policy," *The Annals of the American Academy of Political and Social Science* 499 (1988), pp. 136–147.
36. A trial run was authorized for the first fiscal year after adoption of the amendment, FY 1961, and its full implementation followed in FY 1962.
37. Samuel P. Huntington, *The Common Defense: Strategic Programs in National Politics* (New York: Columbia University Press, 1961). McCubbins and Schwartz ("Congressional Oversight Overlooked: Police Patrols versus Fire Alarms") argue that fire-alarm oversight is an effective method of oversight (see 171–173). But their case seems to assume, at least some level, conflict between the legislative and executive branch. In this case, the decision rules adopted by committee members, reinforced in the 1950s by anticommunist fervor, limited the willingness of committee members to question the president or the Pentagon on its policy decisions.
38. Barry M. Blechman, *The Politics of National Security: Congress and U.S. Defense Policy* (New York: Oxford University Press, 1990), pp. 30–31.
39. Among others see Kenneth R. Mayer, *The Political Economy of Defense Contracting* (New Haven, CT: Yale University Press, 1991).
40. Quoted in John M. Goshko, "Virtuoso Performance Surprises Hill," *Washington Post*, 3 November 1985, p. A-12.
41. The current requirement proscribing the use of any funds appropriated to the Department of State without specific authorization is at 22 U.S.C. 2680.
42. On postwar developments in the foreign policy committees see James M. McCormick, "Decision Making in the Foreign Affairs and Foreign Relations Committees," in *Congress Resurgent: Foreign and Defense Policy on Capitol Hill*, ed. Randall B. Ripley and James M. Lindsay (Ann Arbor: University of Michigan Press, 1993), pp. 118–121.
43. The 2000/2001 bill is hardly exceptional. See Helen Dewar, "Bill Gives Senators a Chance to Play Secretary of State," *Washington Post*, 20 July 1989, p. A-6, for an example from a decade earlier.
44. Thomas M. Franck and Edward Weisband, *Foreign Policy by Congress* (New York: Oxford University Press, 1984), p. 84.
45. Reported by Raymond H. Dawson, "Congressional Innovation and Intervention in Defense Policy," *American Political Science Review* 56 (1962), p. 47.
46. On the Court's reasoning in *Chadha* and its aftermath, see Louis Fisher, "The Legislative Veto: Invalidated, It Survives," *Law and Contemporary Problems* 56 (1993), pp. 273–292.
47. For more on changes in the reprogramming regime, see Louis Fisher, *Presidential Spending Power* (Princeton: University of Princeton, 1975), pp. 75–98.
48. On the hearing see Bradley Graham, "Fighter Response after Attacks Questioned; Senators Grill Nominee for Joint Chiefs Chairman on Military Readiness at Home," *Washington Post*, 14 September 2001, p. A-8.
49. McCubbins and Schwartz, "Congressional Oversight Overlooked: Police Patrols versus Fire Alarms," p. 171.
50. Arthur Lupia and Mathew D. McCubbins, "Learning from Oversight: Fire Alarms and Police Patrols Reconstructed," *Journal of Law, Economics, and Organization* 10 (1994), pp. 96–125.
51. This particular committee report offers three categories of hearings: those they appear to regard as routine, those that are event driven (meaning also they were not in the previous

years' oversight plan), and "others." For the 105th Congress there were nine hearings in the first category, ten in the second, and eight in the third. This count does not include subcommittee efforts that were largely in support of the authorization bill. See Committee on National Security, *Report of the Activities of the Committee on National Security for the One Hundred Fourth Congress*, pp. 35–52.

52. Gordon, "The Military Budget: Congressional Phase," p. 698.
53. It was Arthur Schlesinger, of course, who lamented the rise of a powerful presidency in *The Imperial Presidency* (Boston: Houghton Mifflin, 1973).

7

THE REPUBLICAN HOUSE AND FOREIGN POLICY IN THE 104TH CONGRESS AND BEYOND

JONATHAN D. MOTT AND NICOL C. RAE

The electoral earthquake of 1994 was a watershed event in American politics. The Republicans took control of the chamber as well as the International Relations (formerly Foreign Affairs) Committee at a time when U.S. foreign policy lacked a clear consensus or paradigm. We argue that there are several centrifugal forces in contemporary American politics that precluded the emergence of such a paradigm during the following six years of continued Republican control. Two additional conclusions are evident from our study of foreign policy in the House under Republican rule: In the absence of an ongoing international crisis similar to the Cold War, foreign policy conflict in the Republican House has largely centered on "symbolic" issues such as U.S. aid to international family planning bodies; and in situations of armed conflict and the deployment of U.S. forces, the president maintains the upper hand regardless of whether or not his party controls Congress. With unified control of the presidency and both houses of Congress likely to be a brief and intermittent phenomenon, we expect that this general pattern will be maintained in the first decade of the new century.

THE COLD WAR PATTERN

From the end of World War II until the Vietnam War, American foreign policy was characterized by bipartisanship and presidential preeminence. Both were products of a broad political consensus, forged in the late 1940s, that America should commit itself fully to the global containment of Soviet communism. During the twenty years after World War II, when Congress did address foreign policy issues, the Senate, with its constitutional prerogatives on treaties and its powerful Foreign Relations Committee, assumed a much greater role than the House, whose Foreign Affairs Committee lacked substantive subcommittees and concerned itself mainly with passing annual authorizing legislation on foreign aid. One Foreign Affairs Committee member, serving in the mid-1960s, told Richard Fenno that, "Inside the House, we are thought of as a glamorous committee, but not a powerful one. Foreign Affairs, I don't think, carries much weight in the House at all."[1]

After Vietnam, the balance of power between the branches, and between the Houses of Congress, changed significantly. By 1970, majorities in both houses of Congress had turned against the war but still found it difficult to extract America from the conflict when faced by a president who was determined to end the war on his own terms.[2] The ensuing clash between the legislative and executive branches brought an abrupt end to the norm of congressional deference to the president in foreign policy matters and significantly enhanced the position of the Foreign Affairs Committee in the House.

In addition to growing interbranch tensions, the once bipartisan nature of foreign policy making also began to deteriorate toward the end of the Vietnam War. If the containment of Soviet communism was still largely embraced as the primary end of U.S. foreign policy, Vietnam led to a major breakdown in the bipartisan consensus over the means of doing so. Most congressional Democrats became highly reluctant to support any U.S. military interventions abroad. More broadly, the Democratic Congress was increasingly reluctant to concede that the presidency had the constitutional authority to conduct such operations without explicit congressional approval. Consequently, Republicans tended to condemn Democratic misgivings as "congressional meddling" that undermined U.S. interests as determined by the (Republican) White House.

Given Republican dominance of the presidency and Democratic dominance of Congress for most of the post-Vietnam period, a new pattern of partisanship, congressional assertiveness, and interbranch conflict over foreign policy was established. During this same period, the House began to assert itself as a player across the entire spectrum of foreign and national security policy. The most powerful symbol of congressional resurgence and the emergence of the House in foreign policy making was the 1973 War Powers Resolution, which stated that any presidential deployment of U.S. forces abroad must end after sixty days, unless an extension is granted by the explicit approval of *both* houses of Congress.[3] Elsewhere, House Democrats began to exert the power of the purse effectively to defy the president's wishes in foreign policy matters by, for example, cutting off U.S. funds to anti-Communist forces in Angola in 1975.[4] Another measure of Congress's resurgence in foreign policy making was the grueling investigations, conducted in both houses, of the CIA, a key agency in the presidency's conduct of the Cold War. In the wake of these hearings, the congressional role in intelligence gathering and covert operations was substantially enhanced.[5]

Structural changes within Congress also were important in enhancing the authority of the House Foreign Affairs Committee, and the House as a whole, in the area of foreign policy. Reforms of the House committee system undertaken by the House Democratic Caucus between 1971 and 1975 reduced the control of committee chairmen over the staff resources of the standing committees, increased the power and autonomy of subcommittees, and provided for subcommittee staff.[6] On the Foreign Affairs Committee these changes had a marked effect on the vigor and volume of committee and subcommittee activity. During this period, Congress was also increasing the size of personal, committee, and research staffs, which further enhanced congressional expertise and effectiveness *vis-à-vis* the executive in foreign policy.

The arrival of President Reagan in 1980, accompanied by a Republican Senate, facing a persistent Democrat majority in the House, exacerbated interbranch conflict on foreign affairs. While the Reagan administration decided to reestablish an active policy of containing communism in the Third World using pro-U.S. surrogates, or, if necessary, U.S. forces, most House Democrats, led by Speaker Thomas P. (Tip) O'Neill (Mass.) and his successor James C. Wright (Texas), were equally determined to prevent further U.S. support for foreign surrogates with dubious democratic credentials. Conflict was particularly intense over granting U.S. military aid to the right-wing government of El Salvador and the anti-Sandinista "Contras" in Nicaragua. Ultimately, legislative–executive conflict over funding the Contras resulted in the Iran-Contra scandal, which severely undermined the Reagan presidency in its last two years.[7]

Reagan and his successor, George Bush, nevertheless, demonstrated a new willingness to assert U.S. military power overseas, particularly in Grenada in 1983, and Panama in 1989, where they believed particular U.S. interests were at stake and there were overwhelming numerical and technological advantages that virtually guaranteed military success. In addition, both Reagan and Bush (and every other president since 1973) regarded the War Powers Resolution as an unconstitutional violation of the separation of powers. In practice presidents largely complied with the consultation provisions of the resolution, but refused to be bound by the sixty-day limit on further troop deployment without explicit congressional sanction.[8]

Congress was thus much more querulous, more obstructive, far less trusting, much better informed, and far more active in foreign policy after Vietnam, even if it still found it difficult to prevail against a determined commander in chief.[9]

POST COLD WAR: CENTRIFUGAL FORCES
IN AMERICAN FOREIGN POLICY LEADERSHIP

During the 1990s, several developments rendered both the presidency and Congress less capable of decisive action in the foreign policy area. These were a result of centrifugal forces that have dispersed both the authority to act decisively in this area, and the willingness to do so in the first place. The only balance, if any, that these forces have produced since the Republicans took control of Congress in 1994, is an equal degree of impotence on the part of both branches in foreign policy making. Mann has argued that the absence of balance and bipartisanship in foreign policy making stems from three compounding factors: the persistence of divided-party government, the trend toward increased congressional involvement in foreign policy making, and the persistence of the belief that foreign policy is primarily the president's responsibility.[10] These factors can be overcome, Mann suggests, if reforms were instituted that take into consideration the comparative advantages of each branch, that is, Congress's ability to build a national consensus through open deliberation and the president's ability to lead and act decisively. In the broadest terms, Mann argues that such reforms should seek to "substitute early congressional involvement in the setting of broad policy goals for a reliance on detailed, restrictive, often punitive measures after the fact."[11] While this is, no doubt, a laudable objective, Mann's account of the weaknesses of U.S. foreign policy making focuses exclusively on the separation of powers. In reality, centrifugal forces at work in the broader political environment compound the problems of the American separated system, making such goals difficult to realize.[12] In the balance of this chapter, we discuss the centrifugal forces that, together with the constitutional division of authority between the executive and legislative branches, have made decisive foreign policy making increasingly difficult.

Just as a centrifuge disperses heavier objects increasingly further away from the center of a spinning receptacle, the current political environment has dispersed the authority, legitimacy, and capacity for decisive foreign policy making away from the center of the political spectrum and away from the elected officials responsible for making foreign policy decisions. The net result is increased partisanship and heightened interbranch conflict in U.S. international relations policy. The centrifugal forces which have produced the current foreign policy environment include: the instability of traditional party positions on foreign policy and corresponding rise of partisanship in foreign policy making, voters' ambivalence toward political parties and foreign policy, and the end of the Cold War and the absence of a clear paradigm for prioritizing U.S. interests in the international arena.

THE DEMISE OF BIPARTISANSHIP

In the period immediately following the Vietnam War, the traditional attitudes of the parties on foreign policy had reversed. Because of the Soviet threat, and as a reaction against post-Vietnam pacifism, the Republicans had become more internationalist, more interventionist, and more favorable to presidential direction of foreign policy than the Democrats. While this division still characterized the congressional debate on the 1991 Gulf War, there were already signs that it was coming under strain. Conservative commentator Patrick Buchanan vociferously opposed U.S. military intervention in the Gulf, on the grounds that the United States had no vital national interests there. In 1992, under the old isolationist "America First" slogan of the early 1940s, Buchanan challenged President George Bush for the GOP nomination with a full-fledged critique of Bush's concept of a postcommunist "New World Order" presided over by the United States.

At the same time, congressional Democrats were beginning to show indications of a reversion to their pre-Vietnam internationalism, by criticizing the Bush administration for its failure to act against "ethnic cleansing" in the former Yugoslavia, and for failing to confront the still-communist regime in Beijing on the issue of civil rights. Democrat presidential candidate Bill Clinton emphasized both issues in his successful general election campaign against Bush in 1992.

With the entry of a Democrat into the White House for the first time in a dozen years, the new party alignments in foreign policy began to come more clearly into focus. When the UN peacekeeping mission to Somalia began to encounter casualties, Republican voices in Congress were among the loudest raised for withdrawal. The same voices were also raised when Clinton finally sent U.S. troops to Haiti without explicit congressional approval: an action that drew vociferous Republican opposition in the fall of 1994. Formerly noninterventionist Democrats, on the other hand, endorsed President Clinton's "humanitarian" objectives for supporting Haiti's ousted democratically elected president, Jean Bertrand Aristide. As the Democrats were becoming the more interventionist party, reverting to their Wilsonian roots, the Republicans were increasingly influenced by nationalist arguments. A primary focus of the Republican critique of internationalism was the United Nations, a prime instrument of U.S. foreign policy in the post-Soviet era, and the threat that the supranational body posed to U.S. sovereignty. Despite growing partisan conflict in foreign policy, however, the broad center of both congressional parties—encompassing Republican Senate Leader Robert Dole and Democratic House Foreign Policy Committee Chairman Lee Hamilton—continued to support an active global role for the United States in international affairs although neither party was able to provide a clear definition of that role.

After the upset Republican victory in the 1994 House elections, the internationalist balance was somewhat disrupted. While some tensions persisted within the House Republican party between "bipartisan internationalists" and "nationalists" on foreign policy, more pronounced tensions had arisen between Democrats and Republicans in the Congress and between the legislative and executive branches. As foreign policy has become a far less salient component of American politics since the end of the Cold War, the foreign policy cleavages that have emerged are problematic because they further limit the ability of policy makers to act cooperatively and consistently. Under Republican control, congressional debates on foreign policy have become sharply partisan and clashes between the Congress and the president have become more frequent. With a Republican Congress committed to limiting U.S. involvement overseas and a Democratic president supporting a more extended multilateral role for the United States, the lines in the sand were clearly drawn for most of the 1990s.

PUBLIC AMBIVALENCE REGARDING FOREIGN POLICY AND POLITICAL PARTIES

Since the 1960s, the American people have become increasingly ambivalent about foreign policy. This ambivalence has weakened the leadership positions of both the president and Congress in foreign policy making. This mutual weakness has, in turn, contributed to the heightened conflict between the political parties and legislative and executive branches on foreign policy matters.[13] Public ambivalence has had this effect because politicians are well aware of public perceptions of an expansive foreign policy. Both Congress and the president have become reluctant to pursue actively foreign policy agendas that are at odds with public opinion. Most of the House International Relations Committee members we interviewed suggested that their activities on the International Relations Committee were intellectually interesting, but not necessarily helpful to them electorally. In fact, some Republicans on the committee contended that the only electoral benefit they have realized from their committee work has come from their efforts to cut foreign aid or keep the United States out of foreign conflicts. Furthermore, well-informed foreign policy decisions have become increasingly difficult for members of Congress to make, as fact-finding trips to foreign countries have become political liabilities.

While the president has the advantage of having a full-time team of foreign policy advisors to pursue his foreign policy agenda, the president is similarly constrained by public ambivalence about the United States' role in the international arena. The public's growing concerns about the economy and the focus on those concerns in presidential campaigns have made it difficult for the president to pursue a proactive foreign policy agenda and to gain political capital from foreign policy successes. Opinion surveys consistently show that Americans are much more concerned about domestic policy successes and failures than they are about the problems and victories of the United States abroad. The president's position in foreign policy making has become so marginal as far as public opinion is concerned, that foreign policy issues were almost totally irrelevant in deciding the 1992 and 1996 presidential elections.

The overwhelming emphasis on domestic policy in current political debates is no accident, since the public has been largely concerned with domestic policy problems and has also perhaps been complacent about global issues during the protracted economic boom of the 1990s. Furthermore, the electorate is less partisan and, therefore, uninterested in protracted partisan conflict. Ironically, as the parties on Capitol Hill have become more polarized and negative toward each other, parties have become less important to voters.[14] As the most important political manifestation of voters' detachment from parties, the electorate has persisted in granting control of the legislative and executive branches to opposing parties. The net result of this electoral order is that political parties, the president, and Congress have become incapable of mustering the political capital that would be needed to act authoritatively and decisively in foreign policy.

THE ABSENCE OF A POST–COLD WAR PARADIGM

The post-Vietnam era has been characterized by increased partisanship and persistent conflict between the Congress and the president. While most analyses of this conflict have focused on its origins in Vietnam, Watergate, divided government, and the separation of powers, it has been the absence of a unifying American foreign policy paradigm that has fueled these trends. Lacking such a paradigm, the United States is left with no rules of thumb to determine its international interests, when those interests are worth defending, and at what cost. Several competing paradigms have been advanced, but the two dominant paradigms, multilateralism and unilateralism, tend to further split Democrats from Republicans and, under the current electoral order, Congress from the president, rather than unifying them.

The multilateralist approach to U.S. foreign policy, supported by congressional Democrats and most Democratic presidents, since Woodrow Wilson (including Bill Clinton), is centered on the notion that the United States should be an equal participant in a global community of nations, and should cooperate with other nations through international organizations to address world problems. Proponents of this approach argue that it improves foreign perceptions of the United States in the world, while allowing the nation to be active in the international arena without having to be the primary leader or the final bearer of responsibility on foreign policy problems. The unilateralist approach (often mistaken for an isolationist approach), generally supported by congressional Republicans, rests on the alternative notion that the United States should not play an equal role in the community of nations when it is called on to carry an unfairly large share of the burden. Unilateralists argue that the ability to intervene should not be construed as an obligation to intervene, especially where that involvement would reduce U.S. control of its troops and resources, and confer the determination of U.S. interests to a supranational body such as the United Nations.

The absence of a shared foreign policy paradigm—and the competing paradigms held by the parties—has made bipartisanship and interbranch cooperation, especially under divided government, scarce commodities in foreign policy making. Operating from their contradictory perspectives, Democrats and Republicans are able to offer internally consistent arguments against each other's foreign policy agendas. However, because neither paradigm has been demonstrably proven superior to the other, and because there is no clear public support for one over the other, the prospects for the emergence of a consensus paradigm are not promising.

FOREIGN POLICY MAKING IN THE 104TH CONGRESS

Members of the first Republican Congress since the early 1950s almost uniformly admitted that it was singularly partisan. One member suggested that the level of partisan bickering in the House was directly due to the 1994 elections which, he argued, made both parties more ideological.[15] By most Democratic accounts, the tension was due, at least in part, to the attitudes of the Republican freshmen. One relatively senior Democrat observed:

> The Freshmen elected in 1994 are different than most members of the House. There's no sense of collegiality among them. We're truly a House divided. I'm a friendly person, by nature. I like to talk to everyone—Democrat or Republican, conservative or liberal. This group won't even respond to a "Hey, howya doin'?" It's very disheartening.

Whatever the role of the freshmen in causing it, the strained relations between Republicans and Democrats in the House are undeniably ideological. Indeed, the conflict between the parties that erupted during the budget debates was not simply about differing opinions on fiscal policy. Much more, it was emblematic of the distance between the two parties in the House on a wide range of issues. In virtually every committee and subcommittee in the House, relations between members of opposing parties chilled during the 104th Congress (1993–1995). This was just as true of the renamed International Relations (formerly Foreign Affairs) Committee as it was for any other.

Democrats on the International Relations Committee complained that the new majority used its proceedings almost exclusively for "political purposes." In the words of a very senior Democratic member of the committee:

> They have used the International Relations Committee politically, and they've not been terribly interested in producing legislation. . . . Their concern to make a political point is a legitimate use of the committee, but it's not one I prefer. And it's not been done a lot of the time in the history of Congress. They want to embarrass the president on an issue by making him take a position on it. Their purpose has not been to enact law. We were told way ahead that the bills would not be enacted into law, and that they didn't even care what the Senate's position was. They didn't even consult the Senate. That's not responsible legislating.

For their part, Republicans contended that they were simply addressing issues that Democrats had kept off the agenda for decades. A senior Republican on the committee argued that the Democrats' complaints about the majority's activities on the committee stemmed from the Democrats' failure to understand their new role:

> They think that just because the Republicans don't go along with everything they propose that we're not being bipartisan. The only reason they think this way is because they're used to getting everything they wanted from when they were in the majority. The Republicans, on the other hand, are used to getting rolled by the majority and now that we're the majority, there's a few things we'd like to do, whether the minority wants to go along with us or not.

In light of the perceptions of committee members, it is clear strained relations between Republicans and Democrats in the House characterized foreign policy making during the 104th Congress. There was also a corresponding lack of civility between the House of Representatives and the White House. In stark contrast to the time when bipartisanship and congressional deference to the executive branch were the norms in foreign policy making, decisive decisions based on consensual policy objectives have become increasingly difficult to achieve. The 1996 Helms-Burton Act, (extending the U.S. trade embargo on Cuba), and the reextension of Most Favored Nation trade status to China, were the very rare exceptions during the 104th Congress when the Clinton administration and House Republicans were in accord.[16]

As we have argued, much of the current discord between the executive and legislative branches on foreign policy making can be traced to the centrifugal forces that have undermined the legitimacy of both branches as authoritative leaders in the international arena. In order to understand better how these forces further weakened bipartisan and interbranch cooperation in foreign policy making, we will briefly review the major foreign policy decisions (or indecisions) made during the 104th Congress, offering additional insights from interviews with members of the House International Relations committee and key committee staffers that illustrate the impact of those forces. Our review will be organized by examining three broad areas of foreign policy: peacekeeping, foreign aid, and the international relations bureaucracy.

U.S. PEACEKEEPING EFFORTS

The Republicans' 1994 *Contract with America* stated that politicians have "taken to raiding the defense budget to fund social welfare programs and UN peacekeeping programs. Our defense forces have been cut so deeply that we risk a return to the 'hollow military' of the 1970s. And for the first time in our history, American troops have been placed under UN command."[17] Republicans promised to change this by limiting the president's authority to place American troops under UN command and by enacting limitations on U.S. involvement in UN peacekeeping efforts. In keeping with this provision of the *Contract*, the House passed legislation restricting the president's ability to commit U.S. troops to UN peacekeeping missions unilaterally. The House also sought to limit the administration's international agenda by authorizing only $225 million of the president's $445 million peacekeeping budget request and by failing to act on a $672 million supplemental request to cover unpaid peace-keeping assessments. When the Clinton administration put troops on the ground in Bosnia, the House quickly voted on a measure to cut off funding for the mission, but the measure was narrowly defeated by a vote of 218 to 210. Having failed to force the withdrawal of U.S. troops from Bosnia, the House approved a measure expressing opposition to the Clinton-inspired mission but support for the troops carrying it out. Despite congressional objections, however, the Clinton administration was able to deploy U.S. ground forces to keep the peace in Bosnia.

At first blush, Clinton's successes in Bosnia, that is, brokering the Dayton Peace Accords and placing U.S. troops in Bosnia to enforce them, suggested that the executive branch was still capable of authoritatively and decisively set-ting U.S. foreign policy. While this is true when U.S. interests are clearly and seriously threatened, the president's ability to involve the United States in peacekeeping missions remains limited in important ways. Specifically, the role of the president has been weakened by the centrifugal forces discussed above, and these same forces have weakened the position of Congress as well.

First, the public's ambivalence toward foreign policy has minimized the range of issues on which the president or Congress can act aggressively in the foreign arena. As one freshman Republican noted, junior Republicans tend to be "populists who represent the masses in their districts" who think foreign aid is a waste of money and that American allies have not carried their fair share of the burden. Public aversion to excessive foreign involvement limits the options of both Congress and the president in establishing peacekeeping policies. In Congress, the importance of this centrifugal force is magnified be-cause members of the International Relations Committee, especially junior Republican members, believe that the only electoral benefit from their com-mittee work is to be realized by minimizing U.S. involvement in potentially disastrous multilateral peacekeeping missions, such as Somalia. As one In-ternational Relations Committee Democrat bemoaned, the only time the com-mittee even discussed peacekeeping during the 104th Congress was when it was criticizing the administration's policies toward Bosnia and the UN. Just as the public's lack of enthusiasm for international adventurism has limited the International Relations Committee's position, the Clinton administration has been similarly limited in its foreign policy prerogatives.

Even in the case of Bosnia, Clinton's successes came much later than they might have if the public were more supportive of U.S. involvement in peace-keeping specifically and international problems more broadly. While Clinton's brokering of the peace in Bosnia was one of the highlights of his administra-tion, it was a hard won and overdue victory. Clinton quickly realized after en-tering the Oval Office that his political capital could not be squandered on building public support for significant U.S. involvement in Bosnia if he also wanted to pursue his domestic agenda. The election Clinton had just won had turned, to a large extent, on Bush's preoccupation with foreign entanglements and Clinton's pledge to refocus the nation's energies on its domestic problems. Coupled with a tenuous electoral mandate of well less than 50 percent of the popular vote, Clinton's "It's the economy, stupid," mantra limited his ability to act aggressively on Bosnia, especially during the first two years of his term. The fact that Clinton's peacekeeping agenda was limited to Bosnia during the 104th Congress further underscores the finite boundaries of his latitude in foreign policy making.

The second centrifugal force limiting the presidential and congressional leadership on peacekeeping is the ambivalence of voters toward foreign policy and political parties. The public's lack of interest in foreign affairs, the volatility of the electorate, and the increasing marginality of party control of both the White House and Congress makes it difficult for either the president or Congress to pursue decisive, that is, risky, foreign policies. As a senior International Relations Committee staffer we interviewed noted, partisan differences on peacekeeping were reinforced by the fact that neither the Republicans nor the Democrats regarded the other's electoral victories in 1992 or 1994 as legitimate. The Republicans contended that Clinton's presidential victory was a fluke, due only to Ross Perot's presence on the ballot. Democrats similarly believed that the Republican congressional victory in 1994 had more to do with the Democrats' own failure to communicate their message than it did with the public's acceptance of the Contract with America. As both parties were thus under the impression that the branch of government controlled by the other party was rightly theirs, the incentive for bipartisan activity within Congress or cooperation between the executive and legislative branches on peacekeeping issues was nonexistent.

The paradox of partisanship in the current political environment is that while party affiliation seems to matter less and less to voters, the electoral volatility caused by the growth of independence among voters has galvanized partisanship in Washington. This odd mix of partisan forces has limited the foreign policy agendas of both the legislative and executive branches by pitting them against each other, as well as by souring relations between the two dominant political parties. The Bosnia case again illustrated the effects of these forces on foreign policy making. Nothing approaching a clear bipartisan policy on Bosnia emerged during the 104th Congress. On the contrary, while a loose coalition of Congressional Democrats and more senior International Relations Committee Republicans—including committee chair Benjamin A. Gilman of New York—in the case of Bosnia, cautiously deferred to the president, the Republican-controlled International Relations Committee and the Republican Congress were opposed to the president on the issue of peacekeeping more broadly. In fact, it was the persistence of opposition to the other side's positions on Bosnia that led to the inability of either branch to act decisively on the matter during Clinton's first two years in office. And, given that the public's ambivalence toward foreign entanglements and political parties was not likely to dissipate in the near future, the absence of bipartisanship and interbranch cooperation on U.S. peacekeeping policy appeared likely to persist.

The third centrifugal force that has limited the ability of both Congress and the president to act decisively and cooperatively on foreign policy matters is perhaps the most intractable of the three. The absence of a post–Cold War paradigm—a framework that defines U.S. interests and establishes the circumstances under which those interests ought to be defended and at what cost—is a serious impediment to foreign policy making. With no rules of thumb akin to those that existed during the Cold War (e.g., support anti-Communist regimes), the Congress and the president are left to make *ad hoc* assessments of U.S. interests when faced with international crises such as the civil war in Bosnia. Moreover, the competing approaches taken by the Republicans and Democrats further undermine the coherence of U.S. foreign policy.

Both the multilateralism of the Democrats and the unilateralism of the Republicans are intended to bring clarity and stability to U.S. policy in the international arena. Congressional Democrats' and the Clinton administration's support for multilateralist approaches, such as current U.S. participation in the multinational peacekeeping operation in Bosnia, compensated for the lack of a clear U.S. foreign policy paradigm by diffusing authority and responsibility across all members of broad coalitions of nations, such as those assembled in U.N. peacekeeping efforts. However, such an approach, critics argue, unacceptably minimizes U.S. control over U.S. troops and resources. Congressional Republicans, on the other hand, are more inclined to pursue a unilateral approach, which compensates for the absence of a paradigm by consolidating and curtailing the control and use of U.S. troops and resources. This approach however is tantamount to withdrawing from the world and diminishing the prestige and importance of the United States in the international community. As the parties' competing views on peacekeeping pull in opposite directions, the consistency and legitimacy of U.S. foreign policy are further dispersed and diminished.

U.S. AID TO FOREIGN NATIONS

The 104th Congress also differed from the administration on foreign aid and U.S. humanitarian contributions to the UN. While Congress declared its intentions to cut back foreign aid and, at best, hold the line on U.S. contributions to the UN, the Clinton administration lobbied for increased spending on both counts, and this issue was a persistent bone of contention between the Republican House and the Clinton White House since 1994. In contrast to the balance of constitutional authority in peacekeeping, in which the president has the upper hand, Congress's control over the federal purse strings gives the legislative branch a decisive advantage in establishing U.S. foreign aid poli-cy. Consequently, Clinton administration efforts to convince lawmakers that the current 1.2 percent share of federal spending allotted for international pro-grams was too small fell on deaf ears. In fact, Congress was able to assert its own position that the nation expends too much of its resources, not too little, on foreign entanglements. As one junior Republican on the International Re-lations Committee pointed out, many of the voters who sent the 1994 fresh-man class to Washington perceive foreign aid as a waste of money, almost without regard to its promised future benefits. Among other specific targets, congressional Republicans set their sights on eliminating U.S. contributions to the International Development Association, the "soft-loan" affiliate of the World Bank that many Republicans believe to be little more than an interna-tional welfare agency.[18]

Nowhere in foreign policy making is the centrifugal force of public am-bivalence more profound than in determining the level of U.S. foreign aid. As a senior International Relations Committee Democrat observed, members' hands are tied on the question of foreign aid in more ways than one. First, members are increasingly unwilling to join with congressional delegations, or "Codels," to visit nations that receive U.S. aid because of the negative pub-licity attached to these so-called junkets. When members fail to go on these missions, they also fail to see firsthand how U.S. foreign aid dollars are being spent. Without primary knowledge of the effectiveness of particular foreign aid expenditures, members are forced to make uninformed decisions on the matter. Furthermore, voters routinely indicate their displeasure with the no-tion of sending money to other countries when the United States has its own problems to solve. These two factors combine to make foreign aid decisions much less rational than they should be. The senior Democrat complains that, "There's a huge gap in knowledge of policy between the member and the or-dinary voter or constituent," that often drives members to vote to cut foreign aid, even when it might be in the best interests of the nation to spend more money abroad. The largely domestic focuses of the 104th Congress and the Clinton administration were reflections of voters' priorities, priorities that present a serious impediment to granting more extensive U.S. financial aid to other nations.

Against the backdrop of public opposition to foreign aid, the heightened partisan tensions in Washington, both within Congress and along Pennsyl-vania Avenue, have made it difficult for either the president or Congress to support increases in foreign aid with any enthusiasm. While the Clinton ad-ministration and Democrats on the International Relations Committee were generally in favor of more foreign aid spending than the Republicans on the committee and the House as a whole, the supporters of foreign aid spending were limited by political realities in the amount of funding they could press for in the highly partisan authorization and appropriations processes. As one committee member has argued, it is easy politics for the Republicans to take aim at arcane sounding foreign programs, such as the World Bank and the International Monetary Fund, while it is equally difficult politics for Democrats to defend such programs. As another committee Democrat observed, when Republicans propose to "cut, cut, cut" away at the foreign aid budget, Democrats are wary of the fact that fighting them on that issue might give Republicans political ammunition for the next election.

The polarizing and destabilizing effects of the public's negative perception of foreign aid spending and the partisan acrimony both within the International Relations Committee and between the legislative and executive branches are again exacerbated by the lack of a clear U.S. foreign policy paradigm. The multilateralist tendencies of the Clinton administration and Democrats in Congress constantly ran headlong into the Republicans' support for a more unilateralist approach. As a senior Republican committee staffer explained, both the Democrats and the Republicans recognize the unique position of the United States in the international community, but they disagree on the frequency and extent to which the United States should get involved simply because it can. In contrast to Republican proposals to reduce foreign aid spending significantly, Democrats believe that foreign aid should be viewed as an investment in more stable and productive relations between the United States and other nations. In fact, this perspective carried the day when moderate Republicans joined with Democrats on the floor to restore funding for aid to Africa in 1995. For the most part, however, bipartisan action has remained elusive. A Republican member of the committee observed the following:

> The philosophical tensions on the committee are exacerbated by party politics. There are obvious political tensions between the Republicans in the Congress and the President that make things even more difficult. There are also some committee members, particularly a few outspoken Democrats, who are very acrimonious. The partisan tensions that have flared on the floor have clearly seeped into the workings of the committees. Members who get in floor fights often bring those into their committee work and the tensions are heightened there as well.

These philosophical tensions are both cause and effect of the absence of a bipartisan foreign policy paradigm to guide foreign aid decisions after the Cold War. Until such a consensus is forged, foreign aid spending is likely to remain a political football.

THE U.S. INTERNATIONAL RELATIONS BUREAUCRACY

Partisan bickering and interbranch conflict also characterized decisions about the U.S. international relations bureaucracy during the 104th and 105th Congresses (1993–1997). Early in 1995, the House International Relations Committee moved to eliminate three foreign affairs agencies: the Agency for International Development (USAID), the United States Information Agency

(USIA), and the Arms Control and Disarmament Agency (ACDA). While Democrats were able to block the move in the Senate; House Republicans were able to approve legislation calling for the action. In a conference version of the bill, a provision was made to allow the president to designate two of the three for elimination.[19] The legislation would have also significantly reduced foreign aid and implemented several policy restrictions and recommendations limiting U.S. involvement overseas.

The Clinton administration, on the other hand, listed its primary objectives in foreign policy as repairing relations with China, integrating more fully the administration's environmental goals into diplomacy, cracking down on illegal drug trafficking, bringing war criminals to justice in Rwanda and Bosnia, putting an end to the Arab–Israeli conflict, and pursuing "initiatives in place" in Northern Ireland, Haiti, Cyprus and elsewhere.[20] Virtually all of these objectives depended on the ability of the president to oversee an effective foreign affairs bureaucracy, an ability that was directly threatened by congressional efforts to restructure the State Department. Once again, tensions between Congress and the president caused by the separation of powers were magnified by centrifugal forces in American politics.

While the State Department is not a hugely negative symbol of the public's views on foreign policy, the agencies of the department that oversee the disbursement of foreign aid are ripe targets for elimination in the current political context. As one International Relations Committee Democrat has observed, Republicans are only too eager to satiate the public's demands for reductions in foreign aid. This, however, the legislator argues, is unwise because it is an oversimplified response to the perceived problem. Restructuring the State Department and eliminating key foreign policy agencies might be appealing to an ambivalent public, but such actions undermine the capacity of the president to make coherent foreign policy decisions. Many of the freshman Republicans in the House, including those on the International Relations Committee, had a much more limited view of how the appropriateness of federal action should be determined. As one committee freshman explained, "I have always done what I believe to be a reflection of what the 'little guy' in the district wants" and not what Washington bureaucrats want, and the "average guy without a voice" in Washington is not excited about supporting bureaucracies, especially when their sole purpose is to administer foreign aid.

The battle between Republicans and Democrats on the restructuring of the State Department was one of the central partisan flash points of the 104th and 105th Congresses. A senior Democrat on the International Relations Committee contended that committee Republicans were more concerned with forwarding their own partisan, anti–White House, agenda than in producing legislation. Indeed, just as Republicans perceived the War Powers Resolution as a partisan attack against Republican presidents, Democrats believed that Republican efforts to eliminate foreign affairs agencies were politically motivated attacks aimed, at least in part, at President Clinton. For their part, the

Republicans insisted that several executive branch agencies were in need of restructuring and reorganization, with the State Department being only one example of that need. Far from being "hijacked" by the Speaker, one International Relations Committee Republican argues, the committee pursued its own agenda, focusing on improving the foreign policy making process both within the committee as well as within the foreign policy bureaucracy.

The underlying partisan tensions in the House during the 104th Congress made bipartisan reform of the State Department impossible. This was also true of cooperation between Congress and the president on the same matter. As each side looked for opportunities to blame the other for failing to cooperate, neither side made serious efforts to compromise on the issue.

Even more than public ambivalence and partisan bickering on the Hill, the lack of a shared foreign policy paradigm made cooperative bipartisan State Department restructuring intractable. Since the advent of Republican control of the House, it has even been difficult, as one committee member noted, to discuss the evolving role of the United States in the world without getting bogged down in petty partisan arguments. The gap between the multilateralism of the Democrats and the unilateralism of the Republicans is so broad that a consensus paradigm has yet to emerge. This lack of agreement regarding the direction of U.S. foreign policy makes it impossible to build a consensus on how the foreign affairs bureaucracy should be organized. If the United States had established specific goals that it seeks to achieve in the international arena, any restructuring of the State Department could reflect those goals. Because no such goals have been articulated, however, such a focused restructuring cannot be undertaken. Once again, the absence of a paradigm exacerbates existing tendencies toward partisan conflict, interbranch deadlock, and paralysis in U.S. foreign policy.

THE STRUGGLE CONTINUES: THE 105TH CONGRESS

The pattern of conflict characteristic of the first Republican House since 1954 continued into the 105th Congress (1995–1997) after the reelection of President Clinton (in a campaign in which foreign policy issues had very low salience) and the Republican House (albeit with a somewhat reduced majority). In the perennial struggle to enact legislation reauthorizing foreign aid and the State Department, International Relations Committee chair Gilman secured his committee's approval for a bill that funded foreign aid programs virtually at the level of President Clinton's request of $16 billion.[21] The House Republican leadership, however, rejected Gilman's bill, and the measure that ultimately passed the House floor on June 11, 1997 included long-standing conservative amendments on State Department reorganization and restrictions on international family planning assistance.[22] While Senate Foreign Relations chair, Jesse Helms (R-N.C.) and the Clinton administration subsequently agreed to a package along similar lines that also included a commitment to pay off America's longstanding debts to the United Nations, the deal was unscrambled in conference by the House Republican leadership's insistence on retaining the prohibitions on U.S. funding of international bodies that advocated or practiced abortion.[23] The Republican leadership waited six months after the authorization bill passed in April to send it to the president on the eve of the 1998 midterm elections, when it was vetoed as expected, although the consolidation of the foreign affairs bureaucracy was finally approved as part of an omnibus spending bill.

On overseas military actions, despite widespread grumbling in Republican ranks, Congress largely deferred to presidential authority. In June 1997, the House rejected a measure intended to force the withdrawal of U.S. troops from their peacekeeping mission in Bosnia, although House Republicans favorably voted 182 to 49. Almost a year later, the American troop deployment in Bosnia was further challenged as a possible violation of the 1973 War Powers Resolution by California Republican Representative Thomas J. (Tom) Campbell who proposed a resolution calling for the immediate return of U.S. troops from Bosnia which, if passed would have set up a test of the 1973 measure before the Supreme Court. However, under pressure from the Secretary of State Madeleine Albright and NATO Supreme commander, General Wesley Clarke, forty-three House Republican internationalists led by Representative Gilman ensured the defeat of the Campbell resolution, although the vast majority of House Republicans voted in favor. Later in 1998, House Republicans followed Speaker Newt Gingrich's (Ga.) endorsement of Clinton's airstirkes against terrorist Osama bin Laden after the President had consulted with the Republican congressional leadership. Nevertheless several House Republicans were deeply skeptical of the timing of the president's actions shortly after his admission of an "inappropriate relationship" with Monica Lewinsky. In rallying Republican support, the role of Defense Secretary and former GOP Senator William S. Cohen (Maine) proved to be crucial.[24] However, when Clinton launched airstrikes against Iraq on the eve of his likely impeachment by the U.S. House in December 1998, similar Republican support was not forthcoming. Yet the most critical actors on foreign policy among House Republicans, including then–Speaker-elect Bob Livingston (R-La.) and International Relations chair Gilman, did rally behind the president once again.[25] In sum, U.S. military interventions during the 105th Congress demonstrated the continuing tensions between the branches on such interventions in conditions of divided government, but also indicated that the president's power of initiative in troop deployments and airstrikes will invariably give the commander in chief the upper hand in such conflicts.

Tensions within the House Republican ranks surfaced on China policy, where a determined minority of religious conservatives joined with liberal Democrats to oppose the continued extension of trade privileges to China, while the party leadership and a majority in GOP ranks adhered to business's preference for free trade.[26] (Later in the year, the Clinton administration effort to obtain presidential "fast-track" authority for trade deals failed to even reach the House floor, as it became evident that overwhelming opposition from House Democrats would doom the measure to defeat.) To assuage the critics of China's human rights record, in late 1997 the House GOP leadership backed a series of symbolic anti-China measures including visa restrictions, enhanced funding for Radio Free Asia, opposition to International Monetary Fund (IMF) subsidized loans to China, and a ballistic missile defense for Taiwan.[27]

The religious right was further influential in sponsoring a religious persecution bill allowing economic and diplomatic sanctions against foreign governments engaged in the persecution of religious groups.[28] While the bill eventually passed the House overwhelmingly in May 1998, the debate over its provisions revealed a continuing spilt between business-oriented and religious Republican conservatives over human rights issues, with the former exceedingly wary of all efforts at economic sanctions threatening foreign trade. A weakened compromise measure was eventually passed by the Senate and signed by the president that allowed the latter to waive any sanctions that he determined would be against the U.S. "national interest."[29] Overall the emergence of the divisions within Republican ranks over the emphasis on human rights issues was the only significant new development in the House's foreign policy activity in the 105th Congress. Deep divisions remained between the Republicans' fundamentally unilateralist approach to foreign affairs and the multilateralism of the Clinton administration, but on crucial questions the more internationalist-minded Republican leadership, including International Relations chair Gilman, sought to broker a compromise with the president, or grudgingly accept presidential authority. In the crunch, however, the House deferred to presidential authority on military interventions, and, demonstrating the influence of religious conservatives, concentrated its opposition to the administration on the international funding of abortion and religious persecution. On China, the Republican leadership and the mainstream of the party were generally more supportive of the administration's free trade position, and it was the opposition of congressional Democrats that doomed "fast track." Despite the contentious atmosphere of executive–legislative relations in the 105th Congress, which eventually impeached the president, there was no significant conflict between the House Republicans and the president on foreign policy, and foreign policy issues continued to possess a relatively low salience in the chamber.

THE 106TH CONGRESS: IMPASSE

The Republican House majority was slightly trimmed in the 1998 midterm elections, held in the midst of impeachment proceedings in the House regarding the president's conduct in the Monica Lewinsky affair. However, the narrower Republican margin did not alter the dynamic of foreign policy debate in the House and the patterns of the 104th and 105th Congresses were largely repeated in the 106th (1997–1999). Reflecting the predominance of unilateralist views in their ranks, House Republicans continued to be highly wary of presidential military interventions abroad where a direct U.S. national interest did not appear to be at stake. On the other hand, the Republican House leadership under new Speaker J. Dennis Hastert (Ill.) also continued to be grudgingly supportive of such actions once American forces were actually deployed, in deference to the president's authority as commander in chief. The perennial battles over foreign aid, abortion, and State Department reauthorization continued, and China policy also continued to throw up unlikely coalitions across partisan lines. So while the Republican House and the Democrat president were probably even more contemptuous of each other than at the outset of GOP House rule in 1995, they managed to find ways to avoid conflict when such conflict would likely damage important U.S. interests or undermine American military forces in the field. Their most bitter battles were thus confined to symbolic issues such as the foreign aid and abortion nexus.

In July 1999, the House finally passed a State Department authorization bill excluding the highly contentious provisions on funding for the UN and aid to international family planning programs, leaving those issues to be settled in conference with the Senate.[30] In November, Clinton eventually endorsed a deal as part of the omnibus FY 2000 budget package that reauthorized the State Department with extra funds to improve security at U.S. embassies and consulates; repaid $926 million in U.S. debts to the UN; and provided some debt relief for poor nations. On the abortion issue, Clinton, fearful that the U.S. might suffer the embarrassment of having to give up its seat in the UN general assembly, agreed to restrictions on aid to international family planning organizations although the president was left with the power to waive the restrictions.[31] A similar deal was worked out for FY 2001 the following year.[32]

The major U.S. military operation during the 106th Congress was the NATO bombing of Serbia to force President Slobodan Milosevic to withdraw Serb forces from the province of Kosovo, followed by the deployment of U.S. ground troops as part of a NATO force to guarantee the security of the ethnic Albanian majority in the province. Even before the military campaign began, Speaker Hastert, with support from traditionally internationalist Republicans such as International Relations chair Gilman and Judiciary chair Henry Hyde (Ill.), secured sufficient Republican votes to pass a resolution supporting the deployment of U.S. troops as part of a proposed NATO peacekeeping operation in Kosovo, although Secretary of State Madeleine Albright had urged him to postpone the vote while she was still negotiating with the Serb government. Once the NATO airstrikes began and with U.S. and NATO prestige at stake, most House Republicans rallied behind the operation, their reasoning being summarized by one of the Clinton administration's most astringent critics on foreign policy, House Republican Policy Committee chair

Christopher Cox (Calif.): "Having committed the prestige of the world's only superpower, the only course now is to defeat Milosevic militarily, and to do so swiftly."[33]

House Republican leaders also worked to block an effort from persistent gadfly Representative Campbell to bring the 1973 War Powers Resolution into operation by either forcing a House vote on a declaration of war against Yugoslavia or setting the resolution's procedures for withdrawing U.S. forces from combat into motion.[34] Campbell's resolutions were eventually defeated on the House floor in early May, but a resolution endorsing the air war was defeated on a tie vote and the House passed by 249 to 180 a resolution requiring congressional authorization for the deployment of any ground troops in the region. Although the overwhelming majority of House Republicans (particularly House Whip Tom Delay [R-Texas]) were skeptical at best about the Clinton policy and had voted against the Clinton administration in the above-mentioned floor votes, the House Republicans did not wish to appear to be undermining the war effort. When the House had the opportunity to exercise its power of the purse by cutting off appropriations, a supplemental appropriations bill to fund the Kosovo operation passed overwhelmingly, and an amendment that would have precluded appropriations for ground forces was even more decisively rejected.[35] The House Republicans' maneuvers during the Kosovo operation demonstrated that while hardly enthusiastic about the motivations for the intervention and highly critical of the Clinton administration policy in the region prior to the war, they were determined not to be seen to be undermining the NATO alliance, U.S. forces in combat, and (with the exception of the maverick Campbell) presidential authority to make such military interventions.

Asia policy including China remained another important area of contention in the House, although as previously, the divisions here did not fall strictly along partisan lines. The most significant congressional action regarding Asia during the 106th Congress was the May 2000 House vote granting Normal Trade Relations (NTR) status to China, thus ending the need for annual votes maintaining China's MFN status and allowing the Chinese to enter the World Trade Organization (WTO). On the key House vote, 164 Republicans (74 percent) voted for the measure while a majority of House Democrats voted against their own president's position. Crucial to the passage of this legislation was the decision of the House GOP leadership to embrace an amendment (authored by Democratic Representative Sander M. Levin of Michigan and Nebraska Republican Douglas K. Bereuter) that proposed a commission to monitor China's labor and human rights practices: a long-term concern in the ranks of both parties in the House.[36]

Elsewhere in Asia policy, House Republican relations with the Clinton administration were not so amicable. When the Clinton administration proved reluctant to send peacekeeping forces in the wake of human rights atrocities in the disputed Indonesian province of East Timor, International Relations

Committee chair Gilman reflected the sentiments of many House Republicans that, after having made such a strenuous effort in Kosovo, the United States was now neglecting an area in which it had a clear national interest:

> Is there a double standard for Europe and the rest of the world? Why is the United States not taking a more leading role in resolving this crisis, which occurs in a region of the world enormously significant to our national security interests?[37]

In the end a token U.S. contingent of 200 was sent to East Timor as part of an Australian-led U.N. force. House Republicans were also unhappy regarding the Clinton administration's increasingly conciliatory stance toward the Communist regime in North Korea. In September 1999, the Clinton administration concluded an agreement with the Pyongyang regime that in exchange for the United States ending Cold War–era economic sanctions, North Korea would stop developing a nuclear missile that might be able to strike parts of Alaska. Republican suspicion of the North Koreans led to House passage of a Gilman-sponsored bill that would strengthen congressional oversight of U.S. nuclear cooperation with the North Koreans.[38] In February 2000, the House also voted overwhelmingly for a bill sponsored by Majority Whip Delay that strengthened U.S. military links with Taiwan, reflecting the House Majority's continuing unease with the U.S.–China relationship. While generally enthusiastic about enhancing trade ties with Beijing, House Republicans remained wary of the human rights record and long-term foreign policy intentions of the still-Communist-led Chinese regime.

Two new issues of contention came to the forefront during the 106th Congress. The first concerned the Clinton administration's request for aid to the fragile and embattled government of Colombia to fight drug traffickers and leftist guerillas. After a speech by Speaker Hastert on January 10 warning of a potential disaster in Colombia, the Clinton administration came up with almost $1 billion in aid.[39] Despite strong support from Hastert and House Appropriations chair C. W. "Bill" Young (R-Fla.), the proposal attracted criticism from Democrats and some Republicans including Representative Herbert L. (Sonny) Callahan of Alabama, chair of the Appropriations subcommittee handling the request. Opponents feared that it would entangle the United States in a Vietnam-type morass and that the money might be better spent on antidrug efforts at home.[40] Toward the end of Congress in November 2000, International Relations chair Gilman withdrew his support from the plan, arguing that the United States was on the brink of "a major mistake," due to concerns about corruption and the human rights record of the Colombian military.[41]

A further issue that evidenced the absence of consensus between the parties and the branches was the area of missile defense. In March 1999, both Houses passed similar bills (with almost unanimous Republican support) calling for a system of missile defenses that could intercept and destroy intercontinental missiles headed for the United States. Such a system had been advocated among Republicans since President Ronald Reagan's "Star Wars" scheme in the 1980s, but had never come close to deployment. Interest in the issue was reignited by the possibility that "rogue" nations such as North Korea might develop weaponry capable of striking the United States. The Clinton administration was wary of such deployments for fear that they would violate existing arms control agreements with Russia, still the power with by far the largest arsenal of missiles capable of hitting the United States. Consensus was never achieved on this issue by the end of the 106th Congress, and the Clinton administration ultimately decided to defer to the next administration on whether and when to deploy such a system.

In short, the 106th Congress did not come close to resolving any of the contentious issues between the Republican House and the Democratic president, with the exception of the China trade issue on which divisions did not fall neatly across party lines. With both the president and Congress having an eye to the next administration, there was little incentive for cooperation on foreign and defense policy and more incentive to clearly stake out contrasting positions. Yet while the rhetoric remained harsh and the political atmosphere sour in the wake of the Clinton impeachment, the pattern of continuing cooperation in matters involving the actual deployment of the U.S. forces provided some grounds for hope. At least on the issue of presidential authority to deploy U.S. forces, a *de facto* consensus, first evident in the 104th and 105th Congresses, seemed to have been maintained.

CONCLUSION

On the surface, our account is bleak; however, given the current state of affairs in international relations, the lack of balance, consensus, and leadership in American foreign policy making might actually serve U.S. interests. In a world that is much more uncertain than it was during the Cold War era, the ability to play Republicans off Democrats and the president off the Congress allows the United States to, in some instances, have it both ways. For instance, the United States can participate in UN missions as in Bosnia on the strength of President Clinton's commitment to do so, but it reserves its right to object and pull out without hesitation, on the strength of Congress's reservations about the mission.

Until the balance of power in the world is more settled, standoffishness might serve U.S. interests better than any other approach, although taking such an approach might annoy its allies. It is clear, however, that even though the United States is uniquely capable of intervening in foreign entanglements, it has little interest in getting involved in every conflict that erupts in the world. Its official ambivalence is a direct reflection of the public's ambivalence toward international affairs.

Having given an account of the disarray of U.S. foreign policy making and its likely causes, however, we believe that it would be premature to suggest that Congress and the president are incapable of developing a more consensual and consistent approach to foreign policy making. As we noted above, there have been exceptions during the three Republican Congresses to the norm of partisan and interbranch conflict, specifically the trade status of China, the passage of the Helms-Burton Act, and congressional acquiescence in overseas military operations initiated by President Clinton. These cases are worth examining because of the potential lessons that can be learned from them for improving the process of foreign policy making in other areas. A cursory examination of foreign policy decisions that have been decisive and bipartisan suggests that there are certain types of foreign policy questions on which consensus and cooperation are easier to come by. For example, foreign policy questions that center on protecting clear, nondebatable American interests, especially economic interests, are more likely to be addressed on a bipartisan basis. For this reason, trade issues tend to be dealt with more cooperatively and consistently across parties and between the branches. Further, foreign policy questions that do not accentuate Democratic and Republican differences on multilateralism and unilateralism are more likely to be solved without partisan bickering. Foreign policy problems that focus exclusively on the relations between the United States and one or two other nations, such as Cuba or Canada, then, are more readily addressed. Also, international policy problems that pose little potential for a constitutional turf war between Congress and the president or that pose no significant tradeoffs between domestic and foreign policy choices can be made more cooperatively and consistently even in the face of the centrifugal forces we have discussed. Finally, it is evident that the Republican Congress has been extremely wary of challenging presidential decisions to deploy U.S. troops in combat situations abroad.

The problem that remains, however, is that the bulk of U.S. foreign policy decisions do not meet the criteria we have just laid out. Rather, foreign policy problems tend to underscore the tensions that lead to partisan and conflictual disputes. Mann has argued, in *A Question of Balance*, that the path to restoring consensus and consistency to U.S. foreign policy making lies in rebuilding strained relationships between the legislative and executive branches.[42] While we agree that much of the current deadlock in foreign policy can be traced to tensions between the branches, mending presidential–congressional relations is only part of the picture. The forces that yield conflict and paralysis in American foreign policy must be addressed as well.

The centrifugal forces that make bipartisan and cooperative foreign policy rare in the current political environment share a common characteristic. Without exception, the effects of these forces could be minimized by improved communication and deliberation. Public ambivalence toward foreign policy and political parties could be alleviated if politicians and voters communicated better. The same freshman on the International Relations Committee that declared his loyalty to the views of the "little guy" also noted that:

> People at town hall meetings think that [foreign aid] takes half of the budget, and to say anything positive about foreign aid is a political liability. On the other hand, foreign aid is the equivalent of fence building between neighbors. A conversation [with voters] would make it easier to resolve our disagreements because there's a value to foreign policy that people don't understand or don't appreciate.

It is likely that improved communication and education could significantly diminish voter opposition to foreign aid and U.S. involvement in foreign affairs. Members of Congress who support such policies bear the responsibility of selling them to voters.

Secondly, increased communication and deliberation between the parties would clearly reduce the partisan conflict in the House and, in turn, the conflict between Congress and the president. If partisan and interbranch conflict has exacerbated the inability of policymakers to act consistently and decisively on foreign policy matters, moderating the partisan tone of House debates would foster more cooperative foreign policy decisions. Unfortunately the course of events during that Congress and its successor has diminished whatever grounds for optimism existed on that score. With the two parties very closely matched nationally, and control of the chamber just within reach, the majority and minority party in the House have little incentive to cooperate, even on foreign and defense issues unless national prestige (as in Kosovo) or national economic interest (as in China) are at stake. Partisanship was the most salient feature of politics in the House during the 1990s, culminating in the largely partisan impeachment of President Clinton by the Republican House in late 1998. The environment of contemporary congressional electoral politics—districts that are overwhelmingly "safe" for one party or the other, the partisan nature of primary electorates, the prominent role of ideological activists, and interest groups in congressional election campaigns—militates against a bipartisan approach. When different parties narrowly control the branches—as has been the norm in recent American politics—the incentives for improved communication and deliberation on foreign policy and other issues are meager at best.

Yet, communication and deliberation are needed if Democrats and Republicans in both the executive and legislative branches are to find common ground on the direction of U.S. foreign policy. Whether or not anything as formal as a paradigm will emerge from the diversity of opinion that currently exists on the matter, more open communication and discussion would foster more cooperative approaches to dealing with foreign policy dilemmas. While inaction and indecision might serve U.S. interests in the short term, it is not a controversial proposition to assert that the nation would be much better off with a clear vision of where it is heading and how it plans to get there.

NOTES

1. Richard F. Fenno, Jr., *Congressmen in Committees* (Boston: Little, Brown, and Company, 1973), p. 225.
2. Arthur M. Schlesinger, Jr., *The Imperial Presidency* (Boston: Houghton Mifflin, 1973).
3. James L. Sundquist, *The Decline and Resurgence of Congress* (Washington, D.C.: Brookings, 1981).
4. Thomas M. Franck and Edward Weisband, *Foreign Policy by Congress* (New York: Oxford University Press, 1979), pp. 13–57.
5. Ibid., pp. 15–34 and Thomas E. Mann, "Making Foreign Policy: President and Congress," in *A Question of Balance: The President, the Congress, and Foreign Policy*, 2nd ed., ed. Thomas E. Mann (Washington: D.C.: Brookings Institution, 1990), pp. 20–22.
6. See Sundquist, *The Decline and Resurgence of Congress*, pp. 67–414.
7. Barry M. Blechman, "The New Congressional Role in Arms Control," in *A Question of Balance: The President, the Congress, and Foreign Policy*, 2nd ed., ed. Thomas E. Mann (Washington, D.C.: Brookings Institution, 1990); and Bruce W. Jentleson, "American Diplomacy: Around the World and along Pennsylvania Avenue," in *A Question of Balance: The President, the Congress, and Foreign Policy*, 2nd ed., ed. Thomas E. Mann (Washington, D.C.: Brookings Institution, 1990).
8. Robert A. Katzmann, "War Powers: Toward a New Accommodation," in *A Question of Balance: The President, the Congress, and Foreign Policy*, 2nd ed., ed. Thomas E. Mann (Washington, D.C.: Brookings Institution, 1990).
9. Eileen Burgin, "Congress and Foreign Policy: The Misperceptions," in *Congress Reconsidered*, 5th ed., ed. Lawrence C. Dodd and Bruce I. Oppenheimer (Washington, D.C.: Congressional Quarterly Press, 1993).
10. Mann, "Making Foreign Policy: President and Congress," pp. 28–31.
11. Ibid., p. 31.
12. Charles O. Jones, *The Presidency in a Separated System* (Washington, D.C.: Brookings Institution, 1994).
13. Mann, "Making Foreign Policy: President and Congress," p. 11.
14. Martin P. Wattenberg, *The Decline of American Political Parties, 1952–1988* (Cambridge, MA: Harvard University Press, 1990).
15. In the remainder of the chapter we refer to interviews conducted with members of Congress and their staffers in January to August 1996, particularly with members of the House International Relations Committee. Where appropriate, we give some indication of the members' status in the House. However, we deliberately avoid giving enough detail to identify the members we interviewed. In return for ensuring members that we would use their comments anonymously and for academic purposes, we were afforded more candor than we would have otherwise been. In all, we interviewed nearly sixty members of Congress in 1995–1996 for this and other projects, while we both served as APSA Congressional Fellows. Among this group were two freshman members of the International Relations Committee, two senior Democrats and one senior Republican on the committee. We also interviewed several member and committee staffers, including a very senior Republican staffer on the International Relations Committee.
16. The Clinton administration was initially cool toward the Helms-Burton law, but the president agreed to sign it after the Cuban military shot down a civilian plane on February 24, 1996, piloted by Cuban exiles attempting to rescue seaborne refugees from Castro's regime. Out of deference to the wishes of America's NATO allies who trade with Cuba, President Clinton backed away from full implementation of the legislation in early 1997.
17. Republican National Committee, *Contract with America: The Bold Plan by Rep. Newt Gingrich, Rep. Dick Armey and the House Republicans to Change the Nation* (New York: Times Books, 1994).
18. Carroll J. Doherty, "Function by Function: International Affairs," *Congressional Quarterly Weekly Report*, 23 March 1996, pp. 769–770.
19. Carroll J. Doherty, "Conferees Agree on Bill to Abolish an Agency," *Congressional Quarterly Weekly Report*, 9 March 1996, p. 634.
20. Thomas W. Lippman, "Christopher Sets Assertive U.S. Goals," *Washington Post*, 19 January 1996, p. A-25.
21. Carroll J. Doherty, "Clinton Wins First Round in House on Money for Programs Abroad," *Congressional Quarterly Weekly Report*, 10 May 1997, pp. 1084–1085.

22. Carroll J. Doherty, "GOP Leaders Scuttle Bipartisan Bill in Nod to House Conservatives," *Congressional Quarterly Weekly Report*, 7 June 1997, pp. 1324–1325.
23. Donna Cassata, "Bill Blessed by Helms Falls Prey to Naysayers in the House," *Congressional Quarterly Weekly Report*, 11 October 1997, pp. 2493–2494.
24. Chuck McCutcheon, "Lawmakers Back Missile Strikes Despite a Bit of GOP Skepticism," *Congressional Quarterly Weekly Report*, 22 August 1998, pp. 2289–2290.
25. Miles Pomper, Chuck McCutcheon, and Pat Towell, "GOP Leaders Refuse to Close Ranks With Clinton on Bombing of Iraq," *Congressional Quarterly Weekly Report*, 22 December 1998, pp. 3359–3361.
26. Carroll J. Doherty, "Critics of China Lost Trade Vote, But other Bills Wait in Wings," *Congressional Quarterly Weekly Report*, 28 June 1997, pp. 1536–1537.
27. Donna Cassata, "House Vents Anger at China in Largely Symbolic Bills," *Congressional Quarterly Weekly Report*, 8 November 1997, pp. 2777–2778.
28. William Martin, "The Christian Right and American Foreign Policy," *Foreign Policy* 114 (1999), pp. 66–80.
29. Miles Pomper, "Religious Persecution Bill Overcomes 11th-Hour Snags on Way to Enactment," *Congressional Quarterly Weekly Report*, 10 October 1998, p. 2757.
30. Miles Pomper, "House Passes State Department Bill, Leaving Tough Issues of Abortion and UN Debt Until Conference," *Congressional Quarterly Weekly Report*, 24 July 1999, pp. 1806–1808.
31. Miles Pomper, "Foreign Aid Compromise Is a Success for Clinton Team," *Congressional Quarterly Weekly Report*, 20 November 1999, pp. 2791–2794.
32. Miles Pomper, "Foreign Aid Bill Gives Clinton Requested Debt Relief Funding," *Congressional Quarterly Weekly Report*, 28 October 2000, pp. 2552–2554.
33. Pat Towell, "Congress To Resume Kosovo Debate, Its Option Limited by Ongoing Airstrike," *Congressional Quarterly Weekly Report*, 19 April 1999, pp. 849–850.
34. Pat Towell "Congress Set To Provide Money, But No Guidance, for Kosovo Mission," *Congressional Quarterly Weekly Report*, 1 May 1999, pp. 1036–1037.
35. Andrew Taylor, "House Votes to Double Clinton's Kosovo Emergency Spending Request," *Congressional Quarterly Weekly Report*, 8 May 1999, pp. 1071–1073.
36. Bill Ghent, Spencer Rich, et al. "Legislative Session Wrap-Up," *National Journal*, 23 December 2000, p. 3968.
37. Miles Pomper, "Timor Crisis Ignites New Debate on Use of U.S. Troops Overseas," *Congressional Quarterly Weekly Report*, 11 September 1999, pp. 2125–2126.
38. Miles Pomper, "GOP Criticizes U.S. Policy on Aid to North Korea, Demands More Oversight," *Congressional Quarterly Weekly Report*, 15 April 2000, p. 914.
39. Miles Pomper, "Clinton's Billion-Dollar Proposal for Colombian Anti-Drug Aid Fails to Satisfy Republicans," *Congressional Quarterly Weekly Report*, 15 January 2000, pp. 90–91.
40. Pat Towell and Miles A. Pomper, "Hill Balks at Aid to Colombia in Supplemental Spending Bill," *Congressional Quarterly Weekly Report*, 4 March 2000, pp. 484–485.
41. Christopher Marquis with Juan Foreno, "Key House Leader Withdraws Support for Colombia Aid Plan," *New York Times*, 17 November 2000, p. A-10.
42. Mann, "Making Foreign Policy: President and Congress," pp. 28–34.

8

CONTEXT AND DECISION

EXPLAINING U.S. POLICY TOWARD CUBA, 1980 TO 2000

CHRISTINE DEGREGORIO[1] AND DAVID H. RICHARDS

The story of American policy toward Cuba embodies all the hallmarks of the received wisdom on U.S. lawmaking. Years pass with a nearly moribund agenda toward lifting sanctions or promoting democracy. Activity, when it occurs, closely follows dramatic events. A deluge of Cubans seeking asylum at the Peruvian Embassy in Havana (1980) changed the perception that Cuba was a country to be negotiated with to a country that needed to be controlled. The fall of the Berlin Wall (1989) and the breakup of the Soviet Union (1991) prompted renewed efforts to democratize Cuba. And, more recently, the downing over international waters of two planes flown by the Miami-based group Brothers to the Rescue (1996)[2] gave way to the passage of punitive actions toward Castro in the form of economic sanctions (Helms-Burton).

In each of these instances, politicians in Washington responded. Sometimes the actions are swift and clear, as in the case of Helms-Burton. More often, Congress and the president are indecisive, producing partial answers and semidecisions. Over the last several decades, U.S. policy toward Cuba closely fits the characterization of one observer: "It produced some defeats and some successes. But mostly, it has produced a series of half-defeats and half-successes, an unending sequence of decisions that provided temporary pauses on the way to the next decision."[3]

In this chapter, we examine the fits and starts of Cuba policy over a twenty-year period to test the conventional wisdom about the importance of two ingredients to national lawmaking: personal interest and political context. Taking a long view accommodates the realities of our system of government, which is sequential and involves many players and several stages. Ours is a separated system of branches sharing power. Presidents are prevented from strong-arming senators and House members, whose first loyalties reside with the voters who sent them to Washington. Officials in the executive and legislative branches must share information, test ideas, and figure out ways to persuade one another before any changes will be codified into law. Bicameralism also extends the scrutiny that bills undergo and expands the opportunities that interested parties have to express their preferences and hold their representatives accountable.

THEORETICAL UNDERPINNINGS

Any study of congressional policymaking should consider the importance of goals and contexts.[4] Put simply, all members of Congress are rational people who pursue a variety of interests and do so in political environments over which they have limited control. Their capacity to achieve this or that policy outcome is determined in large part by the energy and talent they devote to their cause and the challenges they encounter in the process. This outlook thus directs attention to the personal characteristics of those who enter the policy fray and the circumstances of their intervention.

Individuals' legitimacy to intervene is closely linked to their positions and the resources that attach to their positions.[5] As a consequence, there is a distinct ebb and flow to who predominates at any given time. Assertive presidents may increase their agenda-setting powers through the clever use of the bully pulpit. They may also promote their preferences through the formulation process by carefully managing the prepared statements of senior appointees who testify before House and Senate committees. Presidents are somewhat disadvantaged, however, when members of Congress begin assembling support for one solution over another—what some call legitimation.[6] Presidents can threaten to veto or offer individual legislators special inducements.[7] But in the final analysis presidents are congressional outsiders; they have no vote.

Separation of powers, which prescribes that presidents and lawmakers attend to different sets of voters under different electoral horizons, vastly complicates policymaking.[8] No one person, no one institution, nor one party is in control. Rather, presidents and lawmakers take sides and prepare for battle to win the hearts and minds of the attentive citizens to whom legislators look when casting their votes in the House and Senate. The more attention and conflict a policy attracts, the more grueling is the journey to resolution. This perspective forces students of Congress (and the executive) to broaden their analytical perspective and observe incidents of interbranch cooperation (and competition) and interbranch outreach to organized interests, two phenomena commonly missed when we restrict ourselves to one branch or to one chamber.

Congressional policymaking is also more chaotic and unpredictable than tidy, textbook descriptions generally attest.[9] As one student of the legislative process puts it, "Advocacy of solutions often precedes the highlighting of problems to which they become attached."[10] Agendas are not first set and then alternatives generated; instead alternatives must be advocated for a long period before short-run opportunity presents itself on an agenda. Early actions—decisions and indecisions—critically shape the contexts of current decisions. This outlook requires taking a long view, because investigators can miss an important feature of the policy context when they restrict their attention to the interval between bill introduction and bill signing. In short, individuals' decisions to enter the fray are closely linked to their personal interests and the resources that they can muster, given their institutional positions.

PERSONAL INCENTIVES

Those who come forward to engage in the hard, pick-and-shovel work of policymaking are typically those who see payoffs from their involvement; influence over the policy outcomes, upward mobility within the institution's influence structures, and appreciation from constituents at home are typical.[11] Moreover, there is a bicameral flavor to these tendencies. Owing to their shorter election cycles, House members experience more urgency than do senators to connect their policymaking activities to their constituents' interests.[12] Reliance on committees as policy incubators is also more pronounced in the House than in the Senate. Having the right committee assignments grants House members the legitimacy to intervene and secure leadership recognition from among their peers and in the media.[13] Owing to the Senate's small size (100 members) and broad focus (states), citizens and news people expect senators to have something to say on a wide range of subjects, even those that exceed the boundaries of their committees' purview.[14]

From this collection of insights, with regard to individuals' involvement in policies toward Cuba, House action is more driven by members with a constituent-based justification for their involvement than is Senate action. House action is also more driven by members who operate from a committee with the jurisdiction to intervene than is Senate action. And the media will rely on senators more often than House members for their authoritative sources on Cuba.

INSTITUTIONAL POSITIONS

Individuals with different institutional loyalties must also come together for issues to attract the sustained attention and support needed to become successfully resolved into law. First, leaders from both ends of Pennsylvania Avenue must see eye-to-eye on the nature of the problem and its solution. Second, individuals inside and outside of government need to be willing to take up the charge and engage in lawmaking; they need to educate themselves and their relevant audiences, which include attentive as well as inattentive publics.[15] Issues that have the best chance of surviving the labyrinthine review of the political arenas, after all, have organized advocates with some shared degree of consensus about the wisdom of the solutions under consideration. As responsive as they are to outside interests, members of Congress tend to stalemate when the advocates they work with are also deadlocked.[16] Consensus among opinion elites, such as the president, congressional entrepreneurs, lobbyists, and media spokespeople, bodes well for a policy's survival.

With these insights in mind, events that are important enough to draw presidential attention to Cuba are also likely to turn entrepreneurial members of Congress to Cuba. When it comes to getting major policy initiatives signed into law, there is a higher standard still. Policy achievements ebb as perspectives diverge, and they flow as perspectives converge. And successful legislation shows a high degree of consensus in the views expressed by major players inside and outside of government.

PATHWAYS TO FOREIGN POLICY: THE CUBA EXAMPLE

The past twenty years captures substantial variation on the three relevant dimensions of interest in U.S.–Cuba relations: people, politics, and climate. The most visible protagonists, for example, vary considerably: three presidents (Ronald Reagan, George Bush, and Bill Clinton), five House speakers (Thomas P. "Tip" O'Neill, James C. Wright, Thomas S. Foley, Newt Gingrich, and J. Dennis Hastert) and five Senate majority leaders (Howard H. Baker, Robert J. Dole, Robert C. Byrd, George J. Mitchell, and Trent C. Lott). The committees with jurisdiction, which are determinative in setting House agendas, changed hands several times as well, allowing for the transfer of power among the individuals most equipped to shape the congressional agenda.[17] And while chairmen have less power to control events in the Senate than they have in the House, in this period it is reasonable to expect a change in hearing activity between the periods when the Senate Foreign Relations Committee was chaired by Joseph R. Biden (D-Del.) and when it was chaired by Jesse Helms (R-N.C.).

Additionally, several contextual circumstances are in a flux beyond the Beltway that affect individuals' strategic decisions as to when and how to engage in policymaking.[18] Examples include: attention-getting events, such as Castro's involvement in advancing communism in Central America, the United Nation's decision to reduce its vigilance over human rights violations in Cuba, and the European Union's decision to lower barriers to trade with the island. Other events posed threats that played into the hands of those who called for harshness. At other times, circumstances arose that brought about calm and even hope, which played into the hands of those who called for normalcy.

LEGISLATING FOREIGN POLICY

Congress and the president have been active in formulating policies toward Cuba. During the course of the last twenty years, legislators introduced an average of sixty-two bills per year on the matter, with nine formally making it into law. The vast majority of these proposed measures and laws appropriate funds for projects and agencies dealing with Cuba. Table 8.1 (on pages 170–171) lists House and Senate members who figure prominently in news coverage of Cuba between 1981 and 2000.[19] Table 8.2 (on page 172) presents the subset of measures during this period that attract serious debate on the floor of Congress, withstand deliberation (sometimes becoming law), or become policy by virtue of a presidential order.

Among the twenty-three initiatives listed, twenty-one are bills and three are presidential orders. The actions attend to a variety of policy concerns, with no one type dominant: communications (six), national security (six), human rights (seven) and restrictive sanctions (four). Considerable variation occurs over time, however. Starting with the Presidential Commission on Broadcasting to Cuba (E.O. 1232), the early 1980s dealt mainly with Radio Marti, a foreign policy tactic aimed at exposing the Cuban people to news of freedom and, in so doing, intensifying their desire for change and the subsequent demise of the Castro regime.

In the face of mounting evidence that Castro was using his resources to nurture communism in the hemisphere (e.g., El Salvador and Nicaragua), policy initiatives in the mid-1980s turned to matters of national security.[20] Bill H.R. 2760, for example, was designed to block Cuba's aid to revolutionary forces in Central America.[21] Later in 1985, after a failed attempt on the part of the Senate (S. 185) to clarify our immigration policies and eliminate Castro's capacity to threaten us with Cuban refugees, Reagan issued an executive order (E.O. 5517) to suspend all Cuban immigration to the United States. These actions came after a renewed threat on the part of Fidel Castro to use the uncontrolled emigration of his people as a weapon against the United States.[22]

The foreign policy focus shifted once again in the late 1980s and early 1990s, this time to human rights violations in Cuba. Officials in Washington appeared to respond to a decision on the part of the United Nations to relax its watch on the country.[23] Not until 1992 did members of Congress seriously entertain using sanctions as an approach to overthrow the Cuban government. The practice was in place since the 1960s via executive order but not codified into law until Helms-Burton in 1996.

As is customary with lawmaking, fewer initiatives succeed than fail. Below, we use three bills—two that passed (H.R. 927 and H.R. 4461) and one that failed (H.R. 5323)—to examine more closely the way consensus affects the policies' fates.

TABLE 8.1   CONGRESSIONAL LEADERS ON CUBAN POLICY, 1981–2000

NAME	CHAMBER	STATE/DISTRICT	AGRICULTURE (PERCENTAGES)	CUBAN AMERICANS (PERCENTAGES)[a]
DeLay	House	TX/22	.01	.01
Sanford	House	SC/1	.01	.01
Diaz-Belart	House	FL/21	.01	.44
Ros-Lehtinen	House	FL/18	.01	.44
Nethercut	House	WA/5	.02	.01
Fascell	House	FL	.01	.01
Menendez	House	NJ/13	.00	.08
Burton	House	IN/6	.01	.01
Rangel	House	NY/15	.00	.02
Torricelli	House	NJ/9	.00	.02
Berman	House	CA/26	.01	.01
Serrano	House	NY/16	.00	.01
Dorgan	House	ND	.01	.01
Dodd	Senate	CT	.01	.01
Roberts	Senate	KS	.02	.01
Kennedy	Senate	MA	.01	.01
Torricelli	Senate	NJ	.00	.01
Warner	Senate	VA	.01	.01
Helms	Senate	NC	.01	.01
Gramm	Senate	TX	.01	.01
Graham	Senate	FL	.01	.05
Dole	Senate	KS	.01	.01
Luger	Senate	IN	.01	.01
Mack	Senate	FL	.01	.05
Simpson	Senate	WY	.03	.01
Hawkins	Senate	FL	.01	.01
Moynihan	Senate	NY	.01	.01
Pell	Senate	RI	.01	.01
Percy	Senate	IL	.01	.01
Lott	Senate	MS	.01	.01
Ashcroft	Senate	MO	.02	.01
Daschle	Senate	SD	.06	.01

Notes: Members of the House and Senate who attract three or more mentions in selected media outlets during the study period are identified as leaders. The papers include the *Washington Post, New York Times,* and the *Congressional Quarterly Weekly*. Nexis-Lexis was searched for "representative" or "senator" within twenty-five words of "Cuba."

[a]House and Senate figures are from U.S. Bureau of the Census (<www.census.gov>) 1990 census. Cuban Americans make up less than one half of 1 percent of the total U.S. population.

TABLE 8.1, CONTINUED

Hispanics (Percentages)[b]	Years in Congress[c]	Party	Media Mentions	Member of "Relevant" Committee[d]
.14	15	R	11	No
.01	5	R	3	Yes
.14	7	R	20	No
.14	10	R	24	Yes
.06	5	R	7	No
.14	40	D	3	Yes
.13	7	D	9	Yes
.02	17	R	15	Yes
.14	29	D	4	No
.13	14	D	9	Yes
.30	17	D	3	Yes
.14	9	D	6	Yes
.01	10	D	4	Yes
.08	19	D	12	Yes
.05	3	R	4	Yes
.06	37	D	3	Yes
.12	3	D	14	Yes
.03	21	R	5	Yes
.02	27	R	24	Yes
.29	15	R	4	No
.14	13	D	5	Yes
.04	28	R	10	Yes
.02	23	R	7	Yes
.14	11	R	5	Yes
.06	20	R	3	Yes
.37	30	D	3	No
.14	23	D	3	Yes
.05	38	D	4	Yes
.06	18	R	3	Yes
.01	11	R	7	Yes
.01	5	R	12	Yes
.01	13	D	3	Yes

[b]Data was taken from *CQ Politics in America*. Information was taken from last available year for each member. If member was still in office for the 106th Congress, the 2000 yearbook was used.

[c]Data as of the end of the 106th Congress (or full term of service if member left prior to 106th).

[d]Membership in Committees dealing with: (1) National Security (2) Foreign Relations (3) Judiciary (4) Appropriations (5) Agriculture (6) Finance. Membership on committee in last available year of information on the member per the *CQ Politics in America Handbook*.

TABLE 8.2   MAJOR LEGISLATION CONCERNING CUBA, 1981–2000

DATE OF FINAL ACTION	TITLE	BILL OR EXEC. ORDER #	THRUST	CHAMBER OF ORIGIN	BECAME LAW
9/22/81	Presidential Commission on Broadcasting to Cuba	EO1232	Communication	President	Yes
05/25/82	Increase Membership to Commission (EO1232)	EO2366	Communication	President	Yes
7/29/83	Radio Marti Funding Measure	HR2453	Communication	House	No
8/3/83	Radio Marti Funding Measure	HR300	Communication	House	No
9/22/83	Radio Marti Funding Measure	HR312	Communication	House	No
10/4/83	Radio Marti Funding Measure	S602	Communication	Senate	Yes
10/20/83	Intelligence Authorization Act of FY 83 (Blocking Cuban aid to Central America)	HR2760	National Security	House	No
10/12/84	Admits Cuban and Haitian immigrants	HR4853	Human Rights/ National Security	House	No
4/17/85	Commemorating Bay of Pigs	S113	National Security	Senate	No
4/19/85	Commemorating Bay of Pigs	HJR236	National Security	House	Yes
7/10/85	Promoting Emigration from Cuba	S185	Human Rights/ National Security	Senate	No
9/22/86	Suspension of Cuban Immigration	EO5517	National Security	President	Yes
10/4/88	Release of Cuban Detainees	HR5164	Human Rights	House	No
7/21/89	Creates TV Marti	S1160	Communication	Senate	No
2/22/90	Urging UN to Continue Reporting Cuban Human Rights Violations	S247	Human Rights	Senate	No
5/15/90	Addressing Human Rights Abuses by Cuba	HR381	Human Rights	House	No
2/26/91	Condemning Cuba's Human Rights Record	S65	Human Rights	Senate	No
2/27/91	Condemning Cuba's Human Rights Record	HR88	Human Rights	House	No
9/22/92	Promote Peaceful Dem. Transition in Cuba	HR5323	Sanctions	House	No
3/4/93	Urging UN Human Rights Commission to Support Human Rights in Cuba	S76	Human Rights	Senate	No
12/17/93	Friendship to Emerging Democracies	HR3000	Sanctions	House	Yes
10/4/94	Condemn Sinking of Tugboat by Cuban Navy	HCON279	National Security	House	No
3/12/96	Cuban Liberty and Dem. Solidarity Act of 1996 (Helms-Burton)	HR927	Sanctions	House	Yes
10/18/00	FY 2001 Agriculture Appropriations Bill	HR4461	Sanctions	House	Yes

Source: Congressional Information Service.

In an effort to understand why certain lawmakers emerged to bring resolution to America's longstanding uneasiness with the Castro regime, it is important to consider the responsible players and the evidence of elected officials' entrepreneurial behavior toward Cuba. Because the success of the legislative entrepreneurs rests so strongly on the energies, resources, and perspectives that emerge within the interest group community, we also examine the organized interests that play a prominent part in policymaking toward Cuba. In particular, it is important to observe changes in the number and mix of organizations that participated in congressional hearings. These are, after all, the formal settings where members of Congress educate themselves about viable solutions for addressing the concerns at hand.

PERSONAL INCENTIVES AND POSITIONS

Of the thirty-two lawmakers who have dominated congressional action on Cuba since 1980, a greater share (59 percent) are senators. Five foreign policy leaders (or 16 percent) come from Florida, a state in which a sizable Cuban-American population is keenly interested in U.S. policy toward Cuba. With the exception of Republican Lincoln Diaz-Belart of Florida's 18th district (himself born in Cuba) and Republican Ileana Ros-Lehtinen of Florida's 21st district, none of the leaders come from areas with more than 10 percent Cuban-American populations. Only Representative Robert Menendez, a Democrat of New Jersey's 12th district, represents an area of more than 5 percent Cuban Americans (8 percent). The vast majority of these lawmakers (twenty-four members) come from districts or states with fewer than 1 percent Cuban Americans, in keeping with the national figure (.042).

On average, members of the House represent slightly larger concentrations of the more general ethnic category, that of Hispanic citizens. But the difference of means across chambers is not significant (11.5 and 8.9 respectively). On average, all of these congressional districts and states have merely a 10 percent share of Hispanic citizens. The recurring states, showing more than one leader, are states with a larger than average share of Hispanics, such as Florida, New York, New Jersey, and Texas.

A second, nonethnic measure of constituent interest that conceivably prompts legislators to engage in trade matters with Cuba is the local economy's involvement in agriculture. Like other constituency characteristics, however, this one is so uniform that it cannot easily account for any variation that may exist between House members and their Senate colleagues.

All told, there is little evidence to support the proposition that differences among one's constituencies (district versus state concentrations of ethnic and economic interests) explain House and Senate involvement in policy toward Cuba. Nor are there bicameral differences to note. Something other than the electoral incentive lay behind the vast majority of the officials' decisions to lead in this area. Furthering good public policy is one likely reason. For example, several members listed in Table 8.1 have a strong track record for involving themselves in matters of national security, apart from Cuba. Seven of the key people listed operated from one of the foreign affairs committees. Representative Dante B. Fascell (D-Fla.), and Senators Jesse Helms (R-N.C.), Claiborne de Borda Pell (D-R.I.), and Charles C. Percy (R-Ill.) are included among this group. Six of the leaders operated from one of the Committees on Agriculture, and six are from the Senate Finance Committee. A tiny few in the Senate, including Christopher J. Dodd (D-Conn.), Jesse Helmes, Robert G. Torricelli (D-N.J.), and former Senator John D. Ashcroft (R-Mo.), hold seats on two such major committees, doubling their opportunities for recognition and influence.

The smaller size of the Senate requires that senators serve on more committees than do their House counterparts, and the table reflects the modest difference seen between major committee assignments held by senators and House members. All but two senators operated from committees that dealt directly with jurisdictions bearing on Cuba, and seven senators served on more than one such valuable committee. Included here are those committees with jurisdictions pertaining to defense (National Security), foreign relations (Foreign Relations), human rights and immigration (Judiciary), funding (Appropriations), and trade (Agriculture and Finance). While a majority of House members operate from one of these committees, no one operates from more than one. A noticeable few even operate from positions with no particular vantage point on Cuba at all. These members are Republicans Thomas D. (Tom) DeLay of Texas's 22nd district, Lincoln Diaz-Belart, George R. Nethercut of Washington's 5th district, and Democrat Charles B. Rangel of New York's 15th district. There is no single, obvious explanation for this. Each member may have his own explanation. For his part, Majority Whip Tom Delay holds a leadership position that gives him ample opportunity to get involved.

The senators are slightly more senior than House members in terms of years served in Congress. While these measures of seniority are also not statistically different across chambers, there is a distinction of note within chambers. Senate leaders are eight years more senior than the average senator during this period (18.8 versus 10 on average for the chamber),while House leaders are only four years more senior than their average counterpart (14.2 versus 10 on average for the House).

The party breakdown of the members by chamber shows more Republicans emerging as leaders in the Senate than in the House: eleven of nineteen (58 percent) as compared with five of thirteen (38.4 percent). One explanation for this difference is the smaller Senate, which gives prominence to members of both parties, regardless of their majority or minority status, whereas majority status actually boosts a House member's capacity to be recognized as a leader.[24] Another explanation is that over the past twenty years Republicans controlled the Senate for more years than they controlled the House—twelve and six respectively. Over the ten-year period, the leaders commanded from three to twenty-four mentions in any of three news outlets: the *New York Times*, the *Washington Post*, and the *Congressional Quarterly Weekly*. Contrary to expectation, House members appear in stories about U.S. policy toward Cuba slightly more often than their Senate counterparts, 9.08 and 6.89 respectively.[25]

Assisting elected members of Congress at every step of the way are a host of interested activists who work to foil or promote particular policies, in keeping with their shared views on the issues.[26] One avenue of participation—witness testimony—is broken down in Figure 8.1 into the various types of organizations that participate in national politics. The greatest activity of congressional testimony on Cuba policy occurred in the early 1980s and the mid-1990s. The activity of the three types of groups testifying—executive agency personnel, citizen groups, and occupational groups—roughly parallels the overall distribution. Within the first category are high-level presidential appointees from the departments of state, justice, and defense. The second category is replete with Cuban-American organizations (Cuban-American National Foundation (CANF), the Cuban Committee for Democracy, and the Bridge of Young Cuban Professionals (Puente), human rights groups (International Human Rights Law Group, Amnesty International, and America's Watch), and religious organizations (Puebla Institute, Caribbean Conference of Churches, and the United Church of Christ). Occupational groups vary considerably as well, including rice, wheat, and barley producers, business associations such as the U.S. Chamber of Commerce, and trade groups such as the Association of Broadcasters.

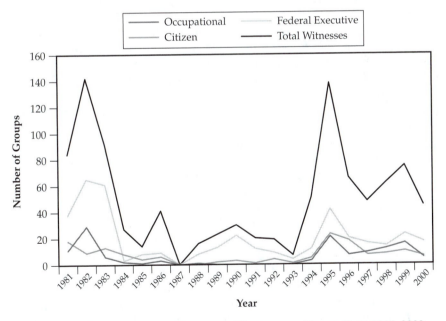

FIGURE 8.1   INTEREST GROUP MAKEUP AT HEARINGS BY GROUP TYPE, 1981–2000

Source: Congressional Information Service, *Congressional Record, 1981–2000.* See text for coding explanation.

The four peak periods of testimony captured in Figure 8.1 (on page 175) correspond with congressional activity and the events of the day, including the end of the Cold War. Witnesses from the executive branch are the most visible of the three, and they are the least susceptible to substantive shifts in hearing focus from one decade to the next. Moreover, citizen groups numerically dominate occupational groups throughout much of the period with the exception of 1982 and 1999, a stark contrast to occupational group dominance that characterizes the advocacy community in domestic policy generally. Additionally, these shifts in the numerical presence of lobbyists on the Hill roughly parallel the substantive shifts in the focus of foreign policy over the last twenty years, with deliberation on economic sanctions dominating the eras when the occupational interests are most visible, and citizen groups surfacing in greater numbers when Radio Marti and immigration policy took center stage. What the distribution does not reveal is the modest difference in the number of hearings the two chambers hosted to focus attention on Cuba. House hearings slightly exceed Senate hearings, with averages of six and four respectively. In any given year, the number ranged from zero to twenty-four in the House and zero to thirteen in the Senate.

CONTEXTUAL CIRCUMSTANCES OF STATUTEMAKING

At the start of the 1980s, the Muriel Boatlift was fresh on the minds of many. Castro opened his prisons and insane asylums, sending a massive influx of "undesirables" to American shores.[27] In the early 1980s, Cuba was used as a staging area, as well, for the spread of communism into Central America. By the middle of the decade, tensions between the United States and Cuba over immigration continued to mount. In 1989 the fall of the Berlin Wall led to increasing uncertainty about the future of the Soviet Union, Cuba's largest patron and trading partner. In 1991, Cuba became more isolated than at any point since Castro took power in 1959, when the Soviet Union collapsed and withdrew funding, sugar quotas, and oil-price supports. In the summer of 1994, Castro precipitated a smaller but equally threatening boat lift. The crises continued almost unabated when in early 1996 the Cuban airforce downed two unarmed civilian aircraft flown by a Cuban-American group of pilots, Brothers to the Rescue. The group had been dropping propaganda leaflets on Havana for several months, but sparks flew when the Cuban airforce shot down the planes while in international airspace. Pressure on Castro to introduce democratizing reforms intensified once again in 1998 following a high-profile visit by Pope John Paul II to the island. The added attention also gave rise to international pressure to lift the U.S. embargo of Cuba.

The presidents' public papers throughout this period contain speech that reflects many of the highs and lows of the era.[28] (See Figure 8.2 on page 178 for a frequency distribution of presidential speech.) The following excerpts illustrate quite distinct ways that presidents spoke about the situation in Cuba.

All mentions of Castro and his government were cast in negative language such as this pronouncement by President Clinton: "During the past two years, the level of Soviet arms exports to Cuba can only be compared to the levels reached during the Cuban missile crisis twenty years ago."[29] Ten years earlier, President Reagan had this to say:

> For twenty-six years, during Republican and Democratic administrations, Castro has kept to his own path of revolutionary violence. Today, Cuba even provides safe passage for drug traffickers who poison our children. In return, of course, Cuba gets hard cash to buy more weapons of war.[30]

References to the people of Cuba are markedly positive by contrast:

> And the beautiful thing about Cuba is because of the industry of those people and because of the affection that a lot of Americans have for the people of Cuba, Cuba, once free and once under democracy, will have a real shot at forward movement in terms of helping their people through a reinvigorated economy. There's no question about that. It could be the success story of the nineties, if Castro would permit the freedom and democracy that the people want.[31]

Concepts about advancing economic and democratic change are sometimes intermingled, as the following excerpt illustrates. As a result, this passage is coded twice. "And I think the policies we are following will hasten the day when that occurs, and we follow those policies because we believe they are the ones most likely to promote democracy and ultimately prosperity for the people of Cuba," declared President Bill Clinton.[32] By way of comparison, the next passage focuses exclusively on democratic advancement:

> Freedom demands sacrifice. And the battle for freedom draws upon people's most heroic instincts and abilities. Jose Marti, a hero of freedom, the father of Cuban independence, said, "To witness a crime in silence is like committing it." So, today we again reiterate unwavering commitment for a free and democratic Cuba. Nothing shall turn us away from this objective.[33]

In the mid-1980s the president's use of the bully pulpit peaks to isolate Castro and eliminate his capacity to aid and abet the spread of communism in Central America. The chief executive's attention to Cuba picks up again in the early 1990s with the fall of the Berlin wall, which brought renewed attention to Castro as one of the few remaining communist dictators. And again in 1996, the president responds with rhetorical force to the downing of the Brothers to the Rescue planes.

Speeches toward Castro and his government frequently entail uniformly negative language, as illustrated in Figure 8.3 (on page 178). These are almost entirely contained in the Cold War period. In contrast, highly positive references to the plight of the Cuban people and their quest for freedom and democracy

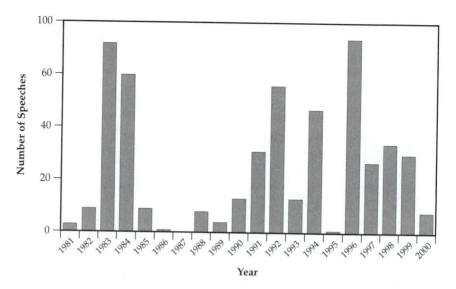

FIGURE 8.2 FREQUENCY OF PRESIDENTIAL SPEECHES CONCERNING CUBA, 1981–2000

Source: The American Reference Library and the National Archives. See text for coding explanation.

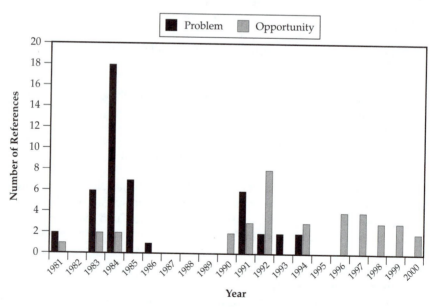

FIGURE 8.3 FREQUENCY OF REFERENCES TO THE SITUATION AS PROBLEM VERSUS OPPORTUNITY, PRESIDENTIAL SPEECH ON CUBA, 1981–2000

Source: The American Reference Library and the National Archives. See text for coding explanation.

occur more frequently in the post–Cold War period. The presidents' positions toward policy approaches can be harsh or supportive, as detailed in Figure 8.4. And these closely correspond to the positive and negative images they paint of Castro and the Cuban people, respectively.

Presidents often express two goals during the time period (see Figure 8.5 on page 180). One pertains to advancement of freedom and liberty, what we label "democratic advancement." The other pertains to encouraging open markets and trade, what we label "economic advancement." As the distributions portray, references to democratic advancement are always two to three times greater than references to the economic theme. From the late 1980s on, roughly starting with the Bush administration, democratic themes are more prevalent, doubling, if not trebling, with the Clinton administration.

Much of the rhetoric offered in congressional hearings and floor speeches by members in their debates prior to votes on Cuba-related legislation (the 1992 Torricelli bill [H.R. 5323], the 1996 Helms-Burton Act [H.R. 927], and the 2000 Agriculture Appropriations Act [H.R. 4461]) portrays Cuba as an economic opportunity for the United States. Several excerpts illustrate this point. "Prior to the imposition of the embargo, Cuba accounted for more than 50 percent of U.S. rice exports," said one lobbyist, who represents the Rice Growers Association, describing Cuba as a potential market. "Today,

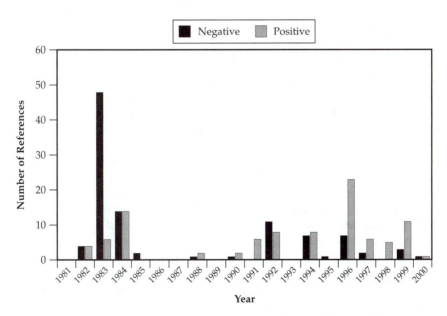

FIGURE 8.4   FREQUENCY OF REFERENCES TO POLICY APPROACHES, PRESIDENTIAL SPEECH ON CUBA, 1981–2000

Source: The American Reference Library and the National Archives. See text for coding explanation.

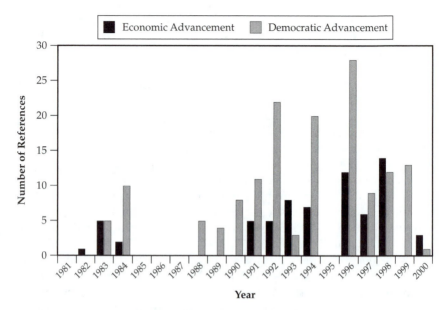

FIGURE 8.5   FREQUENCY OF REFERENCES TO POLICY AIMS FOR ECONOMIC VERSUS DEMOCRATIC ADVANCEMENT, PRESIDENTIAL SPEECH ON CUBA, 1981–2000

Source: The American Reference Library and the National Archives. See text for coding explanation.

Castro is still in power, Cuba is still communist, and the Cuban citizenry consumes 400,000 tons of imported rice, all of which is produced by our competitors."[34] Sometimes the same language portrays Cuba as an insignificant market or urges lawmakers not to think of Cuba in just economic terms. Representative Ros-Lehtinen illustrates this point: "A credible case could be made for some market reforms in other countries. But what reforms have taken place in Castro's Cuba in these forty-one years of tyranny and dictatorship?"[35]

The second line of argument is noneconomic in nature and pertains to rights and needs. Words like *assistance, help, outreach, freedom, liberty, democracy,* and *human rights* illustrate this. "Mr. Speaker, this legislation will put U.S. policy with Castro back on track—back to being tough with concrete action designed to restore democracy and encourage Castro's departure from power," declared Representative Porter J. Goss (R-Fla.).[36] Here, Cuba is portrayed as a humanitarian opportunity, to help it become a democracy, end human rights violations, and allow for more freedoms. Senator Phil Gramm (R-Texas) illustrates another example of this perspective when he says: "Let us restore freedom and democracy to Cuba."[37]

In Figure 8.6 there is one distinction of note: House members and interest groups express modestly different views of the Torricelli bill—a 60–40 split between viewing the bill as democratic advancement rather than economic

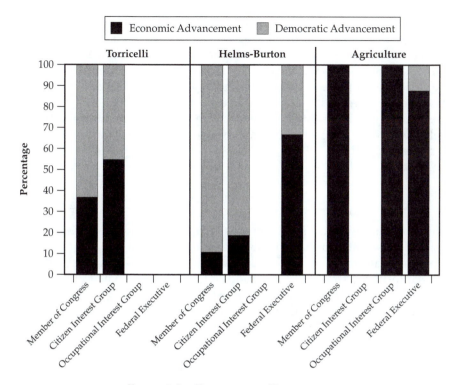

**FIGURE 8.6   FREQUENCY OF REFERENCES
IN TESTIMONY BY GROUP AND BILL (PERCENTAGE)**

Source: Congressional Information Service, *Congressional Record*. See text for an explanation of terms.

advancement. More consensus exists over Helms-Burton and the agriculture bill (and these are the two that passed). In testimony over Helms-Burton, most witnesses regardless of position (interest group or legislator) saw the matter in terms of democratic advancement. Just the opposite occurs over agriculture appropriations. A large majority of participants framed their testimony in terms of economic opportunities.

Not surprisingly, the marked shift in references away from mentions of democracy and towards mentions of trade follow the substantive change in focus that these initiatives entail. Where Helms-Burton called for punitive approaches through economic sanctions, the agriculture policy opened markets for medicine and some basic foodstuffs.

Figure 8.6 makes a further breakdown to observe consensus or lack of consensus between members of Congress and different types of interest groups. It is noteworthy to find no occupational groups in attendance at the Helms-Burton hearings, for example, and no citizens groups at the agricultural hearings. Apparently participation, not just speech, varies with the issues that are under consideration. Last, Figure 8.7 captures speech on the floors of the House and Senate. This shows the same shift across initiatives and no bicameral difference as to the line of argument on the specific issue. The bicameral consensus on the two bills that passed is in keeping with our expectations. Nonetheless, our test is incomplete, because of our comparison case of a bill (Torricelli) that never made it to the Senate floor for debate. Had the Senate and House framed their debate along disparate lines and the bill failed, we would have some preliminary evidence to affirm the importance of congruent speech.

CONCLUSION

There is strong support for the premise that members of Congress and the White House react to changing events on the international stage. There is a marked pattern in the way presidents vary the tone and content of their speech to fit the times. In the period of the Cold War when Fidel Castro threatened American security by assisting the spread of communism in Central America, presidential rhetoric was filled with tough tones and negative images of the Cuban dictator. Since the demise of the Soviet Union

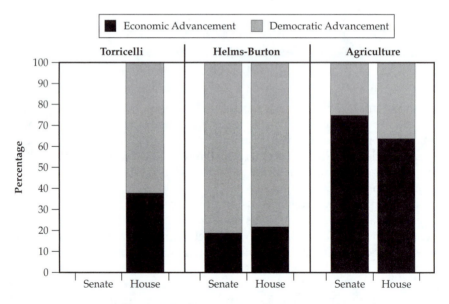

FIGURE 8.7   FREQUENCY OF REFERENCES
IN FLOOR DEBATE BY BILL AND CHAMBER (PERCENTAGE)

Source: Congressional Information Service, *Congressional Record*. See text for an explanation of terms.

and its supportive relationship with Cuba, however, presidential speech has become increasingly positive with frequent references to advancing democracy.

Interest groups, as represented in group attendance at public hearings, are as diverse for this issue as for other issues. Obvious differences pertain to the high concentration of federal executives throughout the last twenty years, not surprising perhaps in the area of foreign policy. Interest groups also maintain a constant presence on the issue of foreign policy toward Cuba. What is atypical compared to some domestic policy is the episodic participation of occupational groups. Most descriptions of the advocacy community acknowledge the numerical dominance of these organizations. Here they emerge and eclipse the citizen groups in only two periods: in the early 1980s with the consideration of Radio Marti and more recently with the consideration of agriculture appropriations. This pattern is consistent with the idea that groups mobilize more often in response to a threat than in response to opportunities. In the case of Radio Marti, for example, broadcasters were concerned that radio signals beamed to Cuba would interfere with the broadcasters' own domestic signals. During the formulation of the agriculture bill, American exporters were concerned that they would lose market share in Cuba to Canada and the European Union.

When one compares how participant groups assess economic impacts of three pending initiatives, there are some differences of note. The 1992 Torricelli bill, which did not pass, attracted more praise than criticism from citizen group witnesses and more criticism than praise from elected officials—a lack of consensus across participants. In contrast, the two bills that passed— one with a tough stance and one with a more open approach toward economic policy with Cuba—showed a consensus perspective among all participants. Members of Congress and interest groups alike expected stronger sanctions from the Helms-Burton bill, so it passed. The agriculture appropriations bill also passed; all parties expected a beneficial effect from the legislation. Admittedly, while we have examined a limited number of bills, nonetheless, there is support for the idea that policies succeed more often than not when participants from different places in the political arena concur over anticipated effects.[38]

There is no evidence to expect prominence with respect to Cuba policy to be attached to House members' more than senators' seat assignments. House members are used as authoritative sources in media accounts of U.S. policy toward Cuba on par with senators, a pattern inconsistent with conventional wisdom on the subject, which usually finds reporters partial to covering senators. Nor is there evidence to suggest that differences in election cycles make House members more attentive to electoral pressures from constituents who follow policies toward sanctions and trade with Cuba. The involvement of a very few number of leaders—from both the House and the Senate—have concentrations of interested citizens as a justification for their prominence. But this finding is the exception, not the rule. More typically, leaders on U.S.–Cuba relations represent states and districts that contain few Cuban Americans and farmers who might prod their legislators into action. On policymaking toward Cuba, at least, there is no particular advantage going to one chamber or the other. House and Senate leaders seem to operate from an equal footing. In both cases they may act more out of a commitment to advance good public policy than out of an electoral need to satisfy constituents.

NOTES

1. With gratitude, we acknowledge William LeoGrande's willingness to read early versions of this chapter and provide many helpful insights. We also thank Gregory Gadren of American University for his valuable assistance with data collection.
2. The group routinely dropped propaganda leaflets over Havana.
3. Richard F. Fenno, Jr., *The Emergence of a Senate Leader: Pete Domenici and the Reagan Budget* (Washington, D.C.: CQ Press, 1991), p. 227.
4. Richard F. Fenno, Jr., *Learning to Govern: An Institutional View of the 104th Congress* (Washington D.C.: Brookings Institution, 1997); Richard F. Fenno, Jr., *The Emergence of a Senate Leader: Pete Domenici and the Reagan Budget*; Richard F. Fenno, Jr., *The United States Senate: A Bicameral Perspective* (Washington, D.C.: American Enterprise Institute, 1982); and Richard F. Fenno, Jr., *Homestyle: House Members in Their Districts* (Glenview: Foresman Scott, 1978).
5. John W. Kingdon, *Agendas, Alternatives, and Public Policies* (Boston: Little, Brown, 1995).
6. Roger Davidson and Walter Oleszek, *Congress and Its Members*, 6th ed. (Washington, D.C.: CQ Press, 1998); and David J. Volger, *The Politics of Congress*, 6th ed. (Madison, WI: Brow and Benchmark, 1993).
7. Sherrod Brown, *Congress from the Inside* (Kent, OH: Kent University Press, 2000); and Nathan Dietz, "Presidential Influence on Legislative Behavior in the U.S. House of Representatives" (Ph.D. diss., University of Rochester, 1998).
8. Charles O. Jones, "A Way of Life and Law," *American Political Science Review* 89 (1995), pp. 1–9; and Samuel Kernell, *Going Public* (Washington, D.C.: Congressional Quarterly Inc., 1986), p. 3.
9. Barbara Sinclair, *Unorthodox Lawmaking* (Washington, D.C.: CQ Press, 1997).
10. Kingdon, *Agendas, Alternatives, and Public Policies*, p. 215.
11. Richard F. Fenno, Jr., *Congressman in Committees* (Boston: Little, Brown, 1973); Gregory Wawro, *Legislative Entrepreneurship* (Ann Arbor, MI: University of Michigan Press, 2000); John W. Kingdon, *Congressmen's Voting Decisions*, 3rd ed. (New York: Harper and Row, 1989); Richard F. Fenno, Jr., *Homestyle: House Members in Their Districts*; and Richard L. Hall, *Participation in Congress* (New Haven, CT: Yale University Press, 1996).
12. Ross Baker, *House and Senate*, 3rd ed. (New York: W.W. Norton, 2000); and David R. Mayhew, *Congress: The Electoral Connection* (New Haven, CT: Yale University Press, 1974).
13. Christine A. DeGregorio, *Networks of Champions: Leadership, Access, and Advocacy in the U.S. House of Representatives* (Ann Arbor, MI: University of Michigan Press, 1997); Timothy E. Cook, *Making Laws and Making News* (Washington, D.C.: Brookings Institution, 1989); and Patrick J. Sellers and Brian Schaffner, "Context, Interest, and Effort: U.S. Senators' Media Activities, 1979–1997" (presented at the annual meeting of the American Political Science Association, Atlanta, Georgia, September 2000), pp. 2–3.
14. Fenno, *The United States Senate: A Bicameral Perspective*; and Baker, *House and Senate*.
15. Kingdon, *Agendas, Alternatives, and Public Policies*; John Krosnick, "Government Policy and Citizen Passion," *Political Behavior* 12 (1990), pp. 59–92; and Steven J. Rosenstone and John Mark Hansen, *Mobilization, Participation, and Democracy in America* (New York: McMillan, 1993).

16. Jeffrey H. Birnbaum and Alan S. Murray, *Showdown at Gucci Gulch: Lawmakers, Lobbyists and the Unlikely Triumph of Tax Reform* (New York: Basic Books, 1987); and Kingdon, *Congressmen's Voting Decisions*.

17. Representatives Dante B. Fascell (D-Fla.), Lee Hamilton (D-Ind.), and Benjamin Gilman (R-N.Y.) surely bring different perspectives, talents, and styles to their management of the House Committee on Foreign Affairs.

18. We omit from this analysis a couple of institutional conditions that bear on domestic policy outcomes in particular. Whether one party controls the executive and legislative branches and the size of the majority's seat advantage in the Congress can certainly affect issues that divide along party lines. When it comes to defending our borders and advancing democracy, we expect these differences to recede.

19. The search protocol requested "representative" or "senator" within twenty-five words of Cuba. The table includes all individuals who received three or more mentions in any one of three media outlets: *Congressional Quarterly Weekly*, the *New York Times*, and the *Washington Post*.

    Member-specific data (e.g., seniority, committee assignments, and party affiliation) are taken from the Library of Congress and the *Almanac of American Politics*. District characteristics are taken from the U.S. Bureau of the Census. We use the Congressional Information Service to retrieve data on the number and type of witnesses who appear before congressional hearings regarding Cuba. We document variations in the chief executives' attentiveness and tone toward Cuba by analyzing presidential papers of the period, assembled by the American Reference Library and the National Archives (www.clerkweb.gov).

20. Daniel Southerland, "Cuba's Welcome Wearing Thin in Several Regions," *Christian Science Monitor*, 7 November 1983, p. 3.

21. We include within this category, as well, two resolutions in 1985 of a more symbolic nature; they recall and commemorate U.S. efforts to block the spread of communism at the Bay of Pigs.

22. For an excellent illustration of the way historical precedent and lingering animosities shape the context of unfolding politics, see William LeoGrande, "Enemies Evermore: U.S. Policy Towards Cuba After Helms-Burton," *Journal of Latin American Studies* 29 (1997), pp. 211–221.

23. Peter B. Gemma, "U.N. Can Hurt Our Role," *USA Today*, 23 September 1991, p. 10-A.

24. DeGregorio, *Networks of Champions: Leadership, Access, and Advocacy in the U.S. House of Representatives*.

25. The difference in means does not reach statistical levels of significance, however, indicating that reporters rely similarly on members from both chambers for their authoritative sources.

26. Jonathan C. Smith, "Foreign Policy for Sale? Interest Group Influence on President Clinton's Cuba Policy, August 1994," *Presidential Studies Quarterly* 28 (1998), pp. 207–220; DeGregorio, *Networks of Champions: Leadership, Access, and Advocacy in the U.S. House of Representatives*; and Philip Brenner, *The Limits and Possibilities of Congress* (New York: St. Martin's Press, 1983).

27. Brian Cody, "Florida Seeks Help with Influx," *Washington Post*, 14 December 1984.

28. The data come from a subset of presidential papers—sixty-nine in all—that contain detailed and explicit mention of Cuba. They include all state of the union messages, presidential orders and proclamations, press conferences, radio addresses, and remarks upon signing public laws when Cuba is a major focus of the address. Below we examine two themes in each of three conceptual categories of speech. They include two aspects of the "situation" in Cuba, references to its leader and its people; two distinguishable "policy aims," one on advancing democracy, and the other on advancing economic opportunities; and two specific "policy approaches," one intoning militaristic and economic sanctions, and the other intoning communication and outreach.

29. President William Clinton, address to the nation on defense and national security, 23 March 1993.

30. President Ronald Reagan, address to the nation on defense and national security, 23 March 1983.

31. President George H. Bush, press conference with foreign correspondents, 19 December 1991.

32. President William Clinton, press conference with foreign correspondents, 19 December 1994.

33. President George H. Bush, message on Cuban Independence Day, 20 May 1991.

34. CIS Congressional Universe: Federal Document Clearing House, Congressional Testimony, 19 July 2000.
35. CIS Congressional Universe: Federal Document Clearing House, Congressional Testimony, 28 June 2000.
36. CIS Congressional Universe: Federal Document Clearing House, Congressional Testimony, 6 March 1996.
37. CIS Congressional Universe: Federal Document Clearing House, Congressional Testimony, 5 March 1996.
38. Because the Toricelli bill was not debated on the floor, we are unable to test the proposition about bicameralism: that successful passage is linked to a circumstance when both chambers demonstrate a common point of reference for arguing the strengths and weaknesses of an issue.

APPENDIX

INTERNET ADDRESSES

American Diplomacy, University of North Carolina
http://www.unc.edu/depts/diplomat

Center for Congress, Indiana University
http://www.congress.indiana.edu

Center for Legislative Archives (National Archives)
http://www.nara.gov/nara/legislative

Congress.org (The Dirksen Congressional Center)
http://www.congress.org

C-SPAN
http://www.c-span.org

Cuba
http://www.state.gov/www/regions/wha/cuba

Federal Election Commission
http://www.fec.gov

Federal judiciary
http://www.uscourts.gov or http://www.fjc.gov

FedNet
http://www.fednet.net

Federal statistics
http://www.fedstats.gov

Gallup Organization
http://www.gallup.com

Latin American and Caribbean Center, Florida International University
http://lacc.fiu.edu

Library of Congress
http://lcweb.loc.gov or http://www.thomas.gov

New York Times
http://www.nytimes.com

Roll Call
http://www.rollcall.com

University of Michigan Documents Center
http://www.lib.umich.edu/govdocs/legishis.htm

U.S. House of Representatives
http://www.house.gov or http://clerkweb.house.gov

U.S. House of Representatives International Relations Committee
http://www.house.gov/international_relations

U.S. Senate
http://www.senate.gov

U.S. Senate Foreign Relations Committee
http://www.senate.gov/~foreign

U.S. State Department
http://www.state.gov

Washington Post
http://www.washingtonpost.com

White House
http://www.whitehouse.gov

INDEX